Kakuriyo
Bed & Breakfast for Spirits

④

Art by
Waco Ioka

Original Story by **Midori Yuma**
Character Design by **Laruha**

CONTENTS

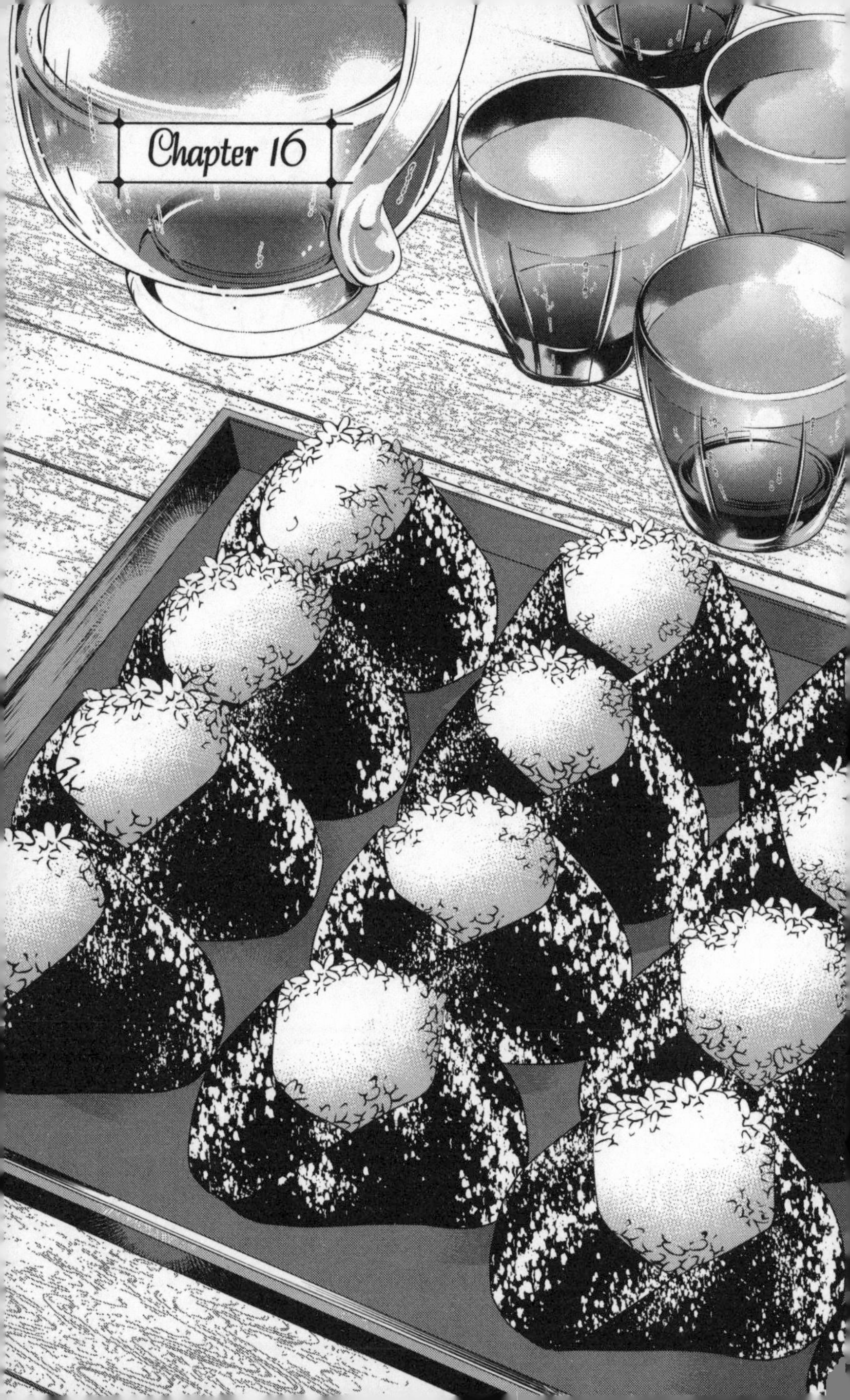
Chapter 16

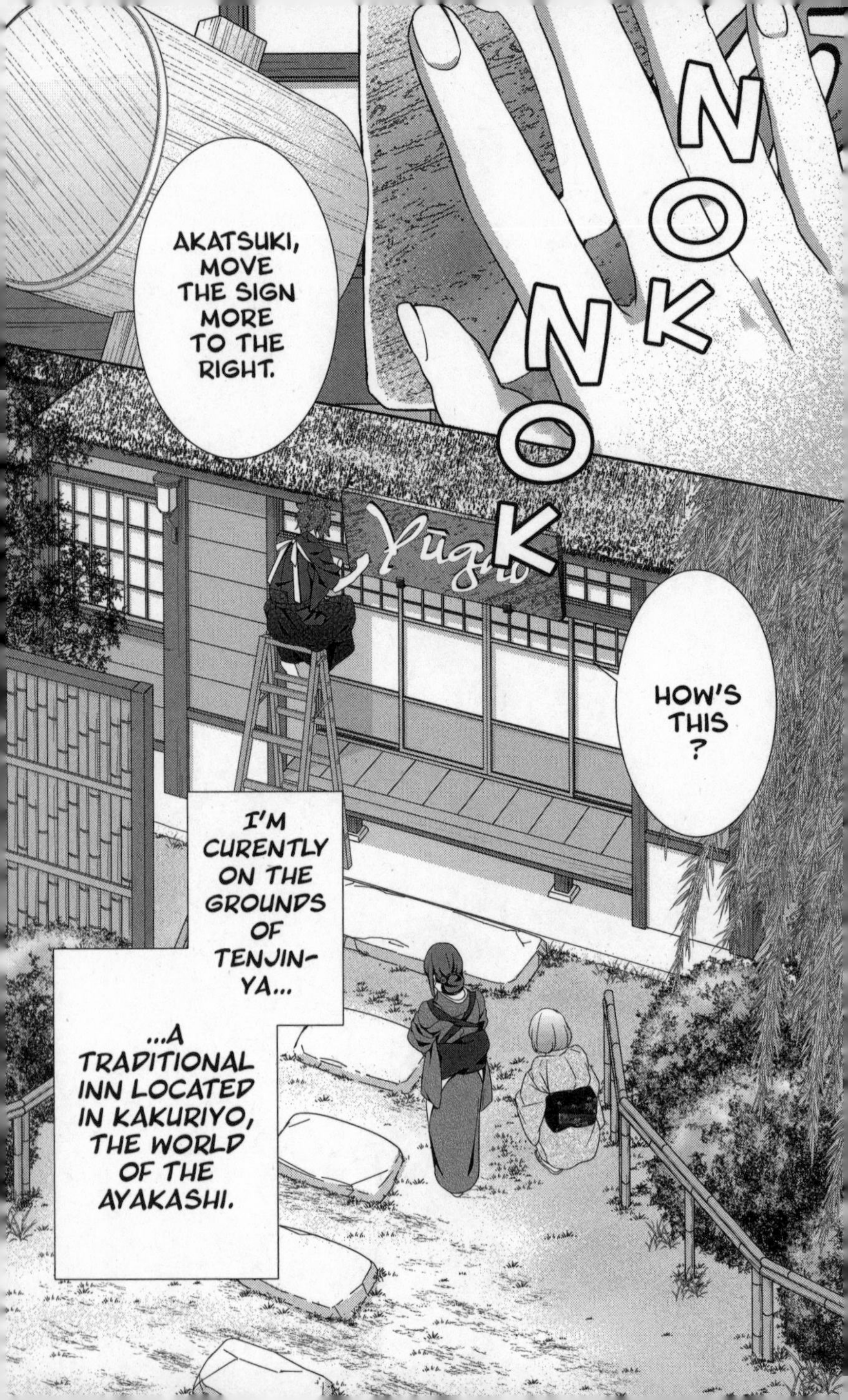
KNOCK KNOCK
AKATSUKI, MOVE THE SIGN MORE TO THE RIGHT.
HOW'S THIS?
I'M CURENTLY ON THE GROUNDS OF TENJIN-YA...
...A TRADITIONAL INN LOCATED IN KAKURIYO, THE WORLD OF THE AYAKASHI.

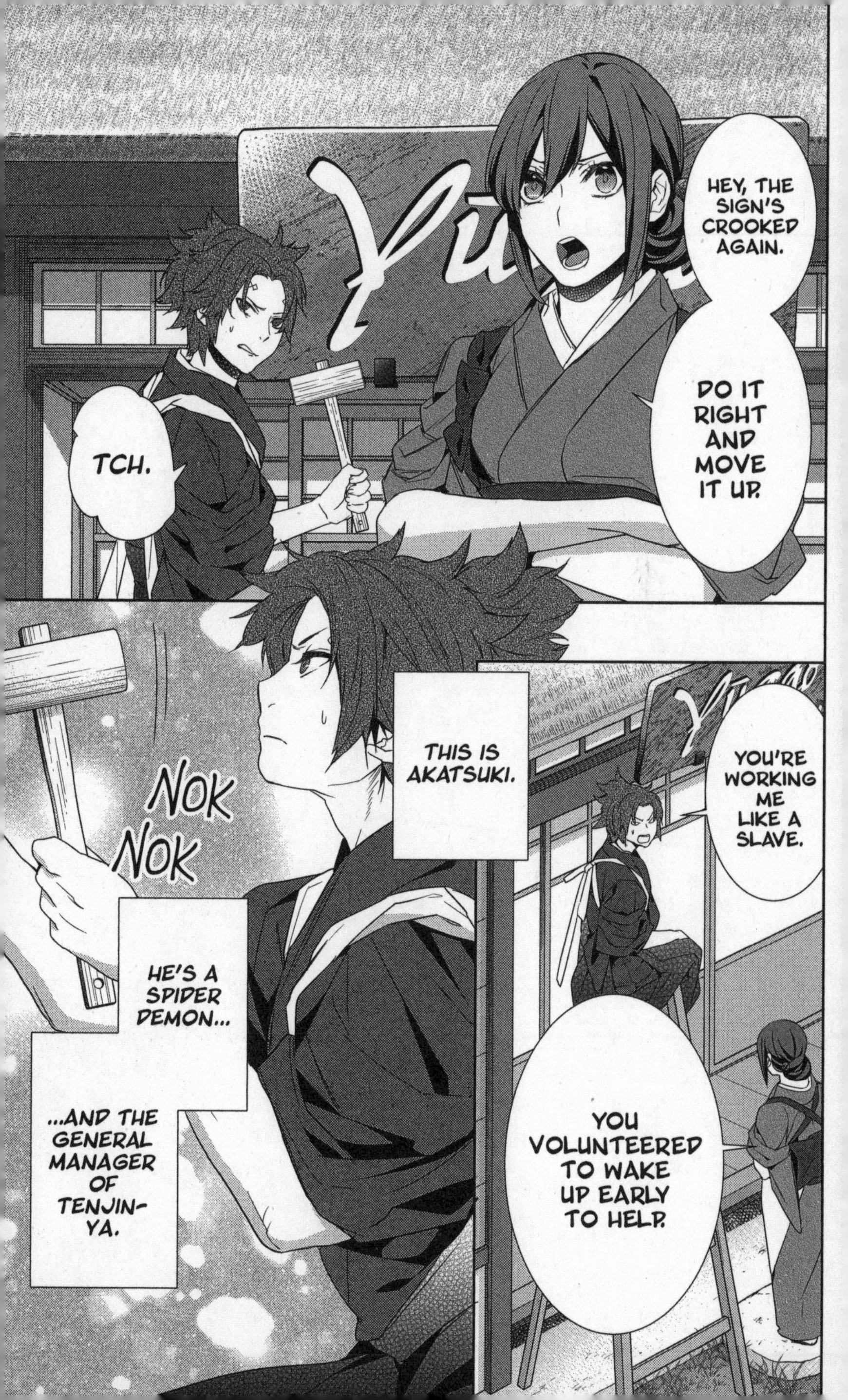
HEY, THE SIGN'S CROOKED AGAIN.
DO IT RIGHT AND MOVE IT UP.
TCH.
YOU'RE WORKING ME LIKE A SLAVE.
YOU VOLUNTEERED TO WAKE UP EARLY TO HELP.
THIS IS AKATSUKI.
NOK NOK
HE'S A SPIDER DEMON...
...AND THE GENERAL MANAGER OF TENJIN-YA.

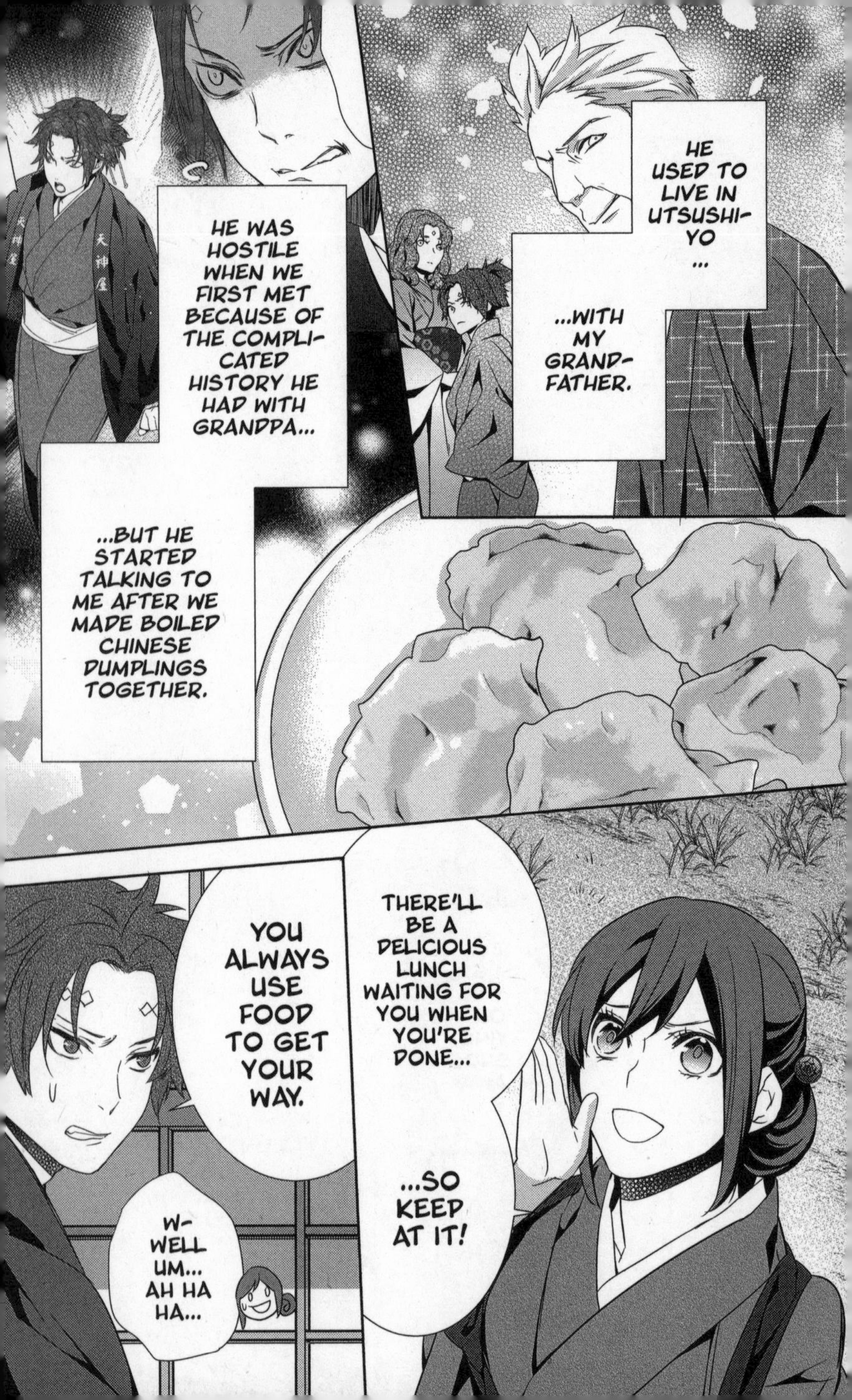
HE USED TO LIVE IN UTSUSHI-YO ...
...WITH MY GRAND-FATHER.
HE WAS HOSTILE WHEN WE FIRST MET BECAUSE OF THE COMPLI-CATED HISTORY HE HAD WITH GRANDPA...
...BUT HE STARTED TALKING TO ME AFTER WE MADE BOILED CHINESE DUMPLINGS TOGETHER.
THERE'LL BE A DELICIOUS LUNCH WAITING FOR YOU WHEN YOU'RE DONE...
...SO KEEP AT IT!
YOU ALWAYS USE FOOD TO GET YOUR WAY.
W-WELL UM... AH HA HA...

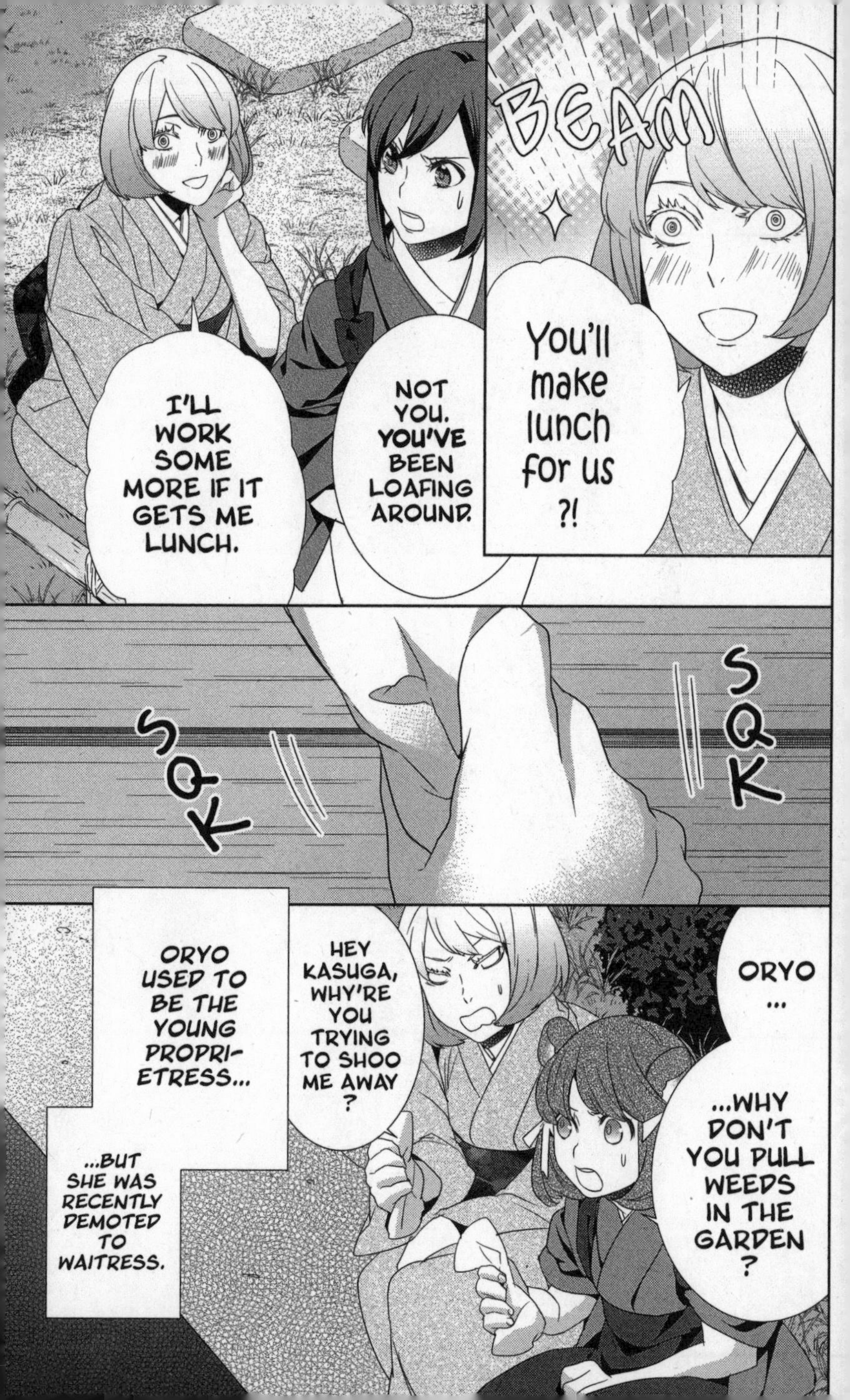
BEAM
You'll make lunch for us ?!
NOT YOU. YOU'VE BEEN LOAFING AROUND.
I'LL WORK SOME MORE IF IT GETS ME LUNCH.
SQK
SQK
ORYO ...
...WHY DON'T YOU PULL WEEDS IN THE GARDEN ?
HEY KASUGA, WHY'RE YOU TRYING TO SHOO ME AWAY ?
ORYO USED TO BE THE YOUNG PROPRI-ETRESS...
...BUT SHE WAS RECENTLY DEMOTED TO WAITRESS.

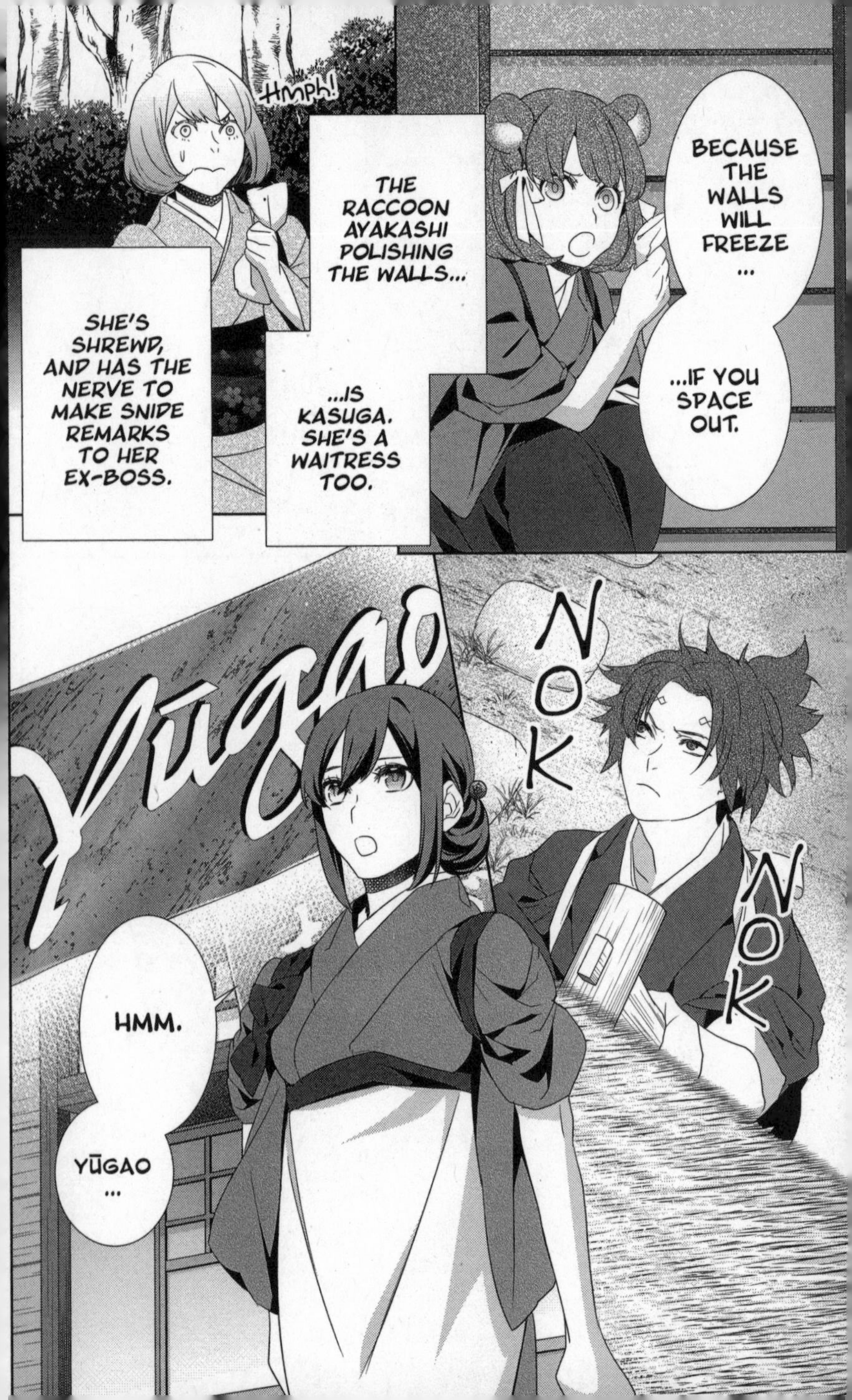
BECAUSE THE WALLS WILL FREEZE...
...IF YOU SPACE OUT.
THE RACCOON AYAKASHI POLISHING THE WALLS...
...IS KASUGA. SHE'S A WAITRESS TOO.
Hmph!
SHE'S SHREWD, AND HAS THE NERVE TO MAKE SNIDE REMARKS TO HER EX-BOSS.
NOK
NOK
Yūgao
HMM.
YŪGAO...

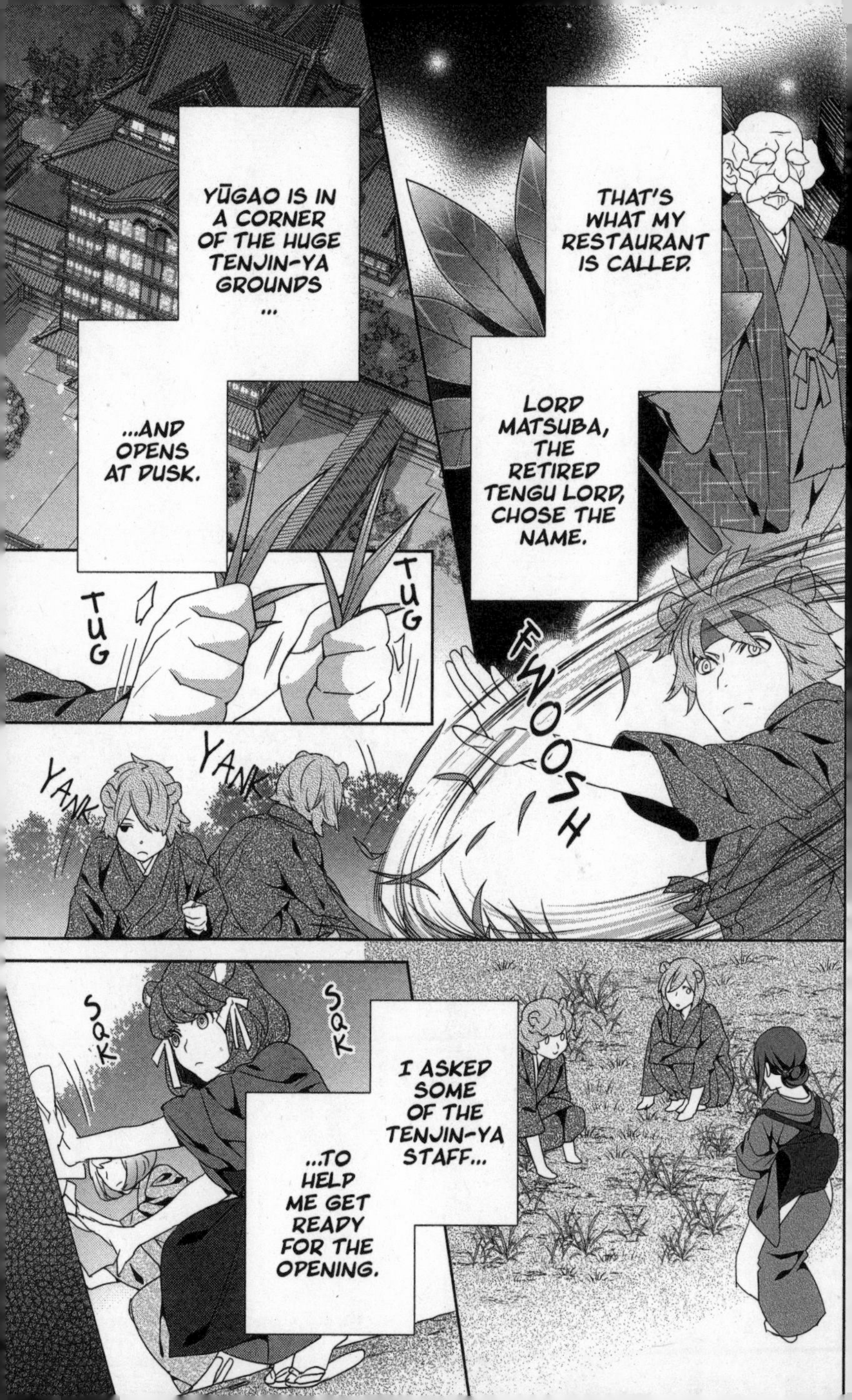
THAT'S WHAT MY RESTAURANT IS CALLED.
LORD MATSUBA, THE RETIRED TENGU LORD, CHOSE THE NAME.
YŪGAO IS IN A CORNER OF THE HUGE TENJIN-YA GROUNDS ...
...AND OPENS AT DUSK.
FWOOSH
TUG
TUG
YANK
YANK
I ASKED SOME OF THE TENJIN-YA STAFF...
...TO HELP ME GET READY FOR THE OPENING.
SQK
SQK

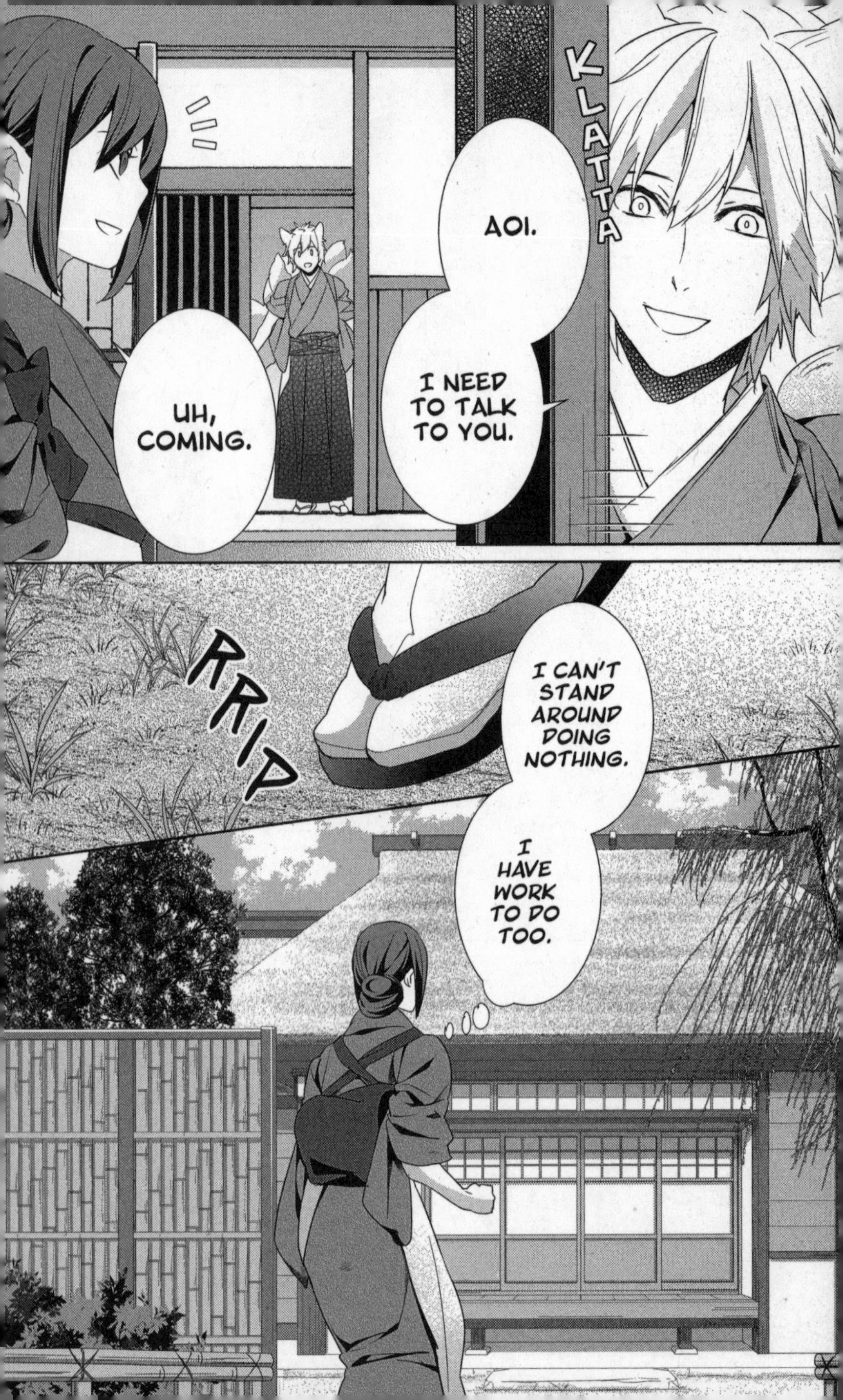
KLATTA
AOI.
I NEED TO TALK TO YOU.
UH, COMING.
RRIP
I CAN'T STAND AROUND DOING NOTHING.
I HAVE WORK TO DO TOO.

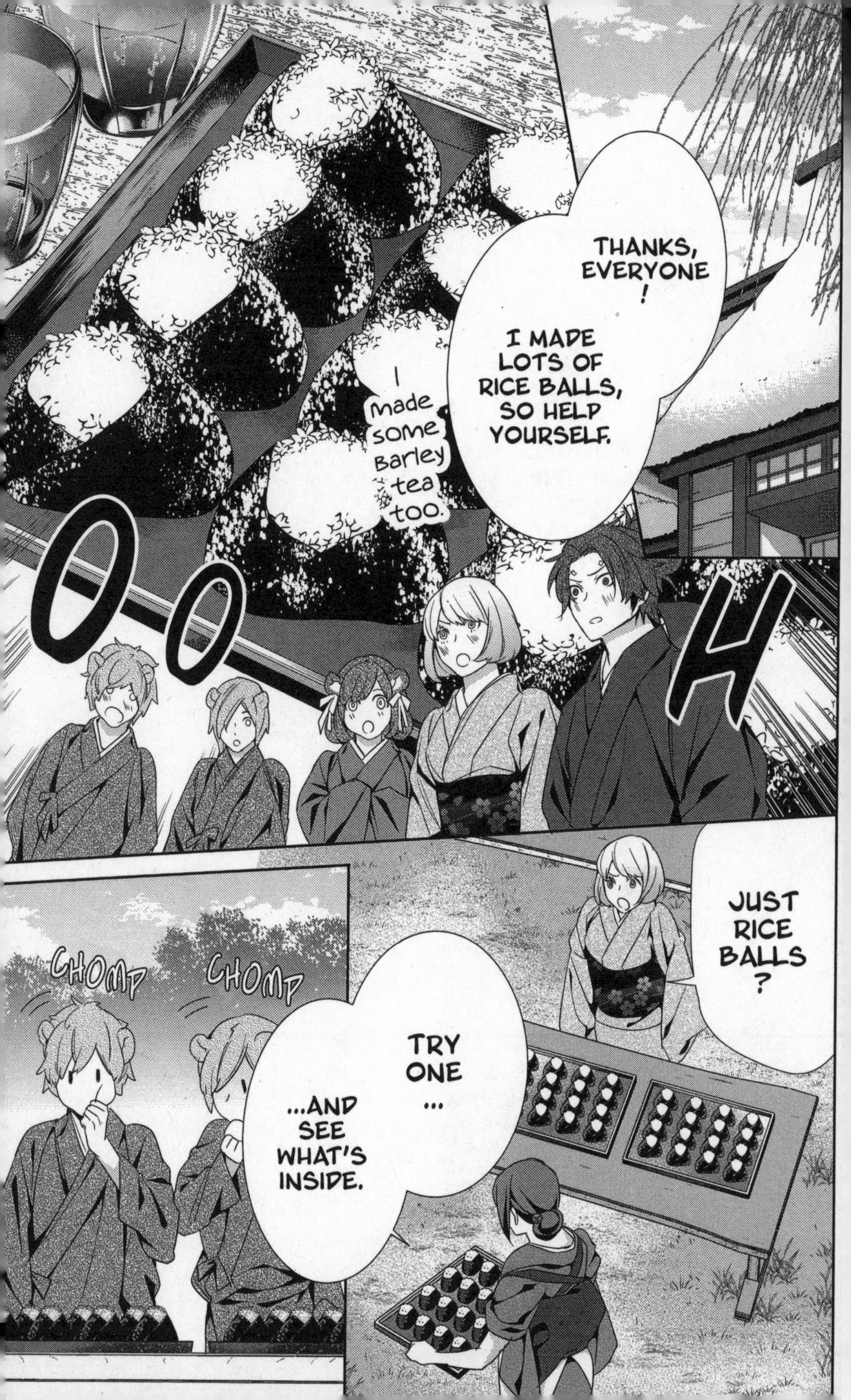
THANKS, EVERYONE!
I MADE LOTS OF RICE BALLS, SO HELP YOURSELF.
I made some Barley tea too.
OOOH
JUST RICE BALLS?
TRY ONE...
...AND SEE WHAT'S INSIDE.
CHOMP
CHOMP

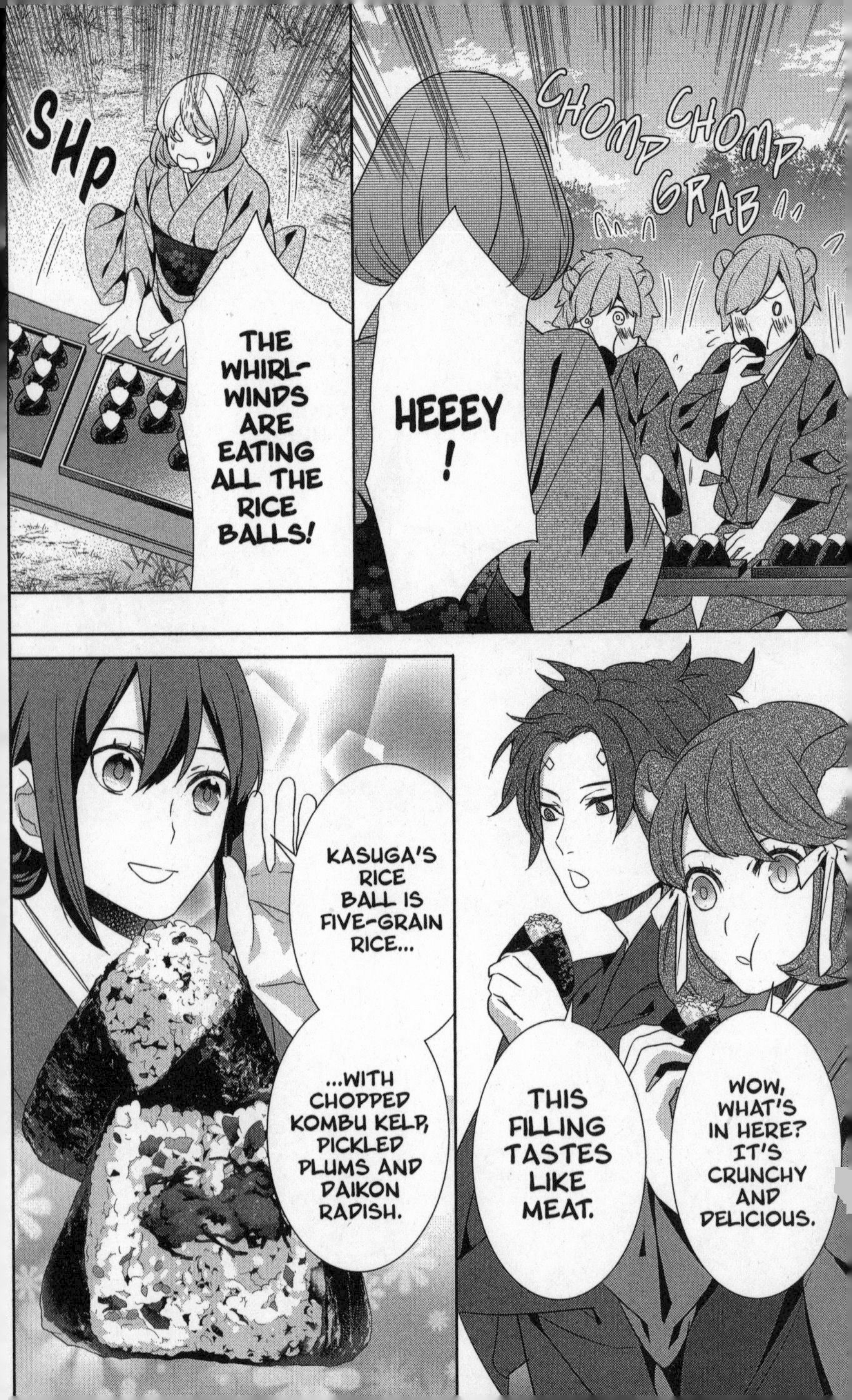
CHOMP CHOMP
GRAB
HEEEY!
SHP
THE WHIRL-WINDS ARE EATING ALL THE RICE BALLS!
WOW, WHAT'S IN HERE? IT'S CRUNCHY AND DELICIOUS.
THIS FILLING TASTES LIKE MEAT.
KASUGA'S RICE BALL IS FIVE-GRAIN RICE...
...WITH CHOPPED KOMBU KELP, PICKLED PLUMS AND DAIKON RADISH.

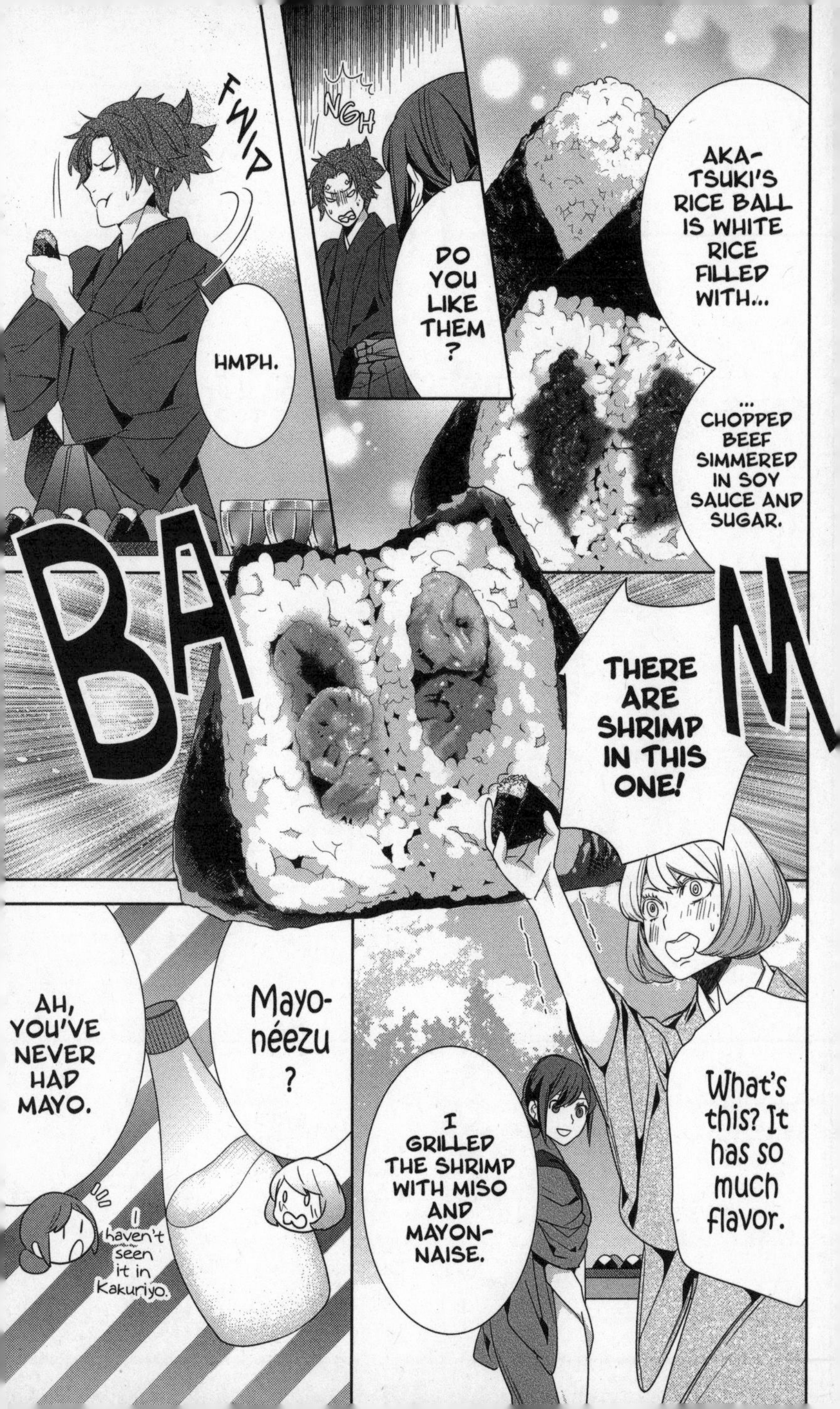
AKA-TSUKI'S RICE BALL IS WHITE RICE FILLED WITH...
...CHOPPED BEEF SIMMERED IN SOY SAUCE AND SUGAR.
NGH
DO YOU LIKE THEM?
FWIP
HMPH.
BAM
THERE ARE SHRIMP IN THIS ONE!
What's this? It has so much flavor.
I GRILLED THE SHRIMP WITH MISO AND MAYON-NAISE.
Mayo-néezu?
AH, YOU'VE NEVER HAD MAYO.
I haven't seen it in Kakuriyo.

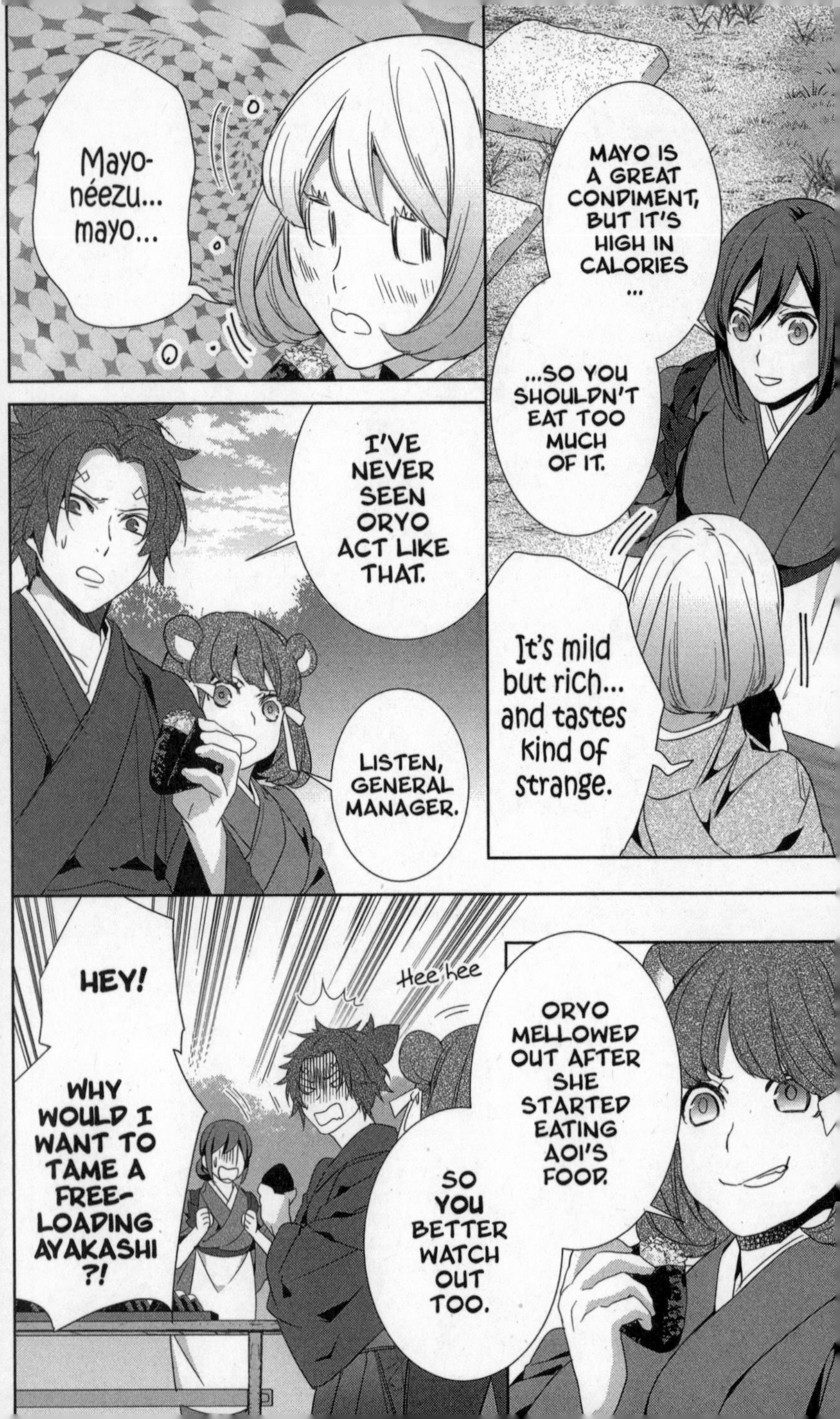
MAYO IS A GREAT CONDIMENT, BUT IT'S HIGH IN CALORIES...
...SO YOU SHOULDN'T EAT TOO MUCH OF IT.
It's mild but rich... and tastes kind of strange.
Mayo-néezu... mayo...
I'VE NEVER SEEN ORYO ACT LIKE THAT.
LISTEN, GENERAL MANAGER.
ORYO MELLOWED OUT AFTER SHE STARTED EATING AOI'S FOOD.
SO YOU BETTER WATCH OUT TOO.
Hee hee
HEY!
WHY WOULD I WANT TO TAME A FREE-LOADING AYAKASHI?!

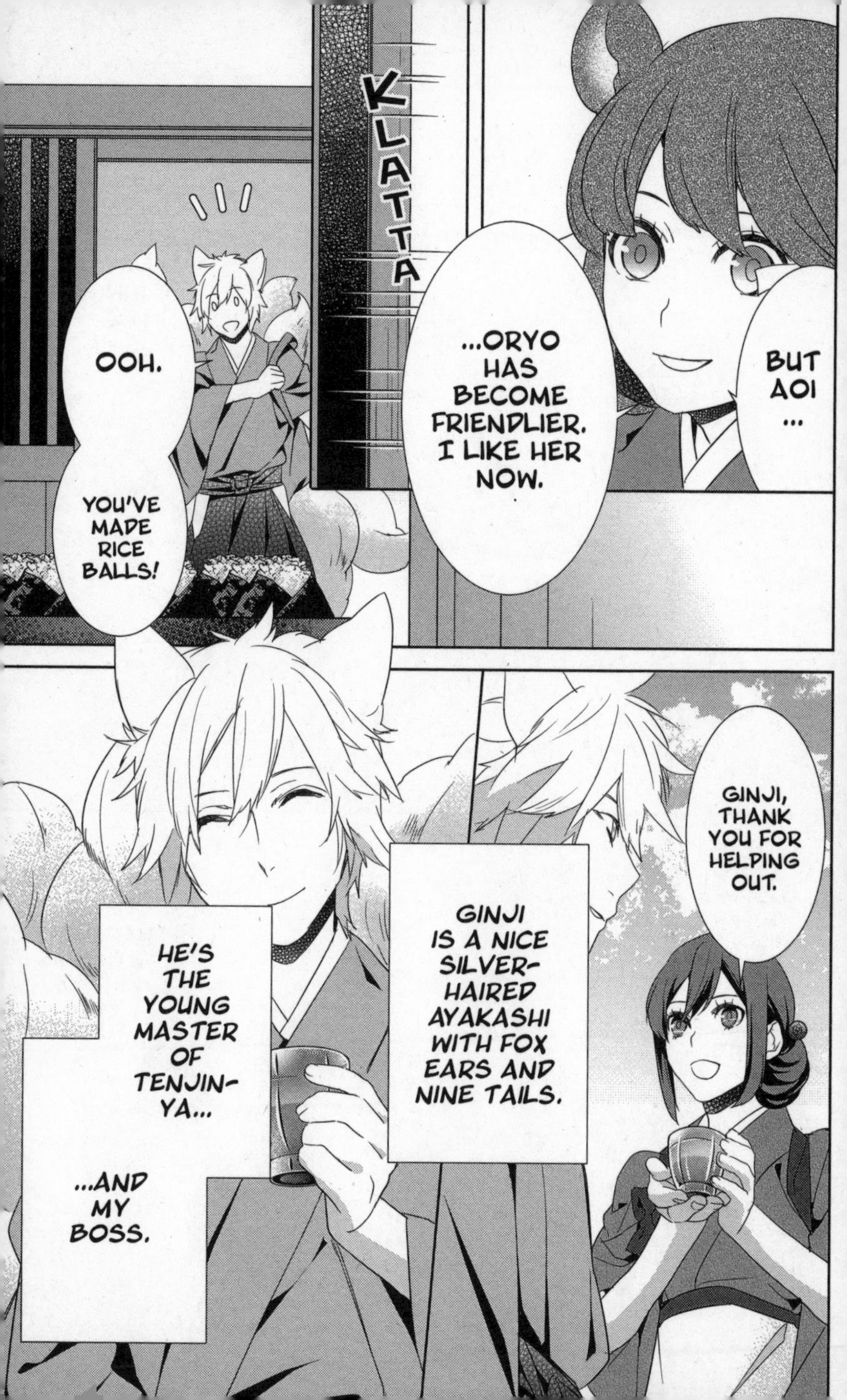
BUT AOI ...
...ORYO HAS BECOME FRIENDLIER. I LIKE HER NOW.
KLATTA
OOH.
YOU'VE MADE RICE BALLS!
GINJI, THANK YOU FOR HELPING OUT.
GINJI IS A NICE SILVER-HAIRED AYAKASHI WITH FOX EARS AND NINE TAILS.
HE'S THE YOUNG MASTER OF TENJIN-YA...
...AND MY BOSS.

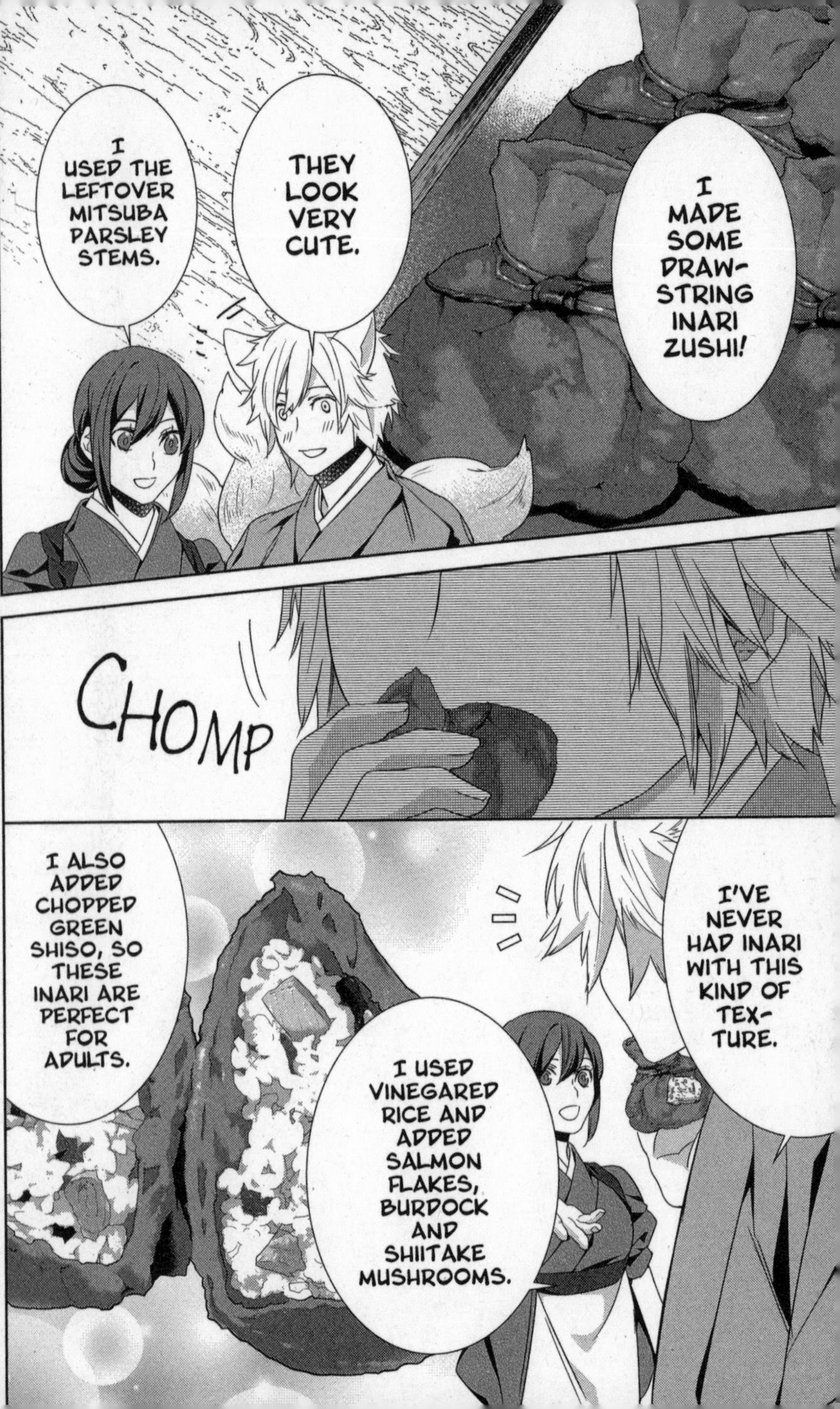
I MADE SOME DRAW-STRING INARI ZUSHI!
THEY LOOK VERY CUTE.
I USED THE LEFTOVER MITSUBA PARSLEY STEMS.
CHOMP
I'VE NEVER HAD INARI WITH THIS KIND OF TEX-TURE.
I USED VINEGARED RICE AND ADDED SALMON FLAKES, BURDOCK AND SHIITAKE MUSHROOMS.
I ALSO ADDED CHOPPED GREEN SHISO, SO THESE INARI ARE PERFECT FOR ADULTS.

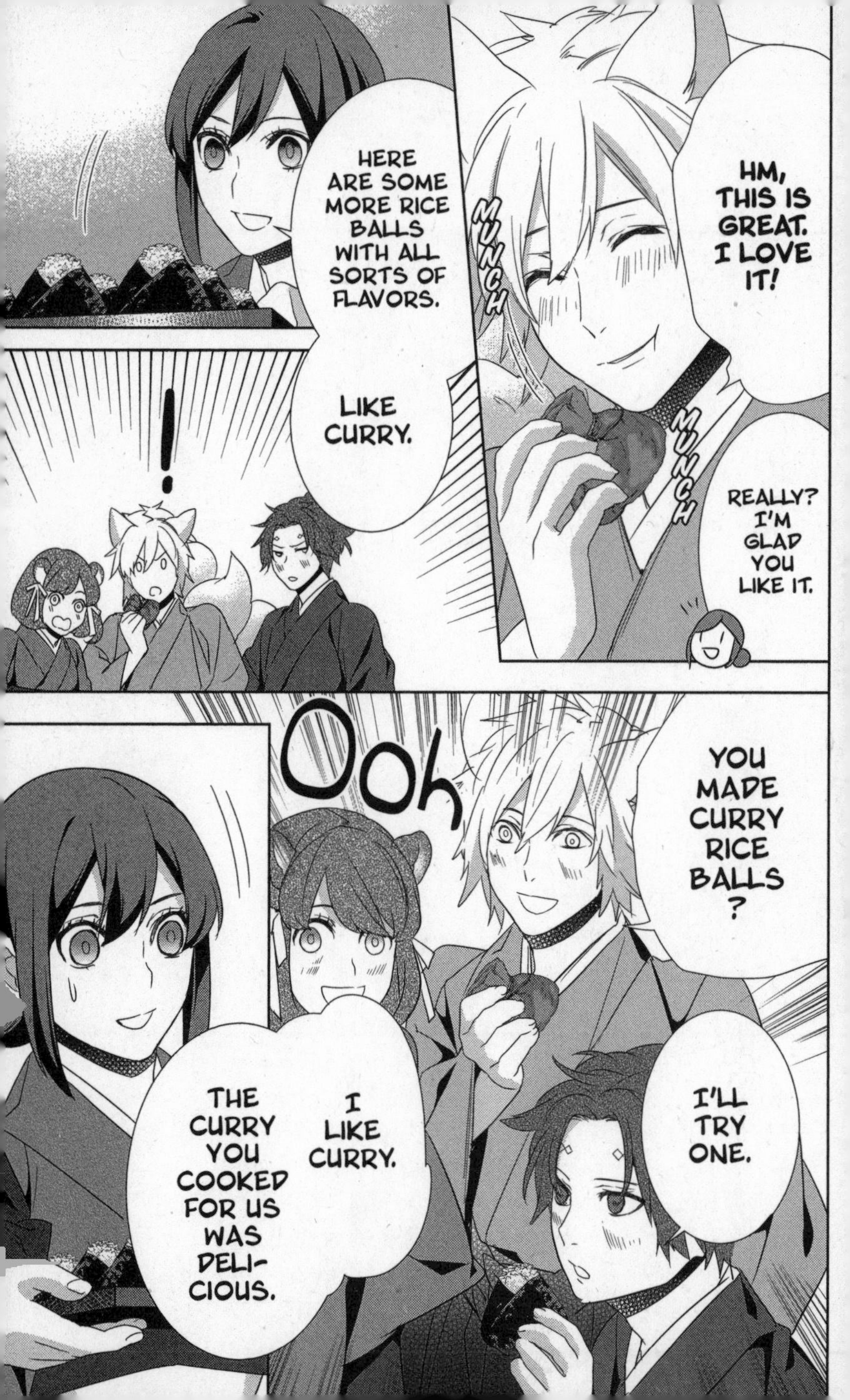
HM, THIS IS GREAT. I LOVE IT!
MUNCH
MUNCH
REALLY? I'M GLAD YOU LIKE IT.
HERE ARE SOME MORE RICE BALLS WITH ALL SORTS OF FLAVORS.
LIKE CURRY.
!
YOU MADE CURRY RICE BALLS?
Ooh
I'LL TRY ONE.
I LIKE CURRY.
THE CURRY YOU COOKED FOR US WAS DELICIOUS.

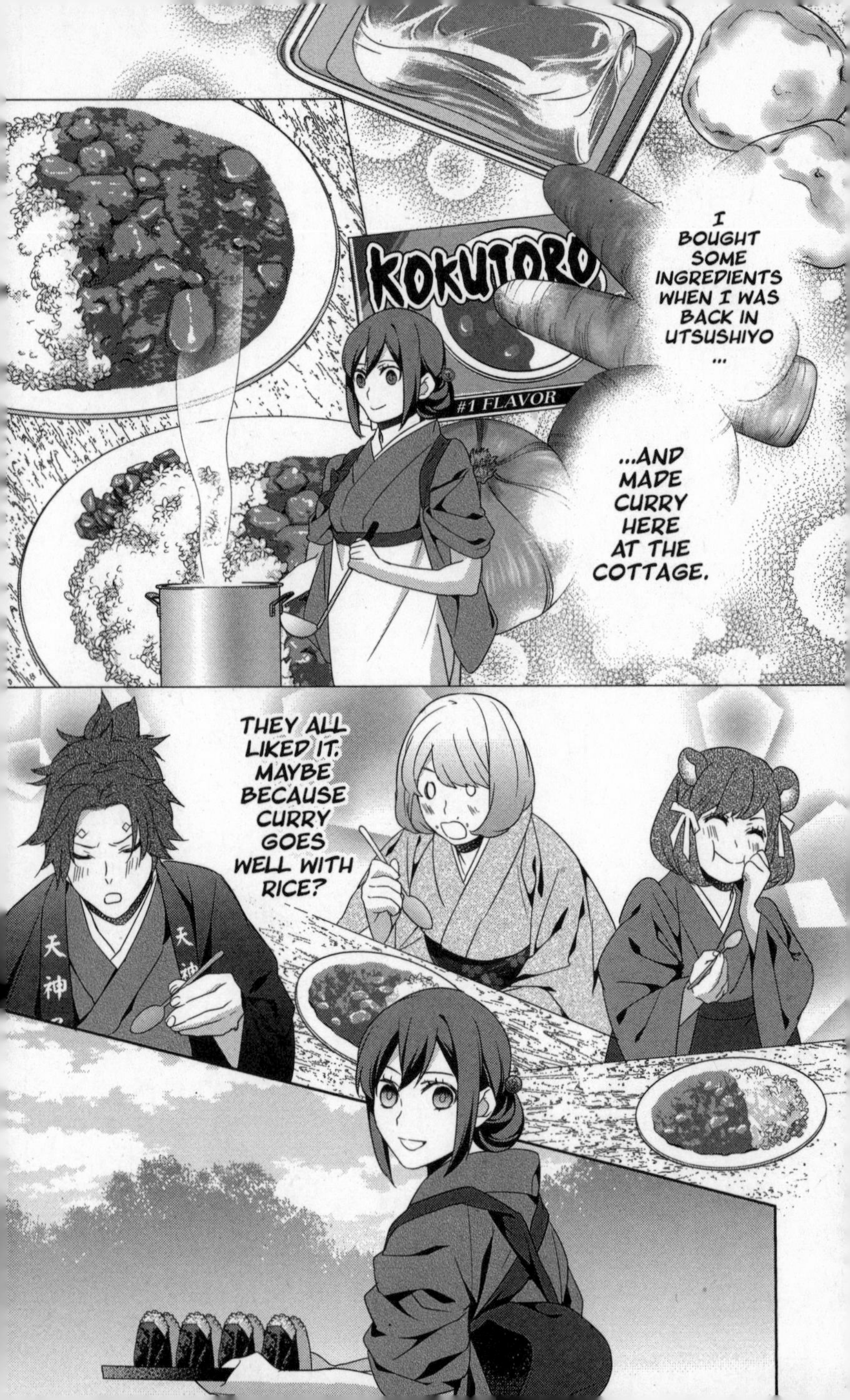
KOKUTORO
#1 FLAVOR
I BOUGHT SOME INGREDIENTS WHEN I WAS BACK IN UTSUSHIYO...
...AND MADE CURRY HERE AT THE COTTAGE.
THEY ALL LIKED IT. MAYBE BECAUSE CURRY GOES WELL WITH RICE?
天神
天神

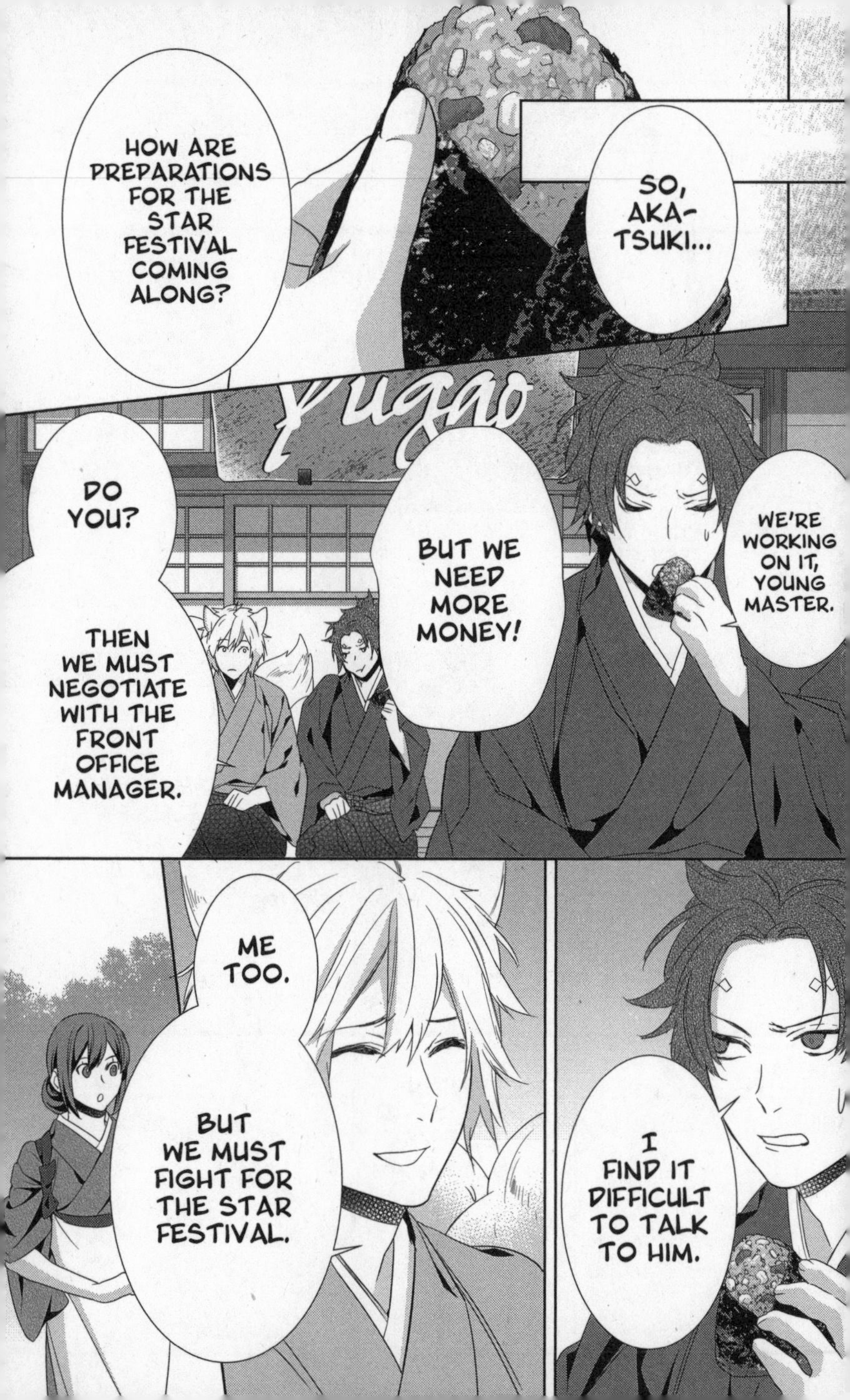
SO, AKA-TSUKI...
HOW ARE PREPARATIONS FOR THE STAR FESTIVAL COMING ALONG?
Yugao
WE'RE WORKING ON IT, YOUNG MASTER.
BUT WE NEED MORE MONEY!
DO YOU?
THEN WE MUST NEGOTIATE WITH THE FRONT OFFICE MANAGER.
I FIND IT DIFFICULT TO TALK TO HIM.
ME TOO.
BUT WE MUST FIGHT FOR THE STAR FESTIVAL.

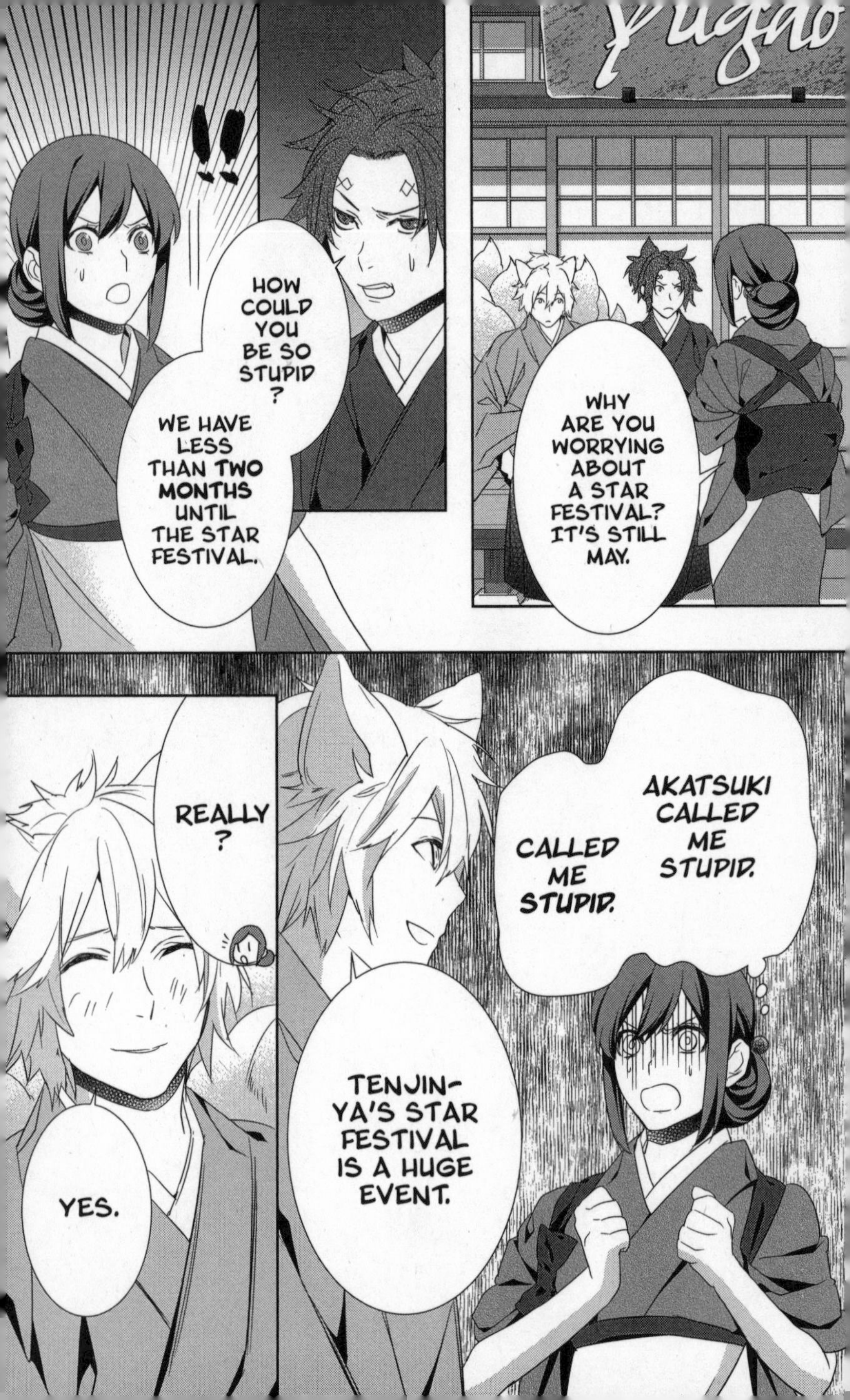
Yugao
WHY ARE YOU WORRYING ABOUT A STAR FESTIVAL? IT'S STILL MAY.
HOW COULD YOU BE SO STUPID?
WE HAVE LESS THAN TWO MONTHS UNTIL THE STAR FESTIVAL.
!!
AKATSUKI CALLED ME STUPID.
CALLED ME STUPID.
TENJIN-YA'S STAR FESTIVAL IS A HUGE EVENT.
REALLY?
YES.

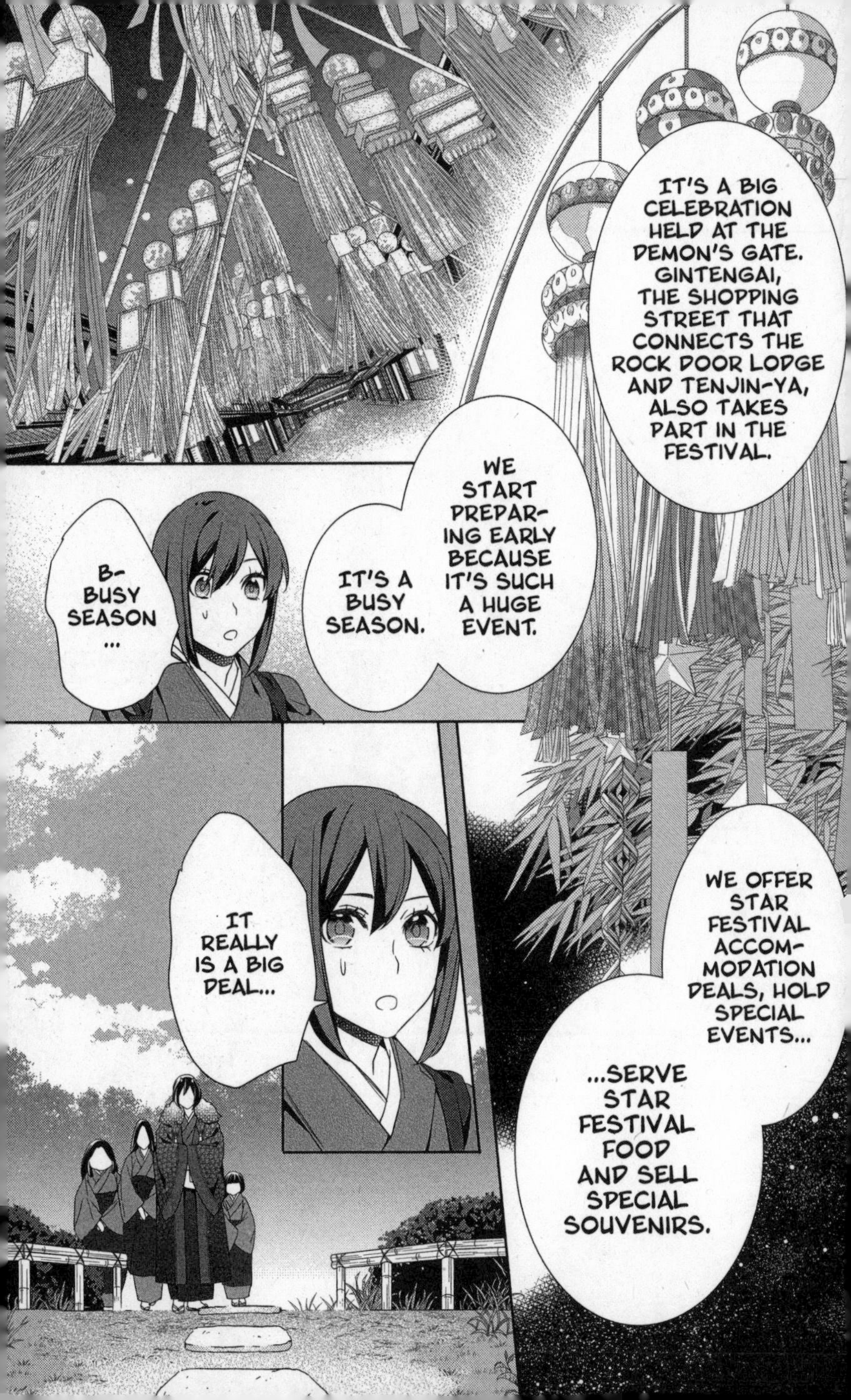
IT'S A BIG CELEBRATION HELD AT THE DEMON'S GATE. GINTENGAI, THE SHOPPING STREET THAT CONNECTS THE ROCK DOOR LODGE AND TENJIN-YA, ALSO TAKES PART IN THE FESTIVAL.
WE START PREPARING EARLY BECAUSE IT'S SUCH A HUGE EVENT.
IT'S A BUSY SEASON.
B-BUSY SEASON...
WE OFFER STAR FESTIVAL ACCOMMODATION DEALS, HOLD SPECIAL EVENTS...
...SERVE STAR FESTIVAL FOOD AND SELL SPECIAL SOUVENIRS.
IT REALLY IS A BIG DEAL...

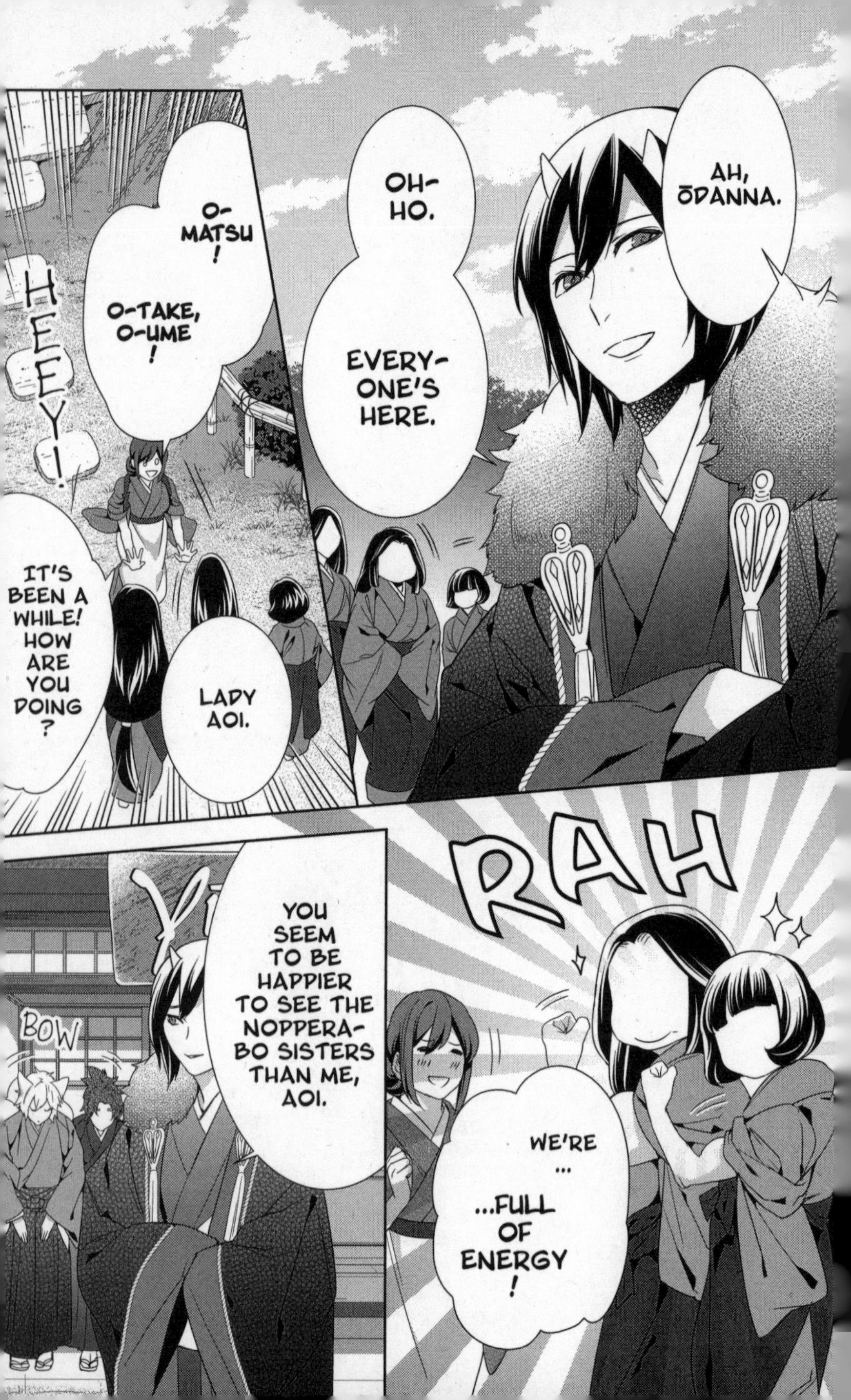
AH, ŌDANNA.
OH-HO.
EVERY-ONE'S HERE.
O-MATSU!
O-TAKE, O-UME!
HEEY!
IT'S BEEN A WHILE! HOW ARE YOU DOING?
LADY AOI.
RAH
WE'RE...
...FULL OF ENERGY!
YOU SEEM TO BE HAPPIER TO SEE THE NOPPERA-BO SISTERS THAN ME, AOI.
BOW

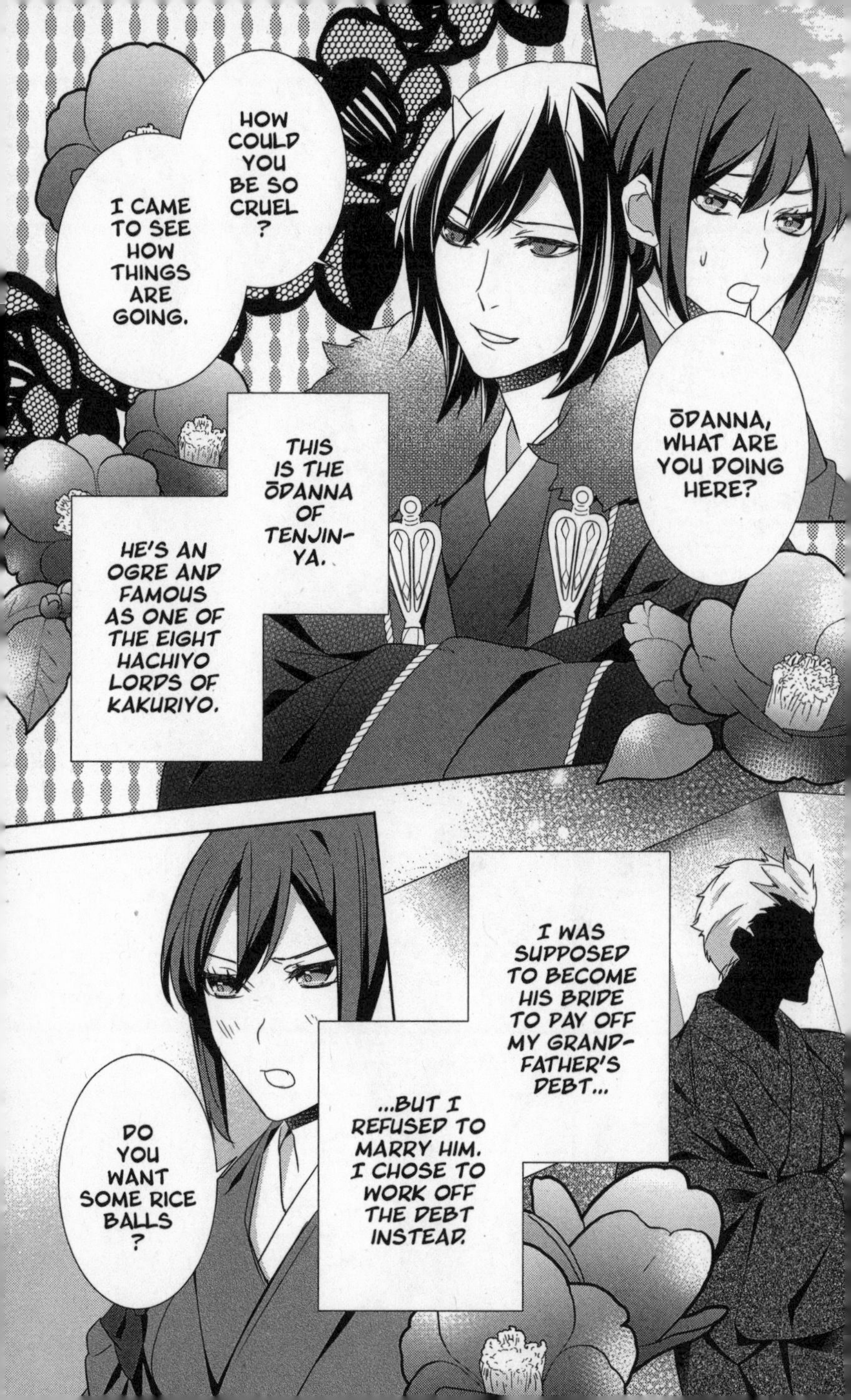
ŌDANNA, WHAT ARE YOU DOING HERE?
HOW COULD YOU BE SO CRUEL?
I CAME TO SEE HOW THINGS ARE GOING.
THIS IS THE ŌDANNA OF TENJIN-YA.
HE'S AN OGRE AND FAMOUS AS ONE OF THE EIGHT HACHIYO LORDS OF KAKURIYO.
I WAS SUPPOSED TO BECOME HIS BRIDE TO PAY OFF MY GRAND-FATHER'S DEBT...
...BUT I REFUSED TO MARRY HIM. I CHOSE TO WORK OFF THE DEBT INSTEAD.
DO YOU WANT SOME RICE BALLS?

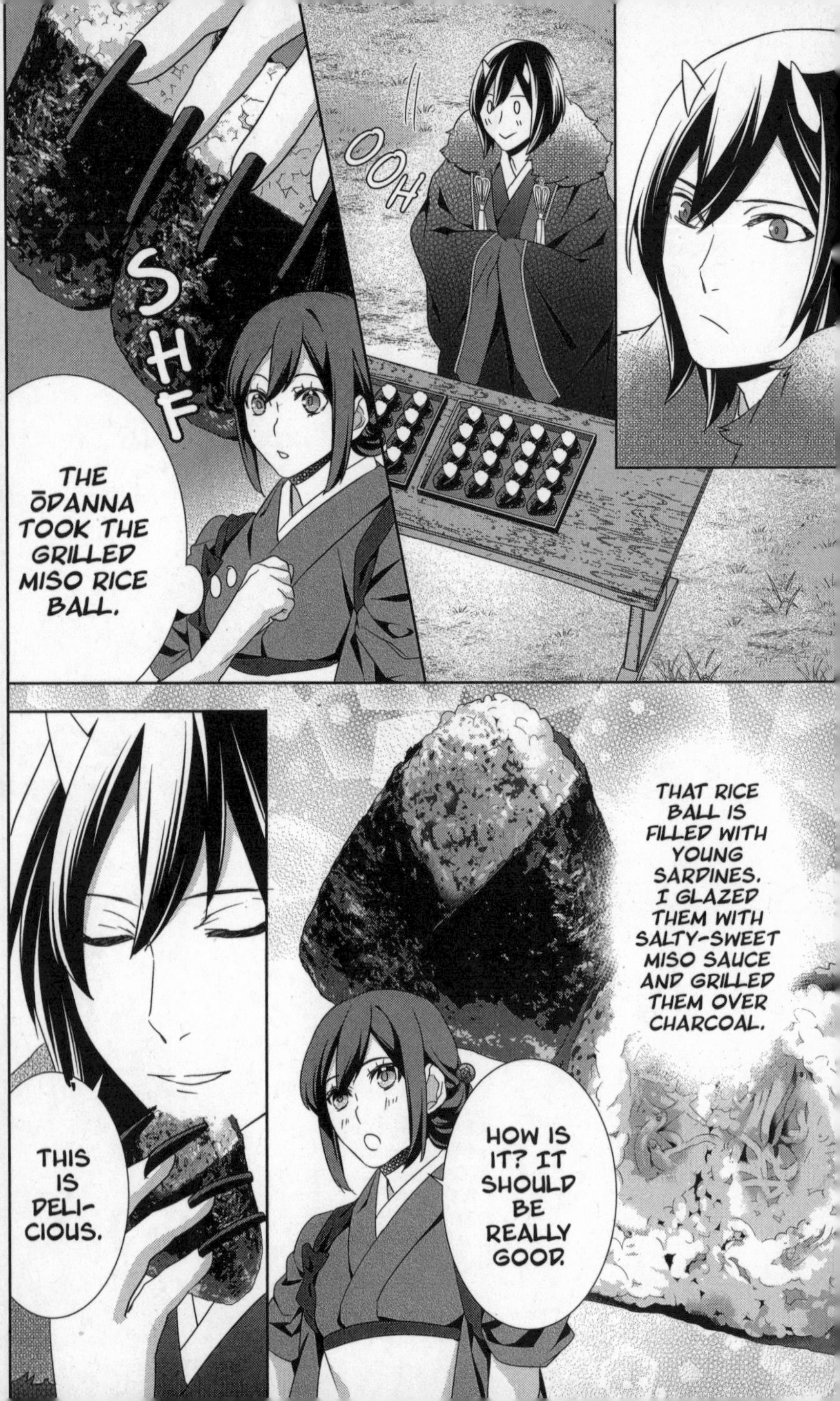
OOH
SHF
THE ŌDANNA TOOK THE GRILLED MISO RICE BALL.
THAT RICE BALL IS FILLED WITH YOUNG SARDINES. I GLAZED THEM WITH SALTY-SWEET MISO SAUCE AND GRILLED THEM OVER CHARCOAL.
HOW IS IT? IT SHOULD BE REALLY GOOD.
THIS IS DELI-CIOUS.

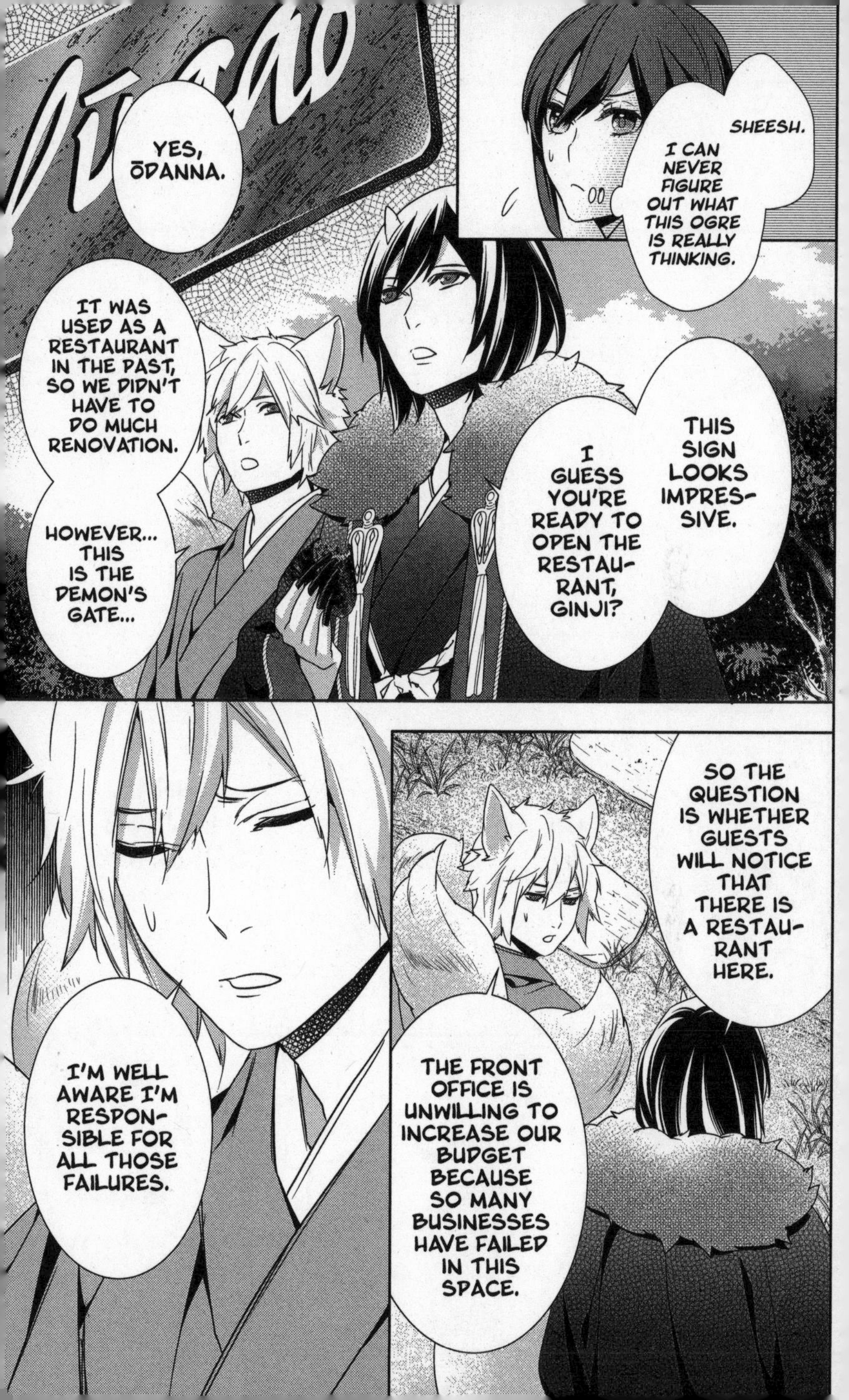
SHEESH.
I CAN NEVER FIGURE OUT WHAT THIS OGRE IS REALLY THINKING.
THIS SIGN LOOKS IMPRES-SIVE.
I GUESS YOU'RE READY TO OPEN THE RESTAU-RANT, GINJI?
YES, ŌDANNA.
IT WAS USED AS A RESTAURANT IN THE PAST, SO WE DIDN'T HAVE TO DO MUCH RENOVATION.
HOWEVER... THIS IS THE DEMON'S GATE...
SO THE QUESTION IS WHETHER GUESTS WILL NOTICE THAT THERE IS A RESTAU-RANT HERE.
THE FRONT OFFICE IS UNWILLING TO INCREASE OUR BUDGET BECAUSE SO MANY BUSINESSES HAVE FAILED IN THIS SPACE.
I'M WELL AWARE I'M RESPON-SIBLE FOR ALL THOSE FAILURES.

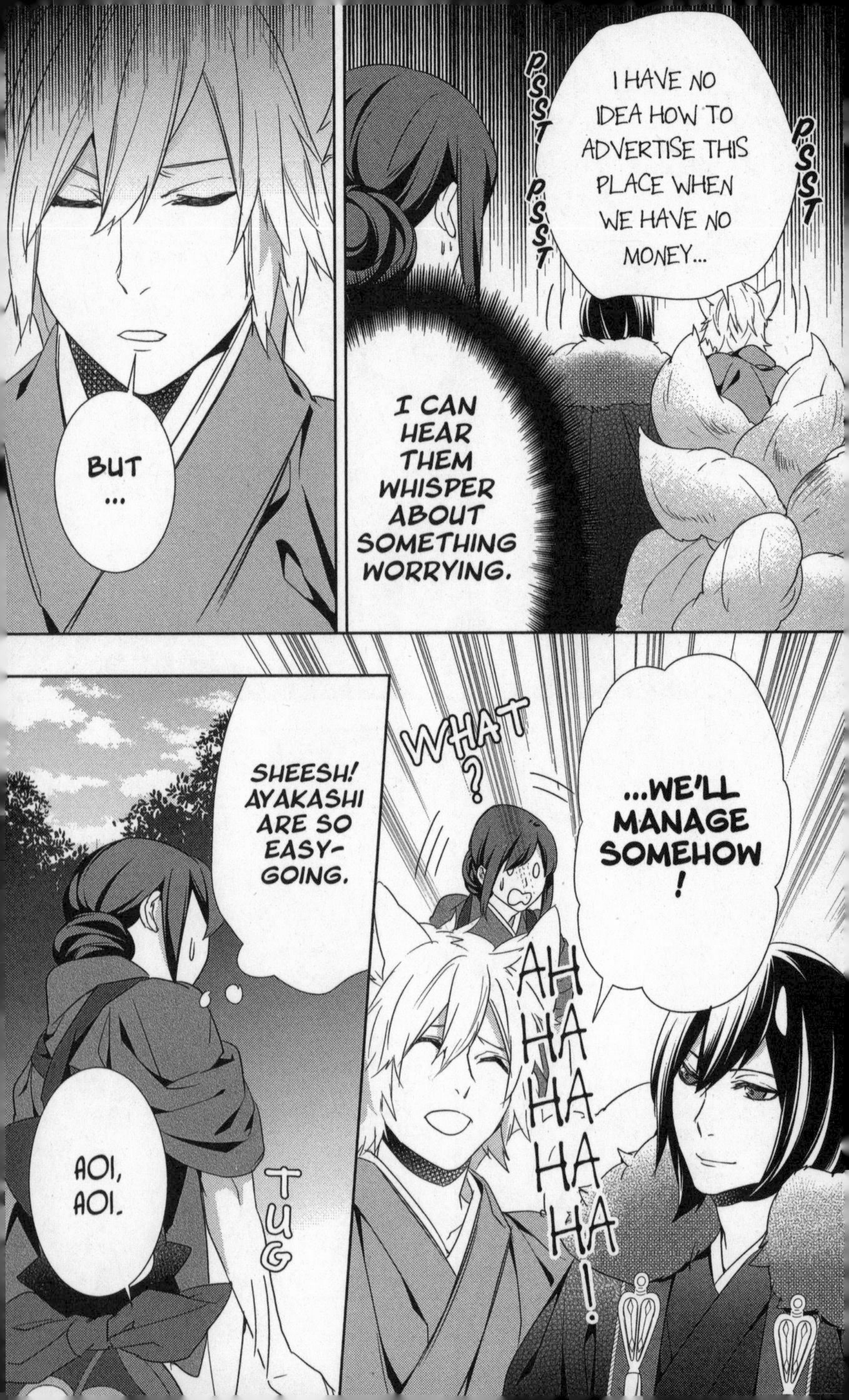
PSST PSST
I HAVE NO IDEA HOW TO ADVERTISE THIS PLACE WHEN WE HAVE NO MONEY...
PSST PSST
I CAN HEAR THEM WHISPER ABOUT SOMETHING WORRYING.
BUT ...
...WE'LL MANAGE SOMEHOW!
WHAT?
AH HA HA HA HA HA HA!
SHEESH! AYAKASHI ARE SO EASY-GOING.
TUG
AOI, AOI.

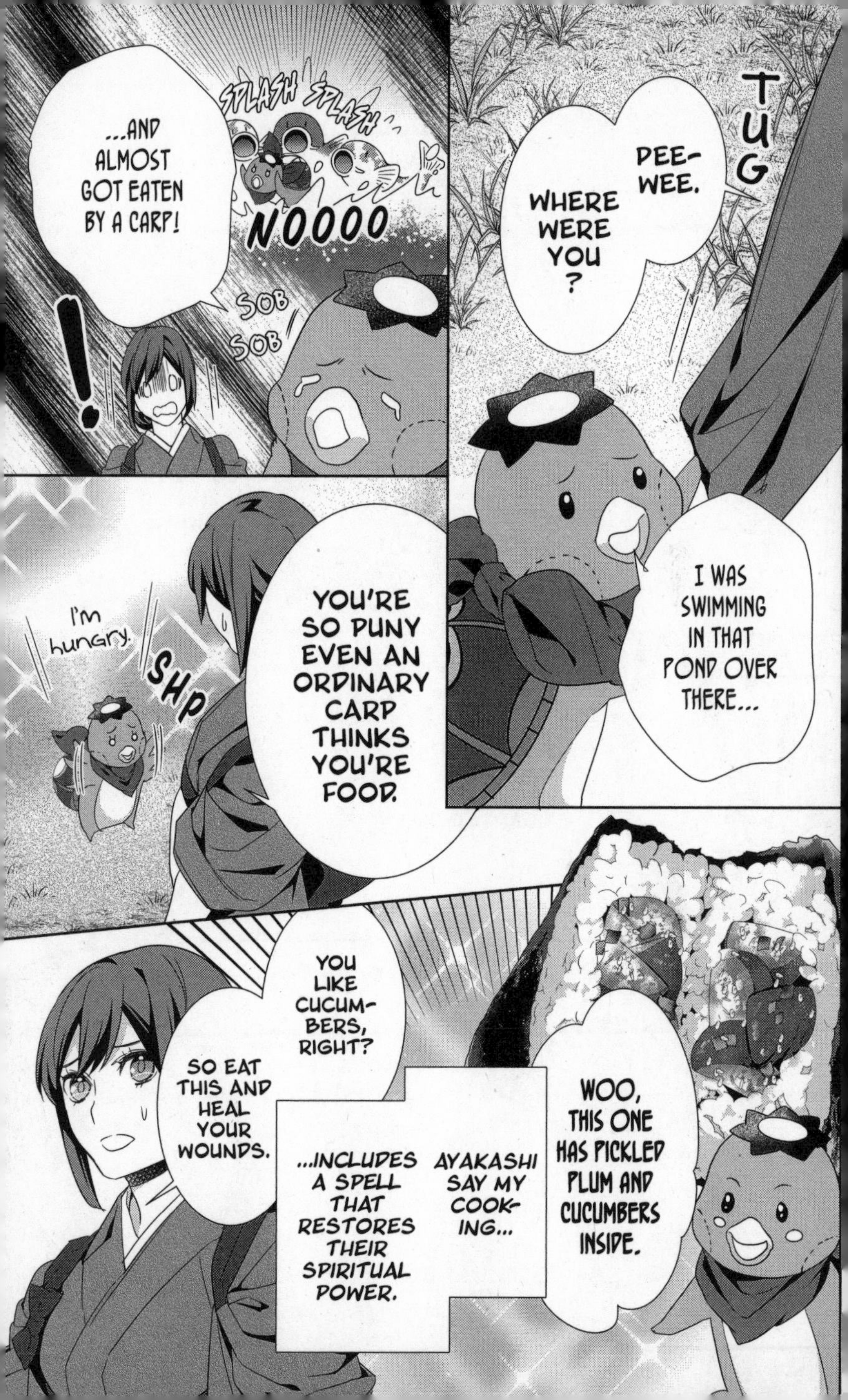
TUG
PEE-WEE.
WHERE WERE YOU?
I WAS SWIMMING IN THAT POND OVER THERE...
...AND ALMOST GOT EATEN BY A CARP!
SPLASH SPLASH
NOOOO
SOB SOB
!
YOU'RE SO PUNY EVEN AN ORDINARY CARP THINKS YOU'RE FOOD.
SHP
I'm hungry.
WOO, THIS ONE HAS PICKLED PLUM AND CUCUMBERS INSIDE.
AYAKASHI SAY MY COOK-ING...
...INCLUDES A SPELL THAT RESTORES THEIR SPIRITUAL POWER.
YOU LIKE CUCUM-BERS, RIGHT?
SO EAT THIS AND HEAL YOUR WOUNDS.

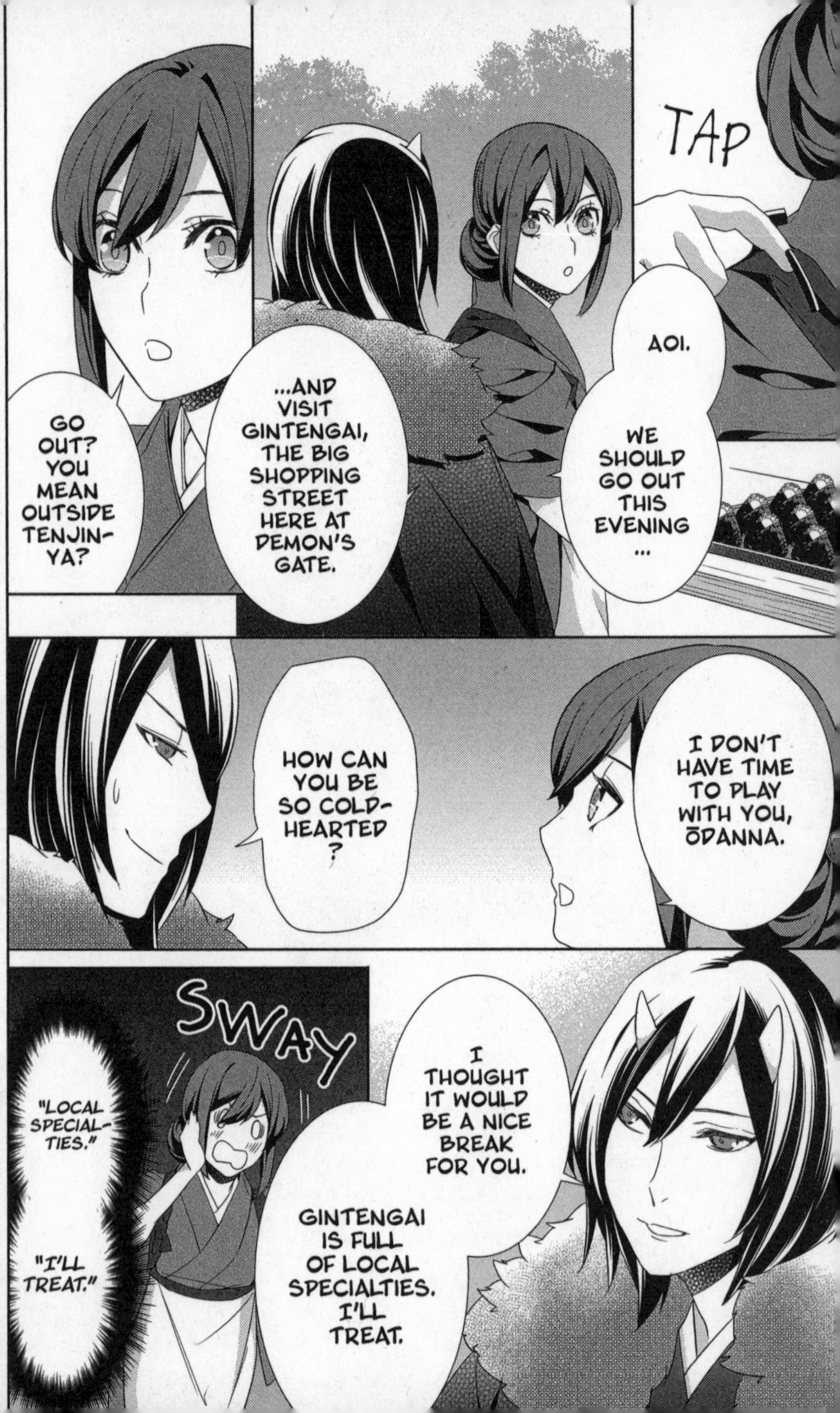
TAP
AOI.
WE SHOULD GO OUT THIS EVENING...
...AND VISIT GINTENGAI, THE BIG SHOPPING STREET HERE AT DEMON'S GATE.
GO OUT? YOU MEAN OUTSIDE TENJIN-YA?
I DON'T HAVE TIME TO PLAY WITH YOU, ŌDANNA.
HOW CAN YOU BE SO COLD-HEARTED?
I THOUGHT IT WOULD BE A NICE BREAK FOR YOU.
GINTENGAI IS FULL OF LOCAL SPECIALTIES. I'LL TREAT.
SWAY
"LOCAL SPECIAL-TIES."
"I'LL TREAT."

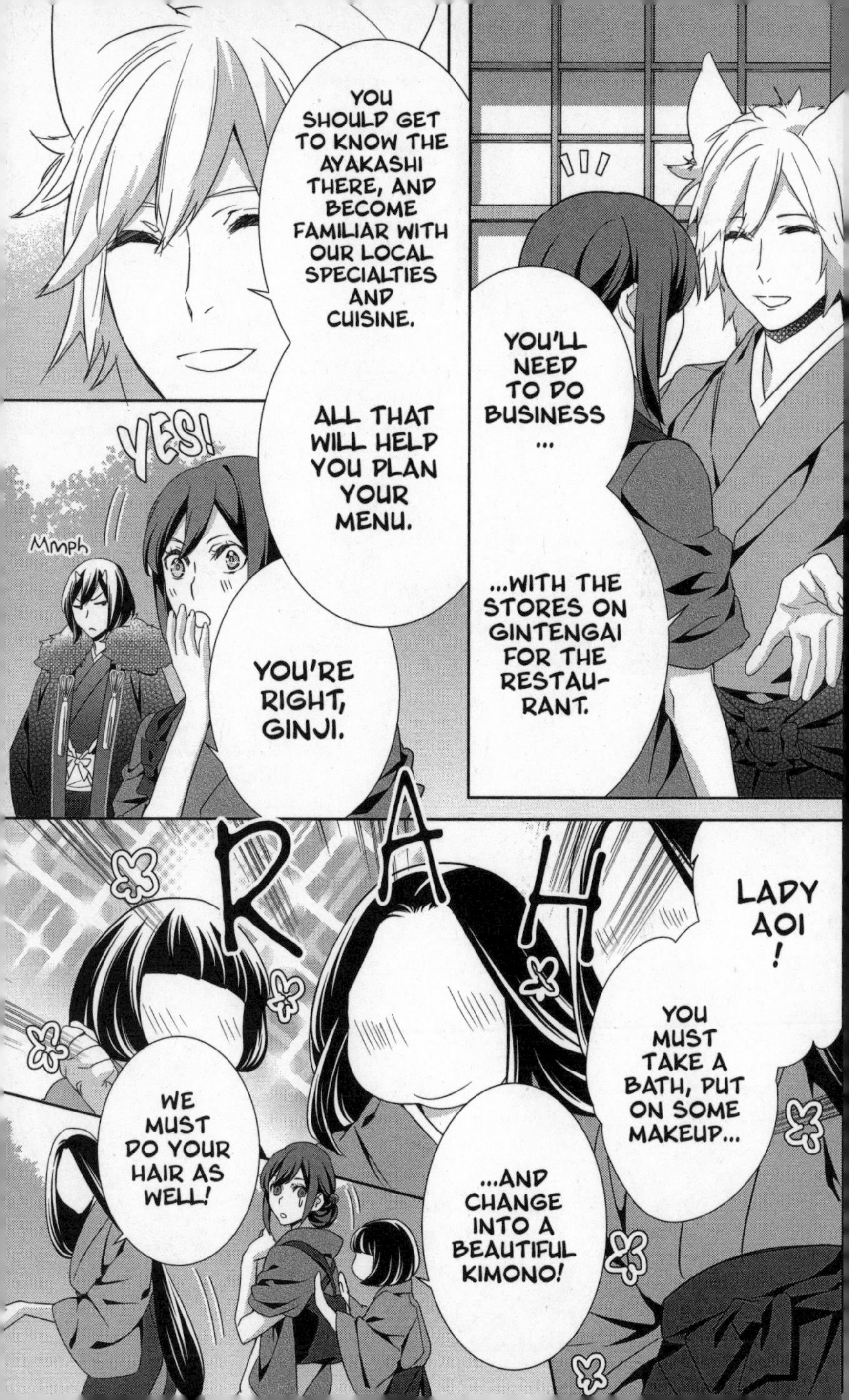

YOU'LL NEED TO DO BUSINESS...
...WITH THE STORES ON GINTENGAI FOR THE RESTAU-RANT.
YOU SHOULD GET TO KNOW THE AYAKASHI THERE, AND BECOME FAMILIAR WITH OUR LOCAL SPECIALTIES AND CUISINE.
ALL THAT WILL HELP YOU PLAN YOUR MENU.
YES!
YOU'RE RIGHT, GINJI.
Mmph
RAH
LADY AOI!
YOU MUST TAKE A BATH, PUT ON SOME MAKEUP...
...AND CHANGE INTO A BEAUTIFUL KIMONO!
WE MUST DO YOUR HAIR AS WELL!

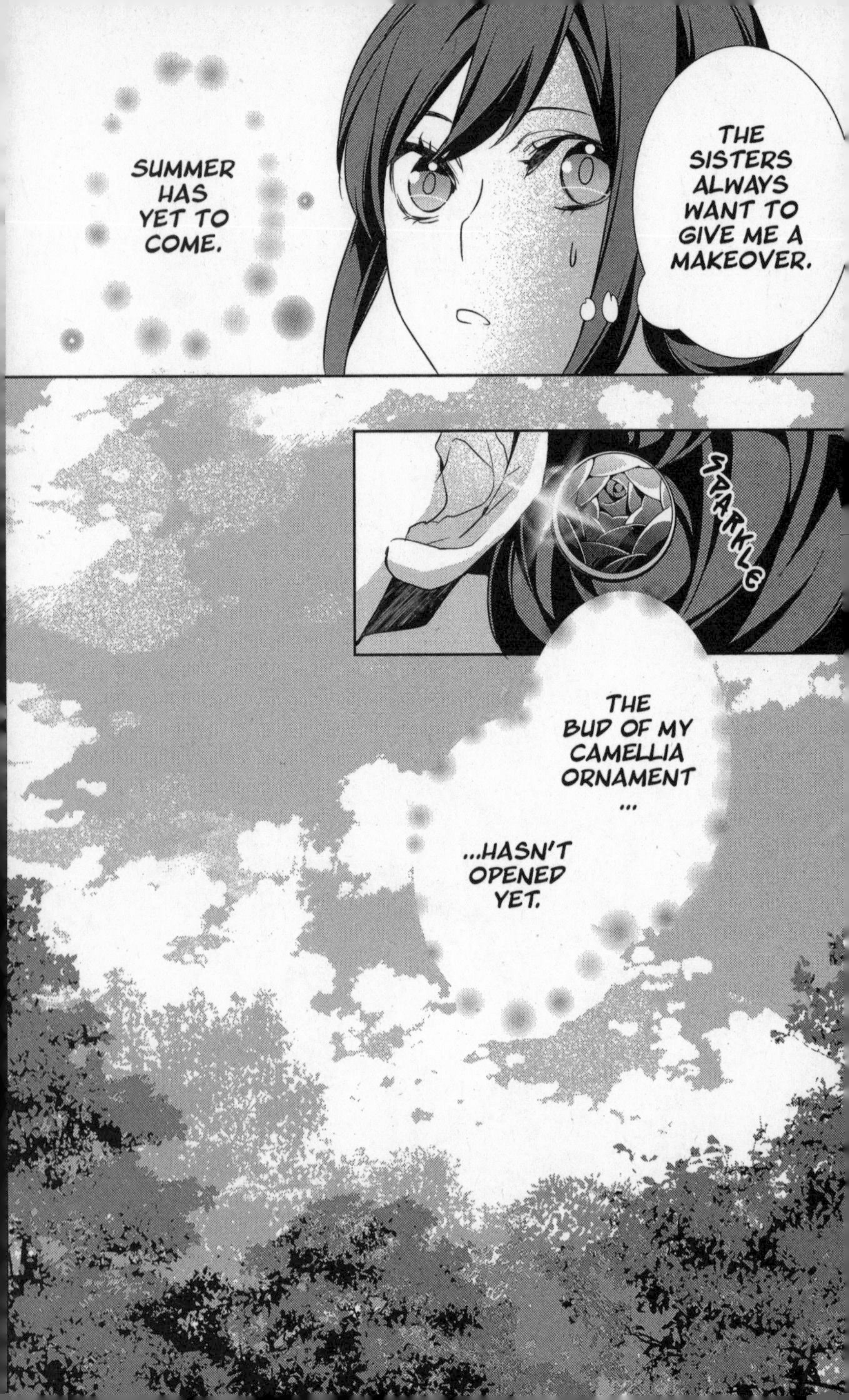
THE SISTERS ALWAYS WANT TO GIVE ME A MAKEOVER.
SUMMER HAS YET TO COME.
SPARKLE
THE BUD OF MY CAMELLIA ORNAMENT ...
...HASN'T OPENED YET.

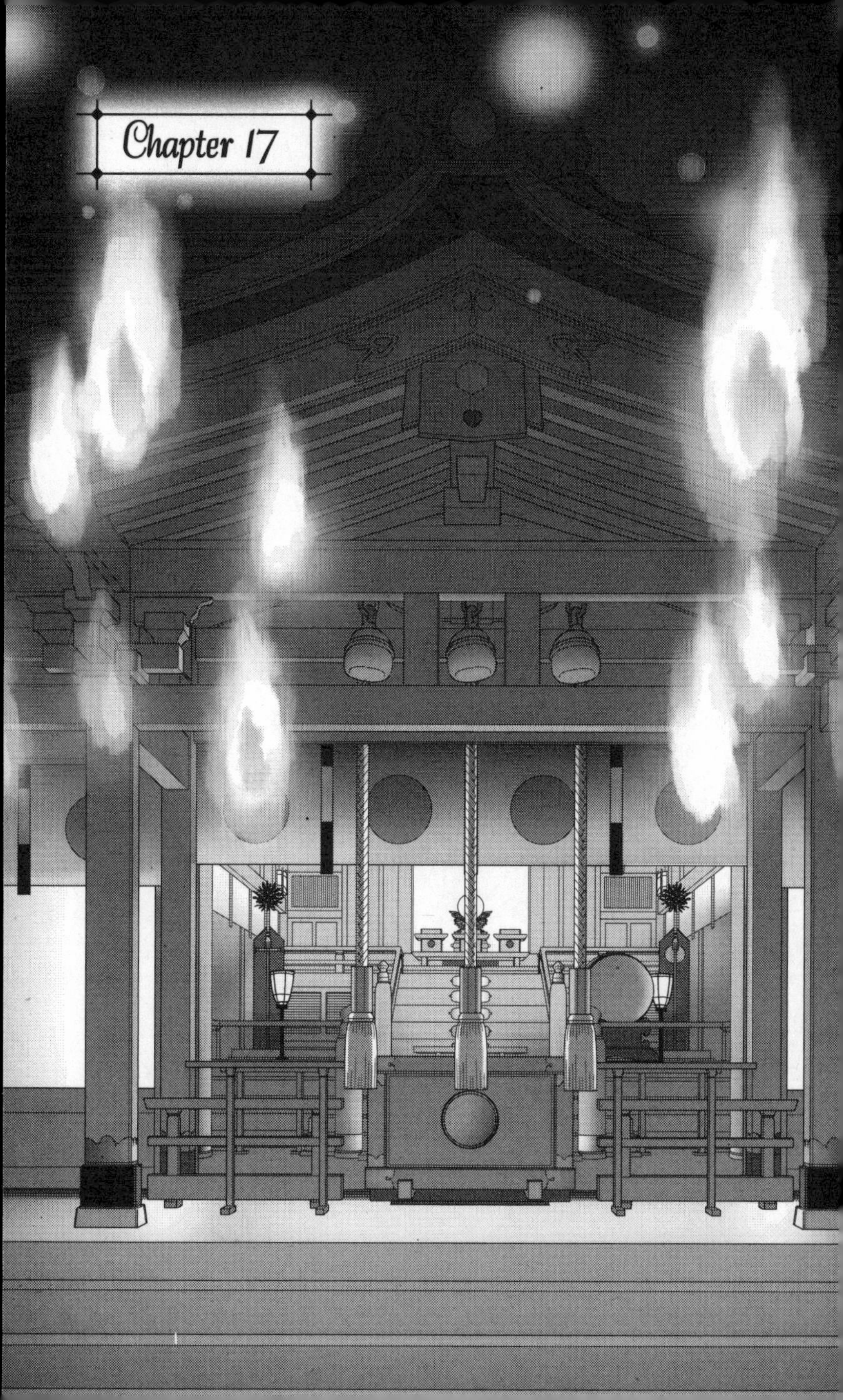
Chapter 17

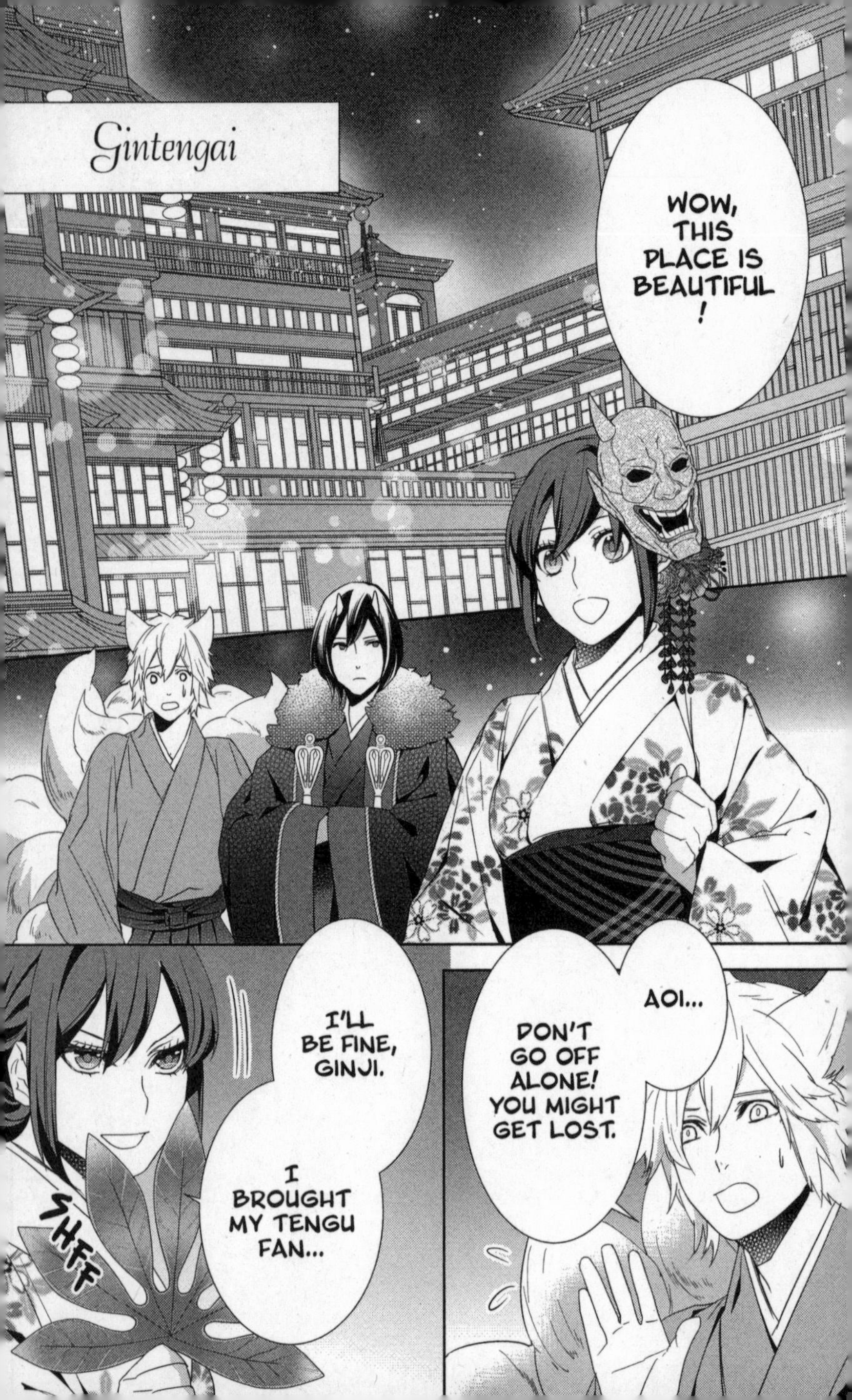

WOW, THIS PLACE IS BEAUTIFUL!
Gintengai
AOI...
DON'T GO OFF ALONE! YOU MIGHT GET LOST.
I'LL BE FINE, GINJI.
I BROUGHT MY TENGU FAN...
SHFF

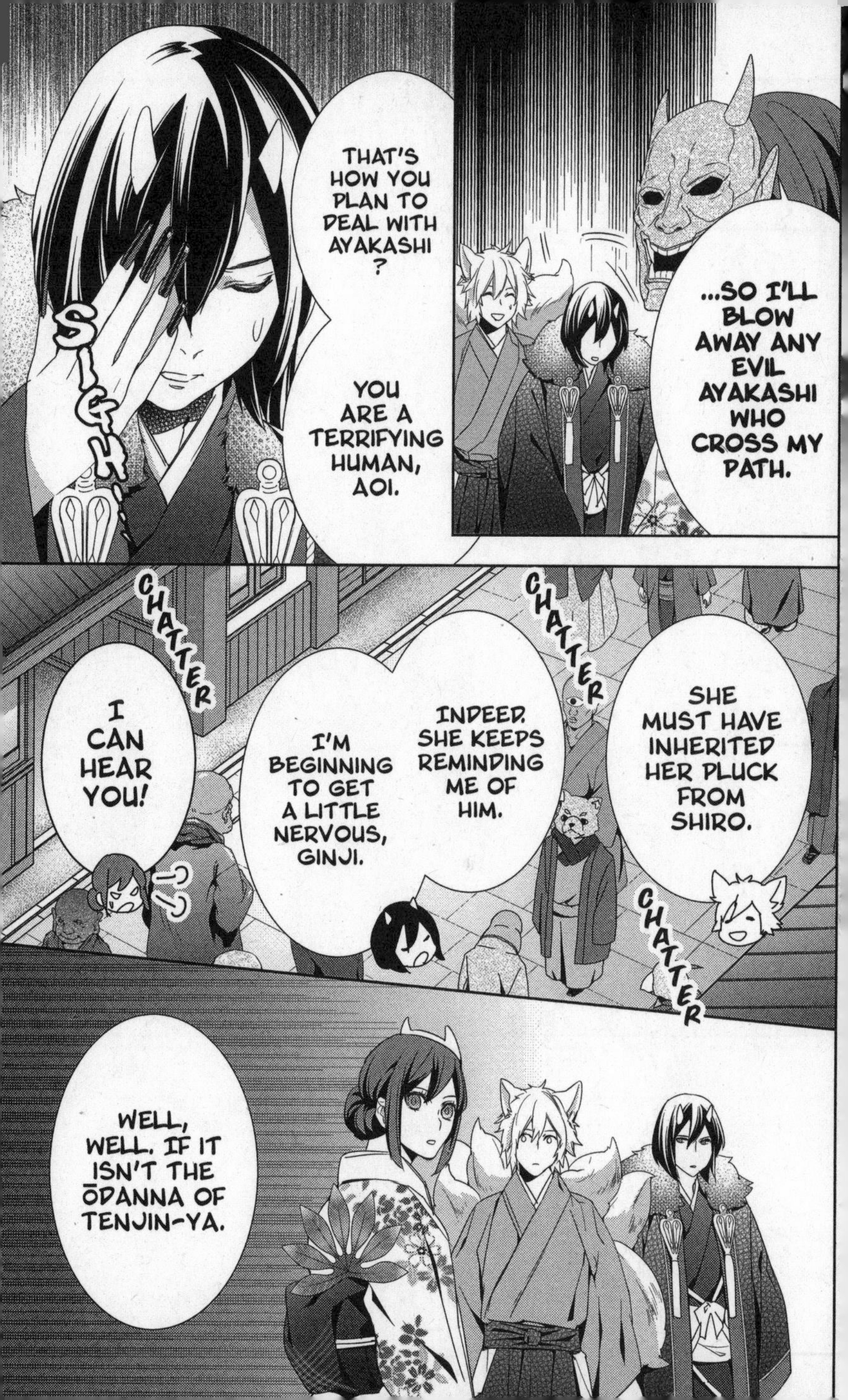
...SO I'LL BLOW AWAY ANY EVIL AYAKASHI WHO CROSS MY PATH.
THAT'S HOW YOU PLAN TO DEAL WITH AYAKASHI?
YOU ARE A TERRIFYING HUMAN, AOI.
SIGH
CHATTER
SHE MUST HAVE INHERITED HER PLUCK FROM SHIRO.
CHATTER
INDEED. SHE KEEPS REMINDING ME OF HIM.
I'M BEGINNING TO GET A LITTLE NERVOUS, GINJI.
CHATTER
I CAN HEAR YOU!
WELL, WELL. IF IT ISN'T THE ŌDANNA OF TENJIN-YA.

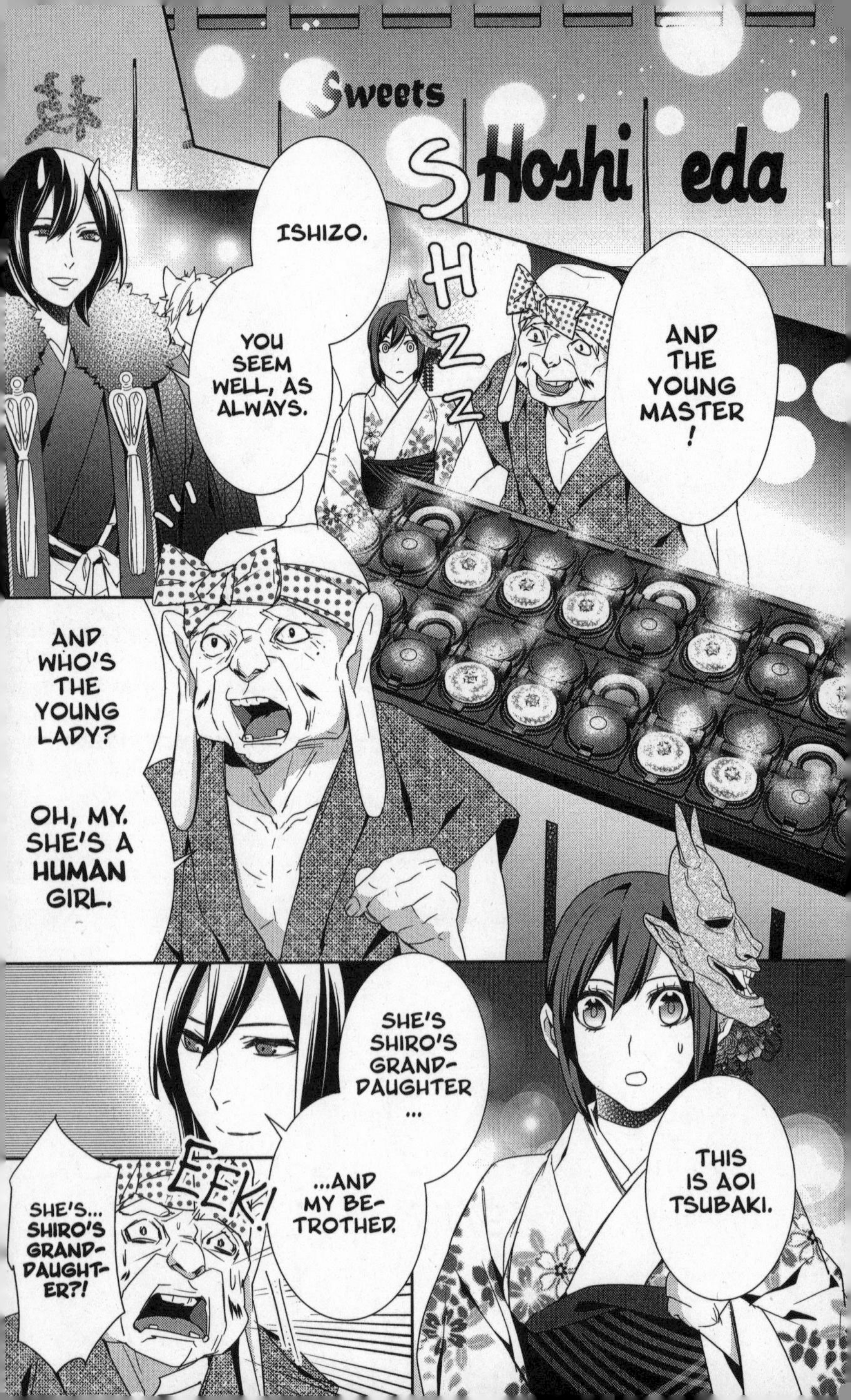
Sweets
Hoshi eda
SHZZ
AND THE YOUNG MASTER!
ISHIZO.
YOU SEEM WELL, AS ALWAYS.
AND WHO'S THE YOUNG LADY?
OH, MY. SHE'S A HUMAN GIRL.
THIS IS AOI TSUBAKI.
SHE'S SHIRO'S GRAND-DAUGHTER...
...AND MY BE-TROTHED.
EEK!
SHE'S... SHIRO'S GRAND-DAUGHT-ER?!

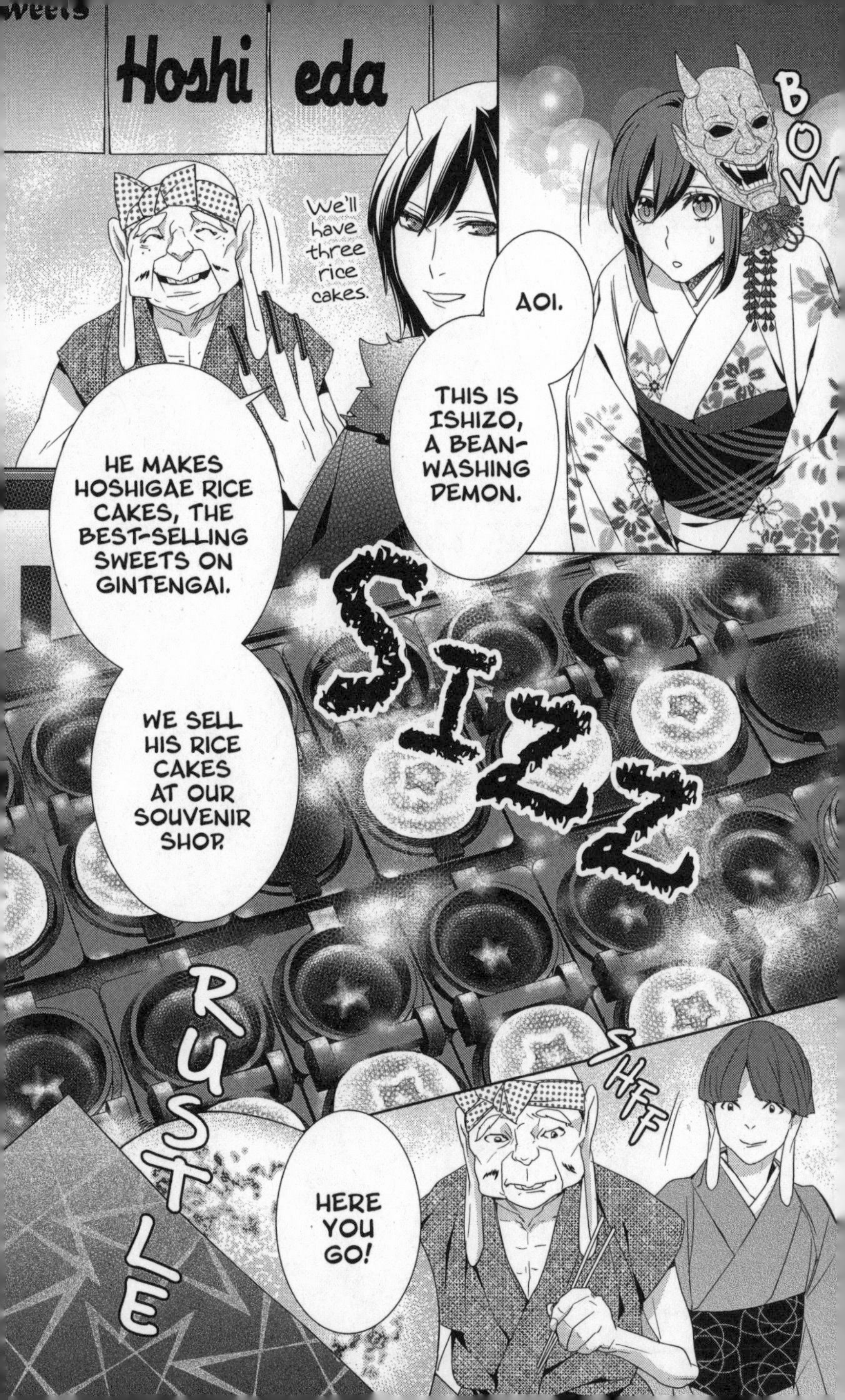
Hoshi eda
BOW
AOI.
THIS IS ISHIZO, A BEAN-WASHING DEMON.
We'll have three rice cakes.
HE MAKES HOSHIGAE RICE CAKES, THE BEST-SELLING SWEETS ON GINTENGAI.
SIZZ
WE SELL HIS RICE CAKES AT OUR SOUVENIR SHOP.
SHFF
HERE YOU GO!
RUSTLE

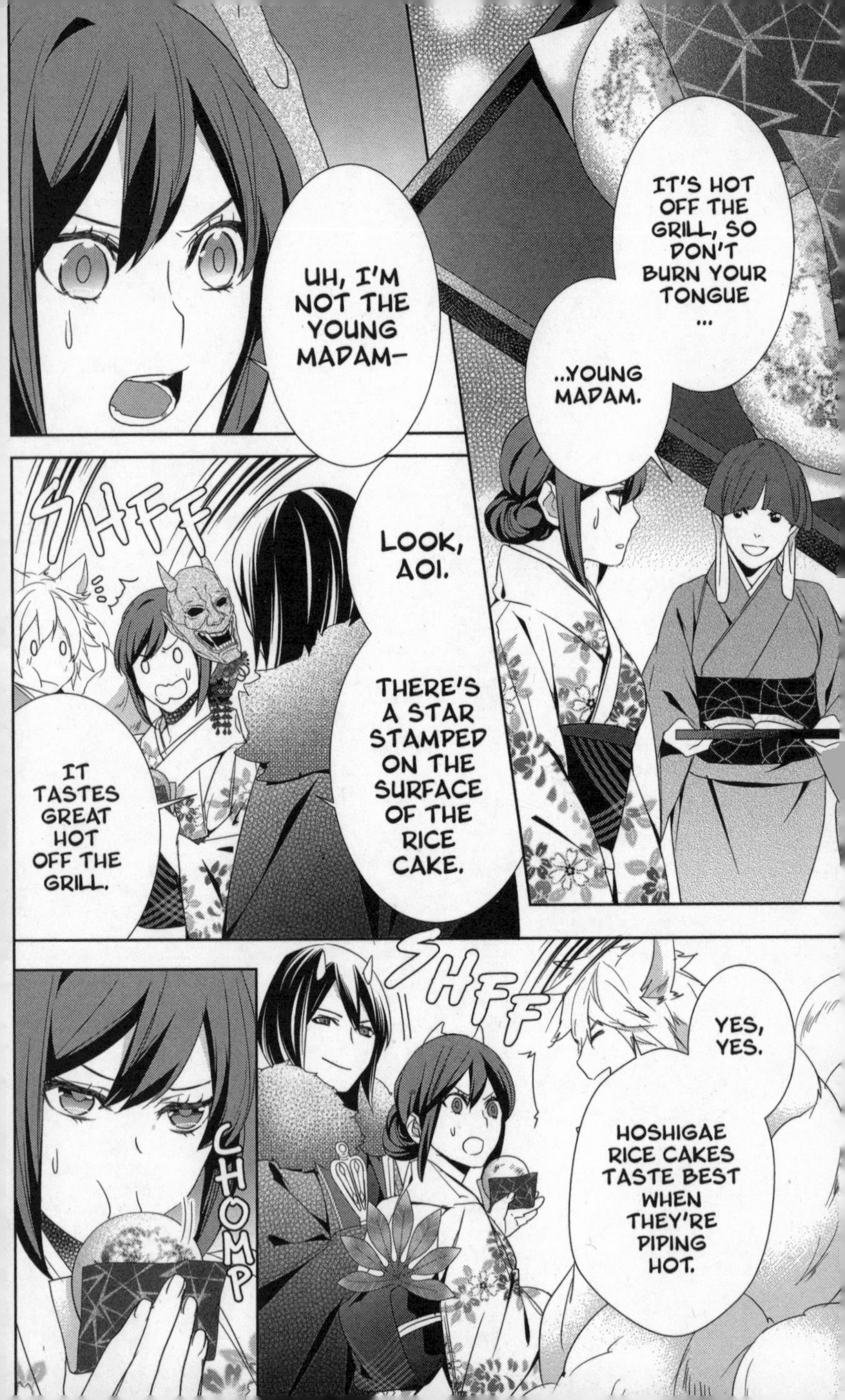
IT'S HOT OFF THE GRILL, SO DON'T BURN YOUR TONGUE ...
...YOUNG MADAM.
UH, I'M NOT THE YOUNG MADAM—
SHFF
LOOK, AOI.
THERE'S A STAR STAMPED ON THE SURFACE OF THE RICE CAKE.
IT TASTES GREAT HOT OFF THE GRILL.
SHFF
YES, YES.
HOSHIGAE RICE CAKES TASTE BEST WHEN THEY'RE PIPING HOT.
CHOMP

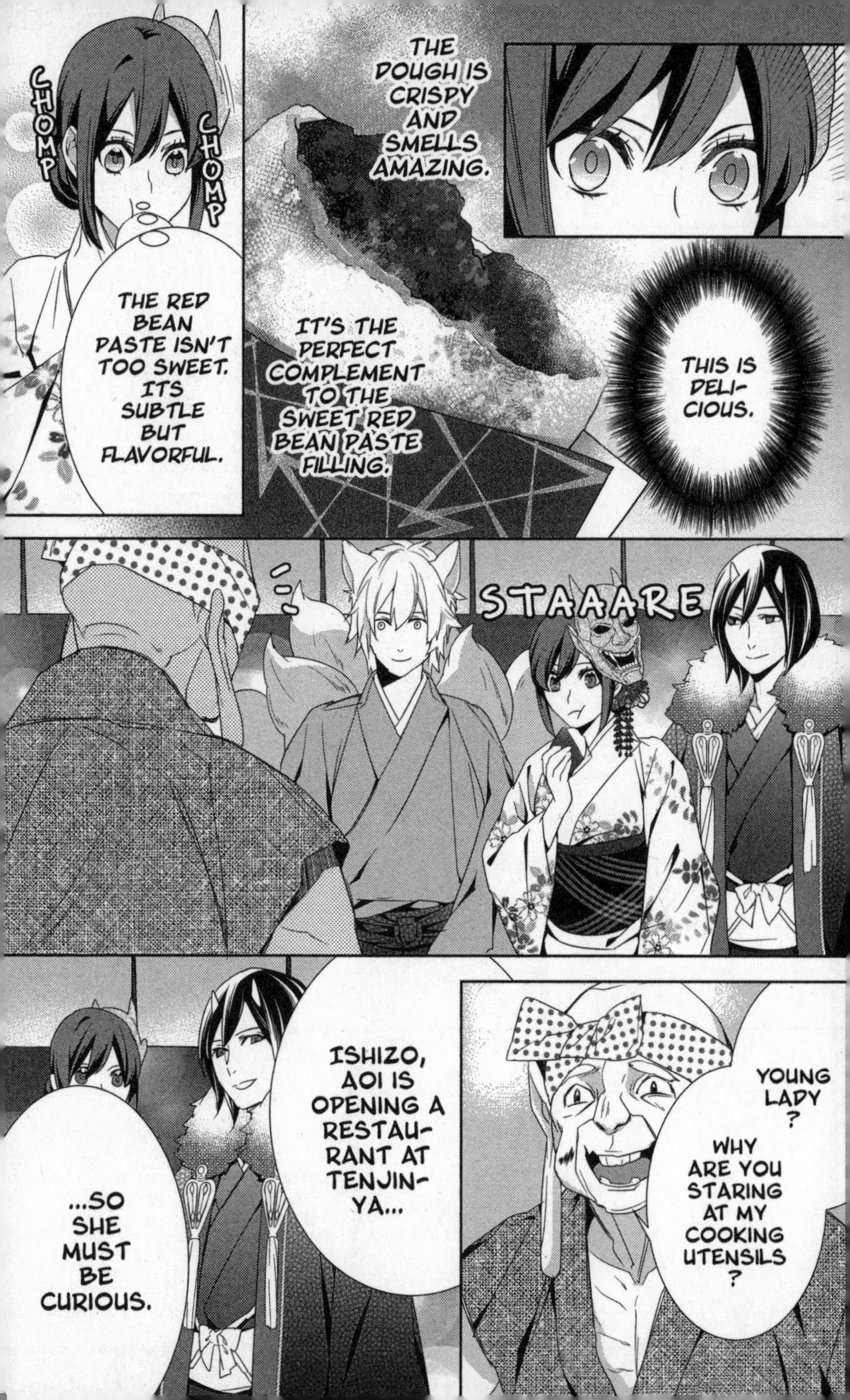
THIS IS DELI-CIOUS.
THE DOUGH IS CRISPY AND SMELLS AMAZING.
IT'S THE PERFECT COMPLEMENT TO THE SWEET RED BEAN PASTE FILLING.
CHOMP
CHOMP
THE RED BEAN PASTE ISN'T TOO SWEET. ITS SUBTLE BUT FLAVORFUL.
STAAARE
YOUNG LADY?
WHY ARE YOU STARING AT MY COOKING UTENSILS?
ISHIZO, AOI IS OPENING A RESTAU-RANT AT TENJIN-YA...
...SO SHE MUST BE CURIOUS.

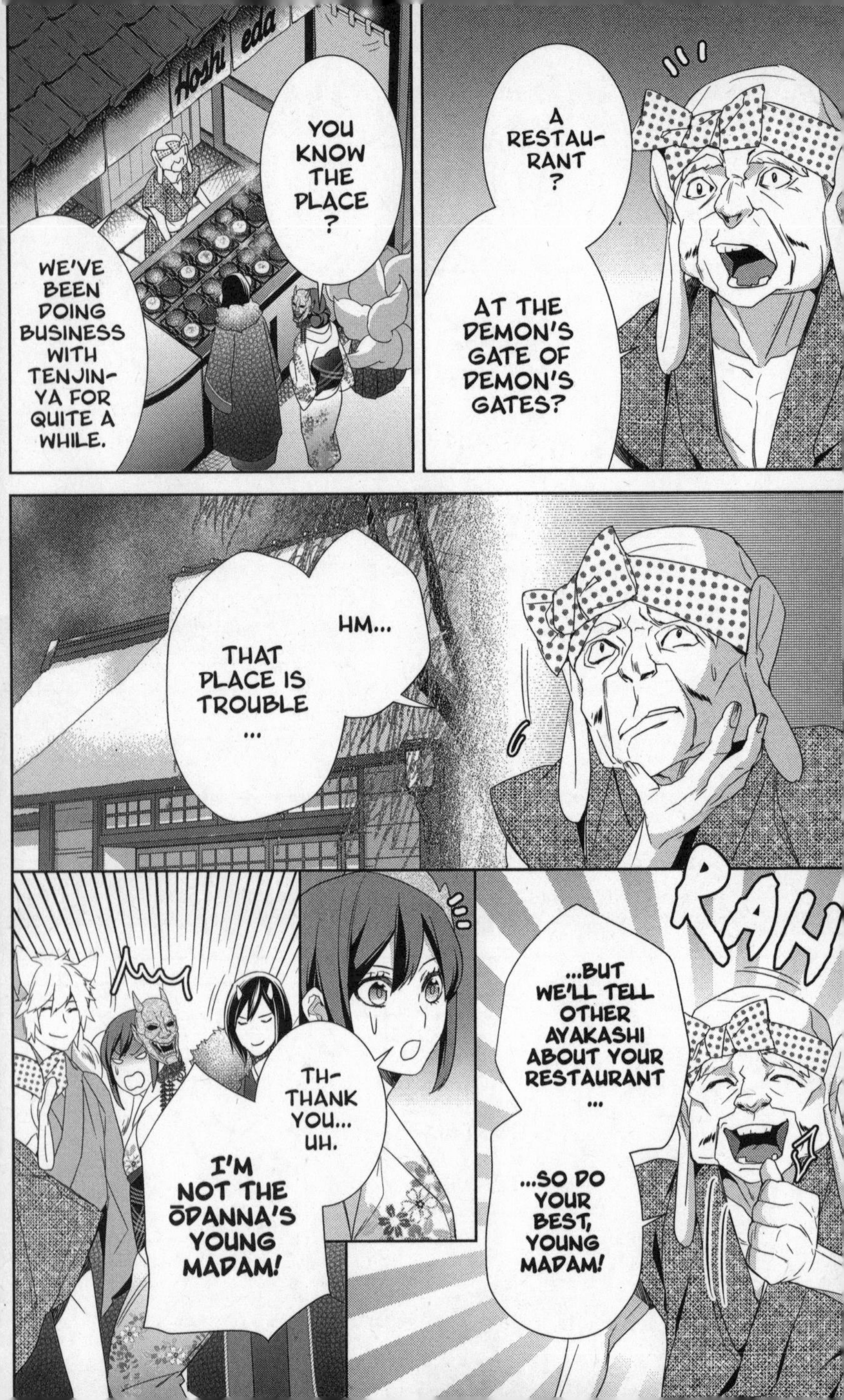
A RESTAU-RANT?
AT THE DEMON'S GATE OF DEMON'S GATES?
Hoshi eda
YOU KNOW THE PLACE?
WE'VE BEEN DOING BUSINESS WITH TENJIN-YA FOR QUITE A WHILE.
HM...
THAT PLACE IS TROUBLE...
RAH
...BUT WE'LL TELL OTHER AYAKASHI ABOUT YOUR RESTAURANT...
...SO DO YOUR BEST, YOUNG MADAM!
TH-THANK YOU... UH.
I'M NOT THE ŌDANNA'S YOUNG MADAM!

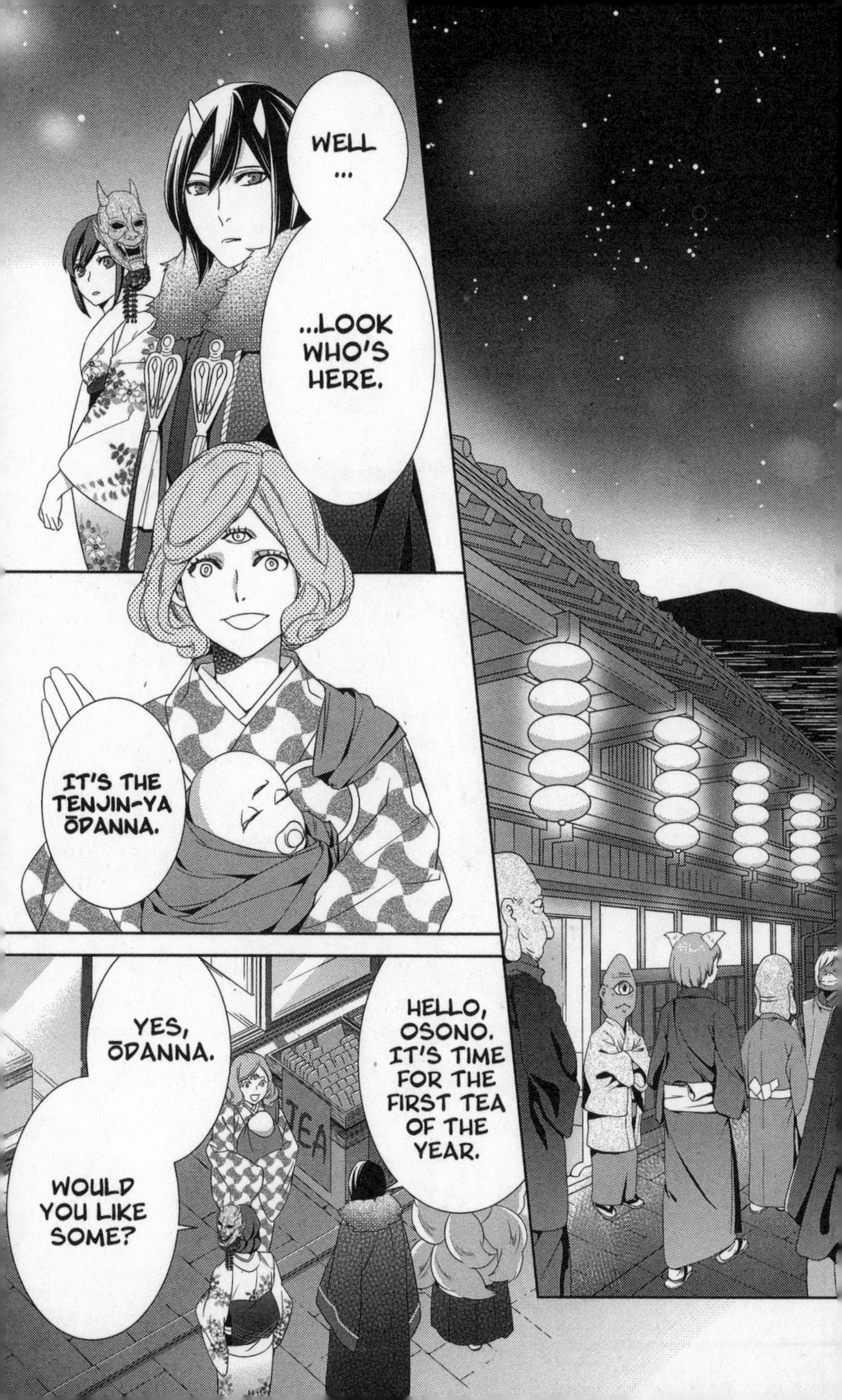
WELL ...
...LOOK WHO'S HERE.
IT'S THE TENJIN-YA ŌDANNA.
HELLO, OSONO. IT'S TIME FOR THE FIRST TEA OF THE YEAR.
YES, ŌDANNA.
WOULD YOU LIKE SOME?
TEA

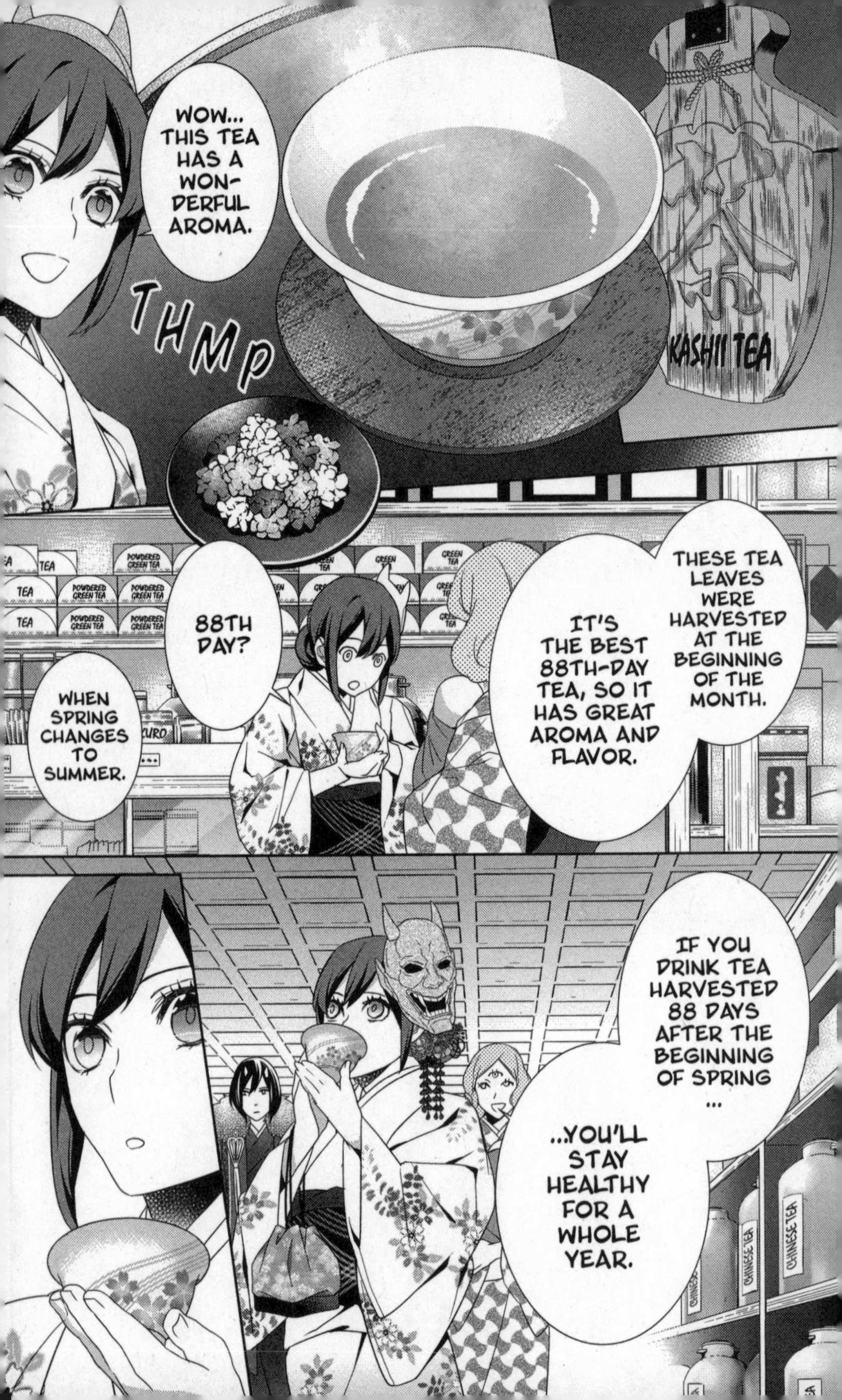
WOW... THIS TEA HAS A WON-DERFUL AROMA.
THMP
KASHII TEA
THESE TEA LEAVES WERE HARVESTED AT THE BEGINNING OF THE MONTH.
IT'S THE BEST 88TH-DAY TEA, SO IT HAS GREAT AROMA AND FLAVOR.
88TH DAY?
WHEN SPRING CHANGES TO SUMMER.
IF YOU DRINK TEA HARVESTED 88 DAYS AFTER THE BEGINNING OF SPRING ...
...YOU'LL STAY HEALTHY FOR A WHOLE YEAR.
CHINESE TEA
CHINESE TEA

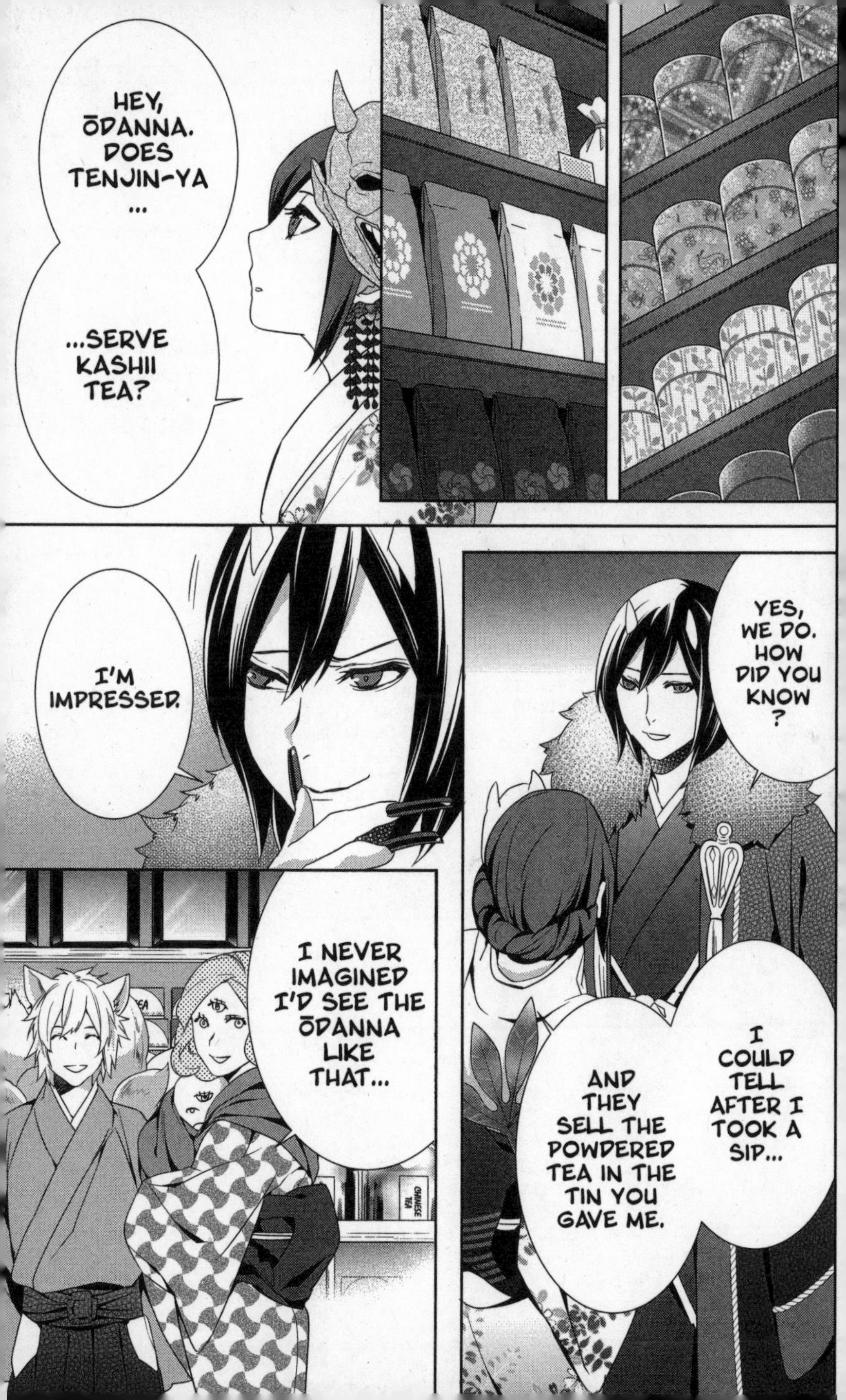
HEY, ŌDANNA. DOES TENJIN-YA ...
...SERVE KASHII TEA?
YES, WE DO. HOW DID YOU KNOW?
I COULD TELL AFTER I TOOK A SIP...
AND THEY SELL THE POWDERED TEA IN THE TIN YOU GAVE ME.
I'M IMPRESSED.
I NEVER IMAGINED I'D SEE THE ŌDANNA LIKE THAT...
CHINESE TEA

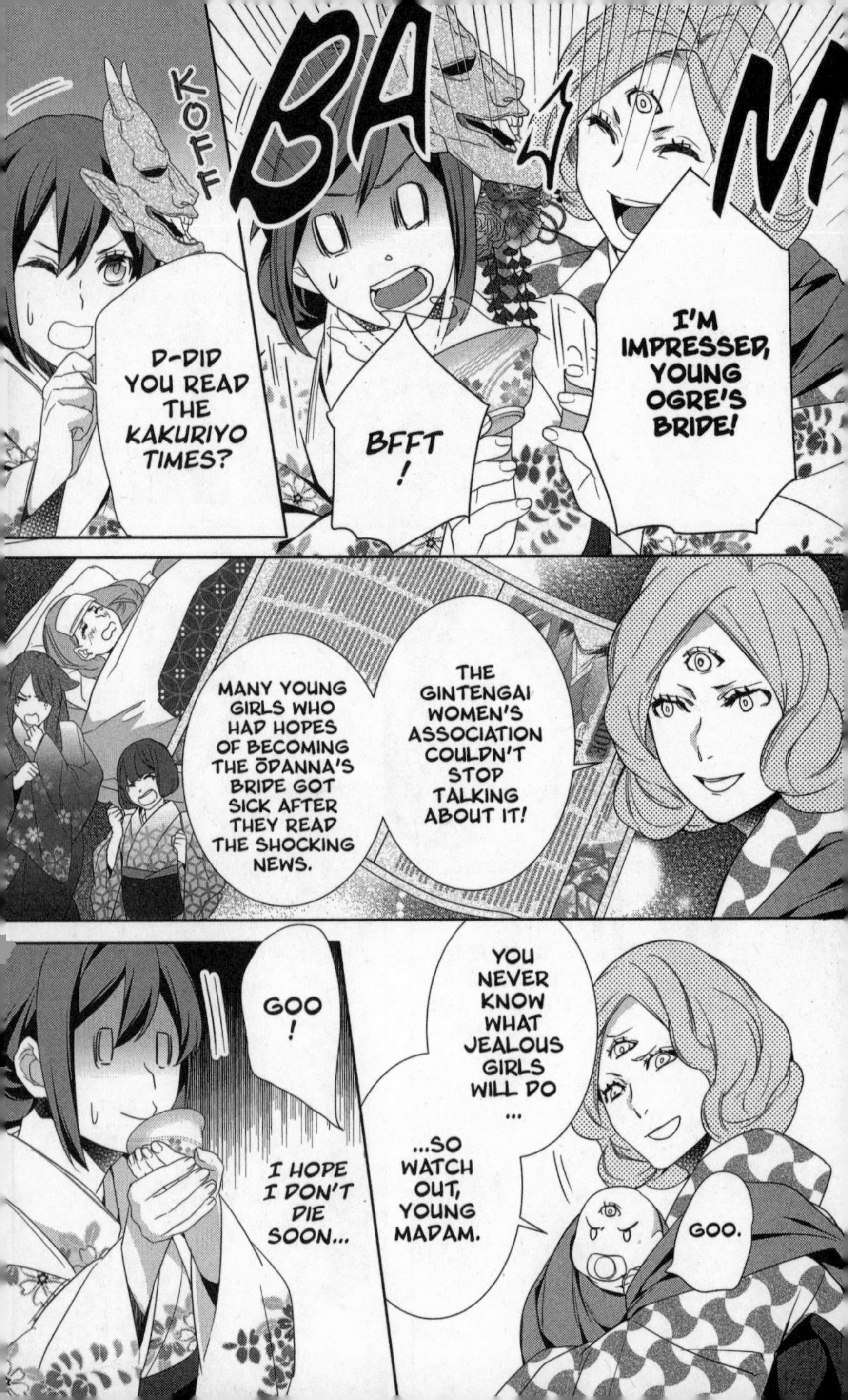

BAM
I'M IMPRESSED, YOUNG OGRE'S BRIDE!
BFFT!
KOFF
D-DID YOU READ THE KAKURIYO TIMES?
THE GINTENGAI WOMEN'S ASSOCIATION COULDN'T STOP TALKING ABOUT IT!
MANY YOUNG GIRLS WHO HAD HOPES OF BECOMING THE ŌDANNA'S BRIDE GOT SICK AFTER THEY READ THE SHOCKING NEWS.
YOU NEVER KNOW WHAT JEALOUS GIRLS WILL DO ...
...SO WATCH OUT, YOUNG MADAM.
GOO.
GOO!
I HOPE I DON'T DIE SOON...

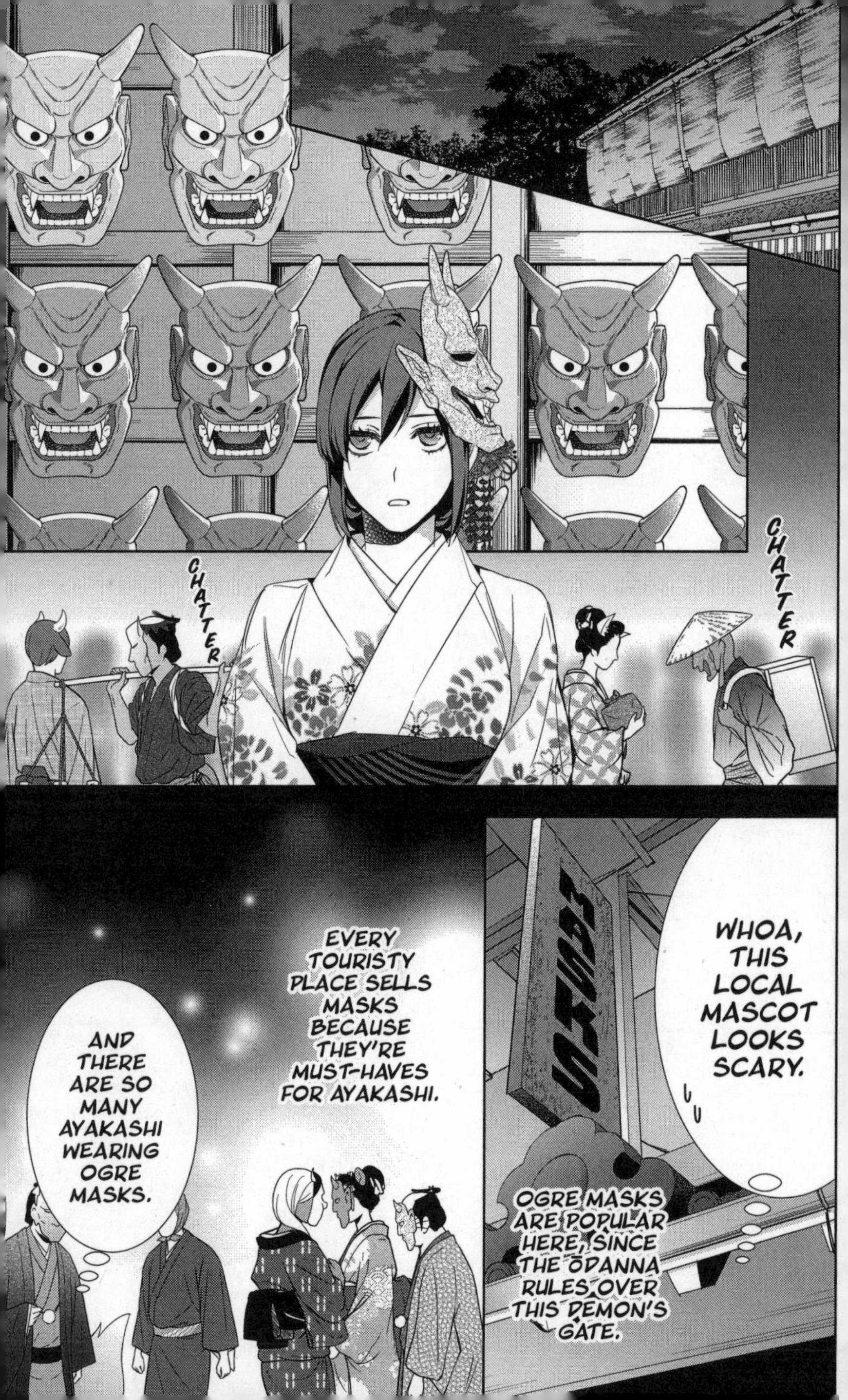
CHATTER
CHATTER
WHOA, THIS LOCAL MASCOT LOOKS SCARY.
OGRE MASKS ARE POPULAR HERE, SINCE THE ŌDANNA RULES OVER THIS DEMON'S GATE.
EVERY TOURISTY PLACE SELLS MASKS BECAUSE THEY'RE MUST-HAVES FOR AYAKASHI.
AND THERE ARE SO MANY AYAKASHI WEARING OGRE MASKS.

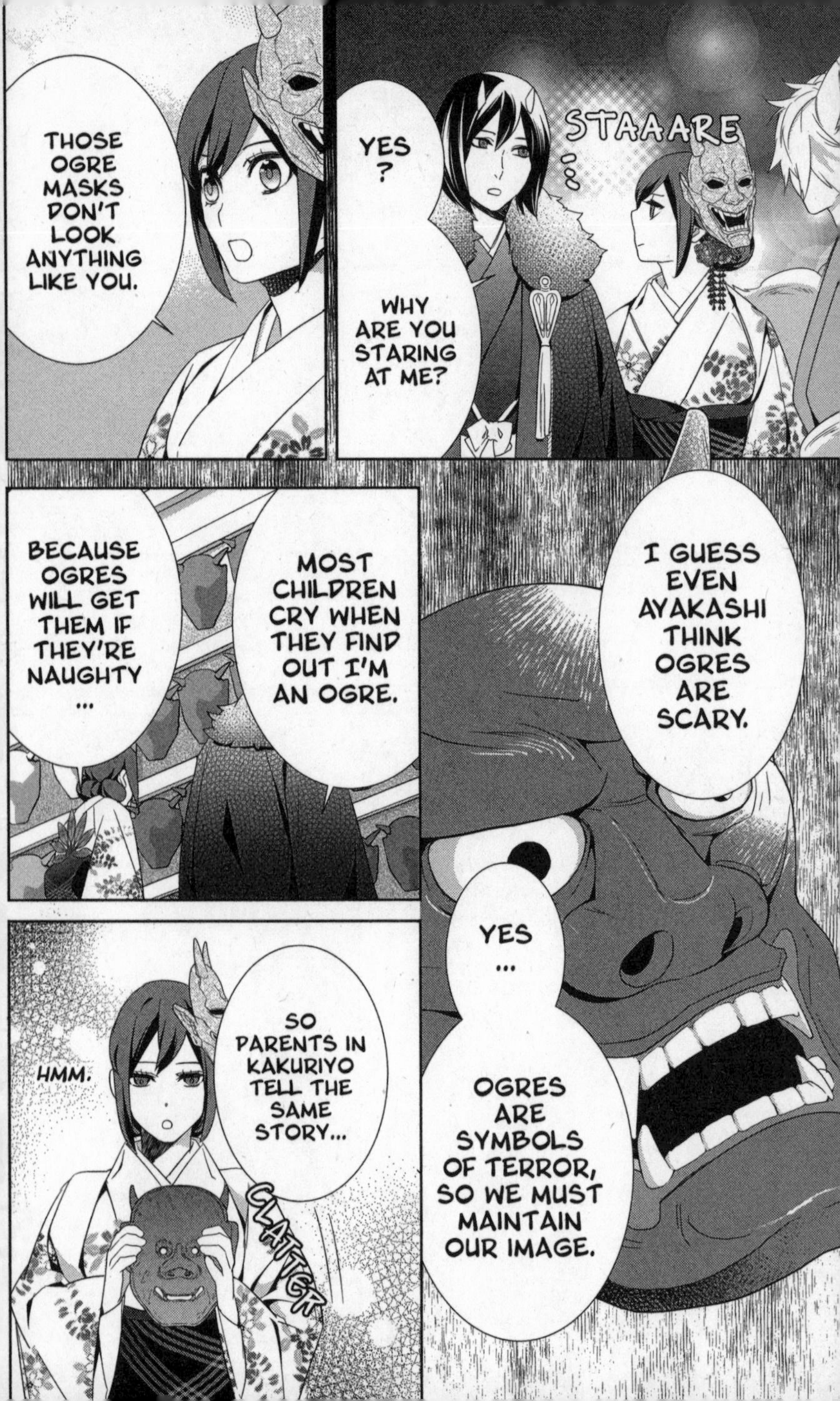
STAAARE
YES?
WHY ARE YOU STARING AT ME?
THOSE OGRE MASKS DON'T LOOK ANYTHING LIKE YOU.
I GUESS EVEN AYAKASHI THINK OGRES ARE SCARY.
YES...
OGRES ARE SYMBOLS OF TERROR, SO WE MUST MAINTAIN OUR IMAGE.
MOST CHILDREN CRY WHEN THEY FIND OUT I'M AN OGRE.
BECAUSE OGRES WILL GET THEM IF THEY'RE NAUGHTY...
SO PARENTS IN KAKURIYO TELL THE SAME STORY...
HMM.
CLATTER

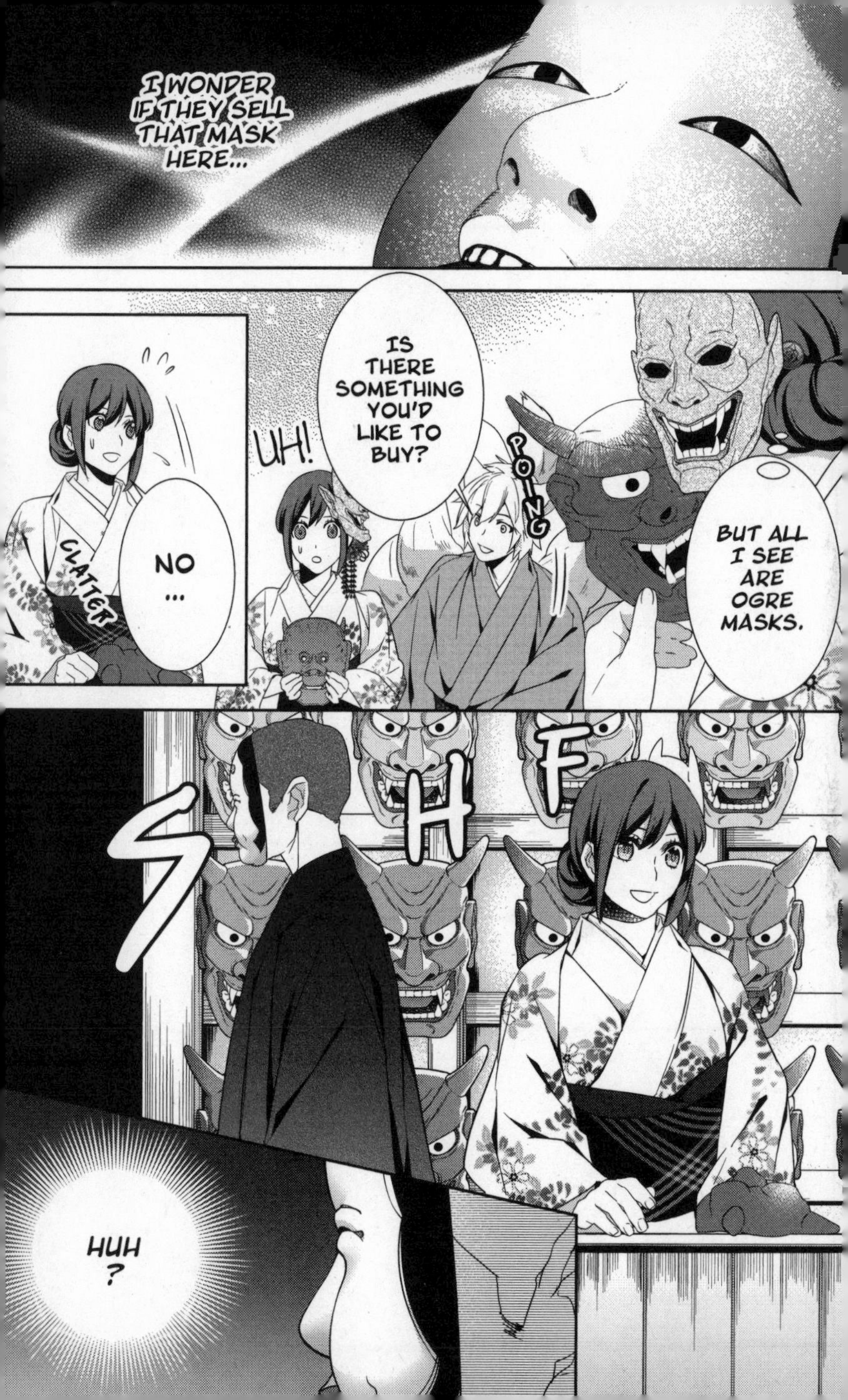
I WONDER IF THEY SELL THAT MASK HERE...
BUT ALL I SEE ARE OGRE MASKS.
POING
IS THERE SOMETHING YOU'D LIKE TO BUY?
UH!
NO ...
CLATTER
SHF
HUH?

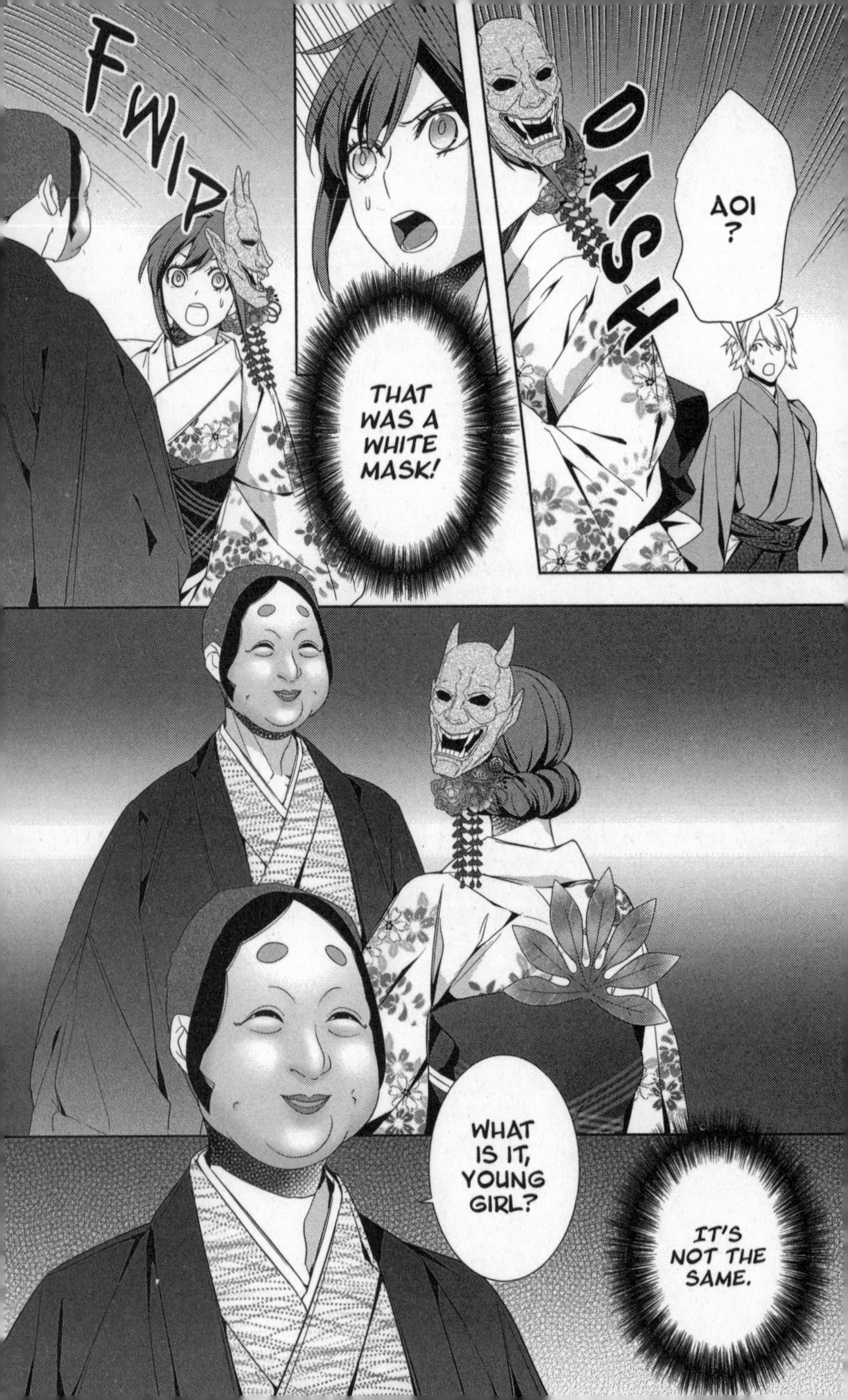
DASH
AOI ?
THAT WAS A WHITE MASK!
FWIP
WHAT IS IT, YOUNG GIRL?
IT'S NOT THE SAME.

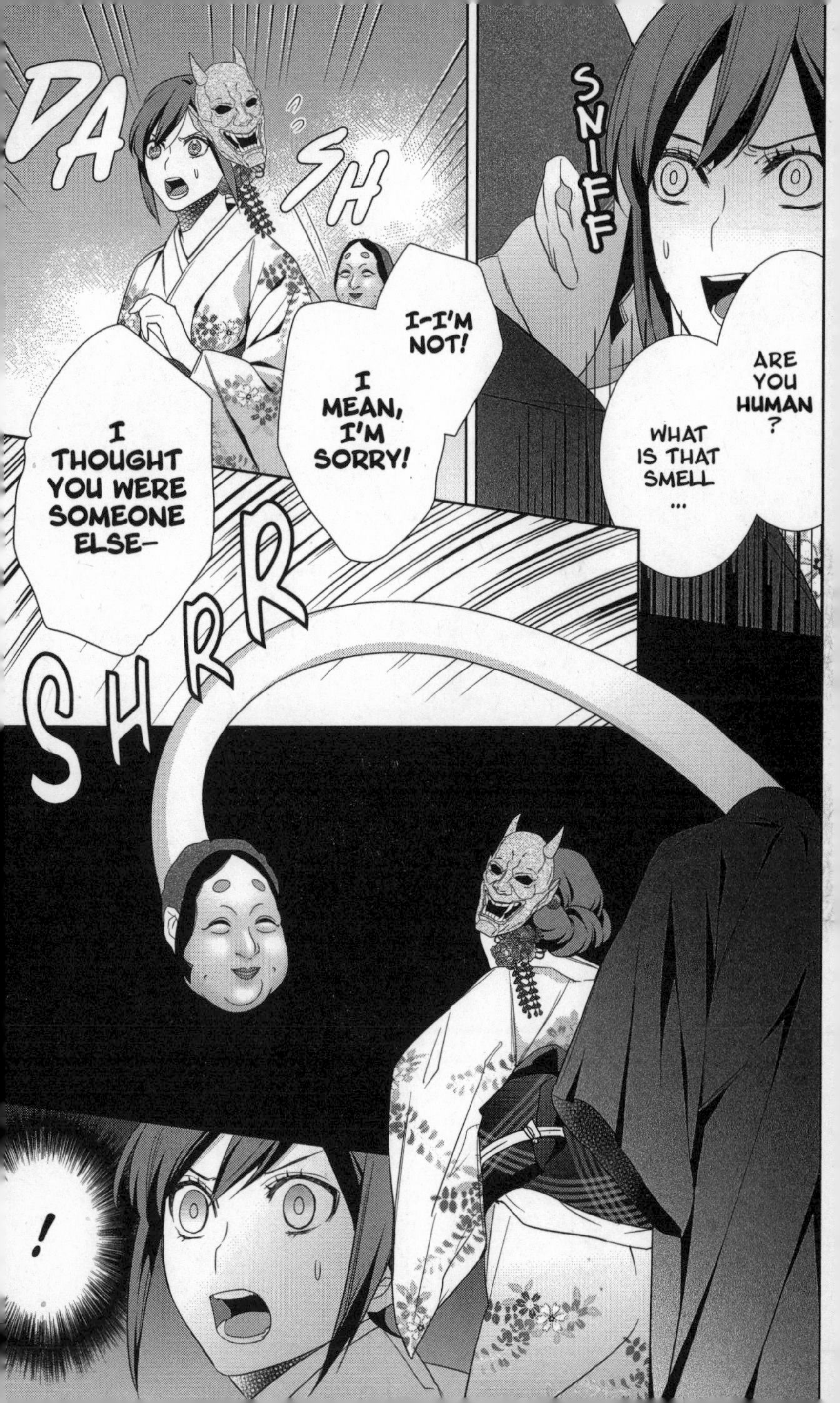
SNIFF
ARE YOU HUMAN?
WHAT IS THAT SMELL...
DASH
I-I'M NOT!
I MEAN, I'M SORRY!
I THOUGHT YOU WERE SOMEONE ELSE-
SHRR
!

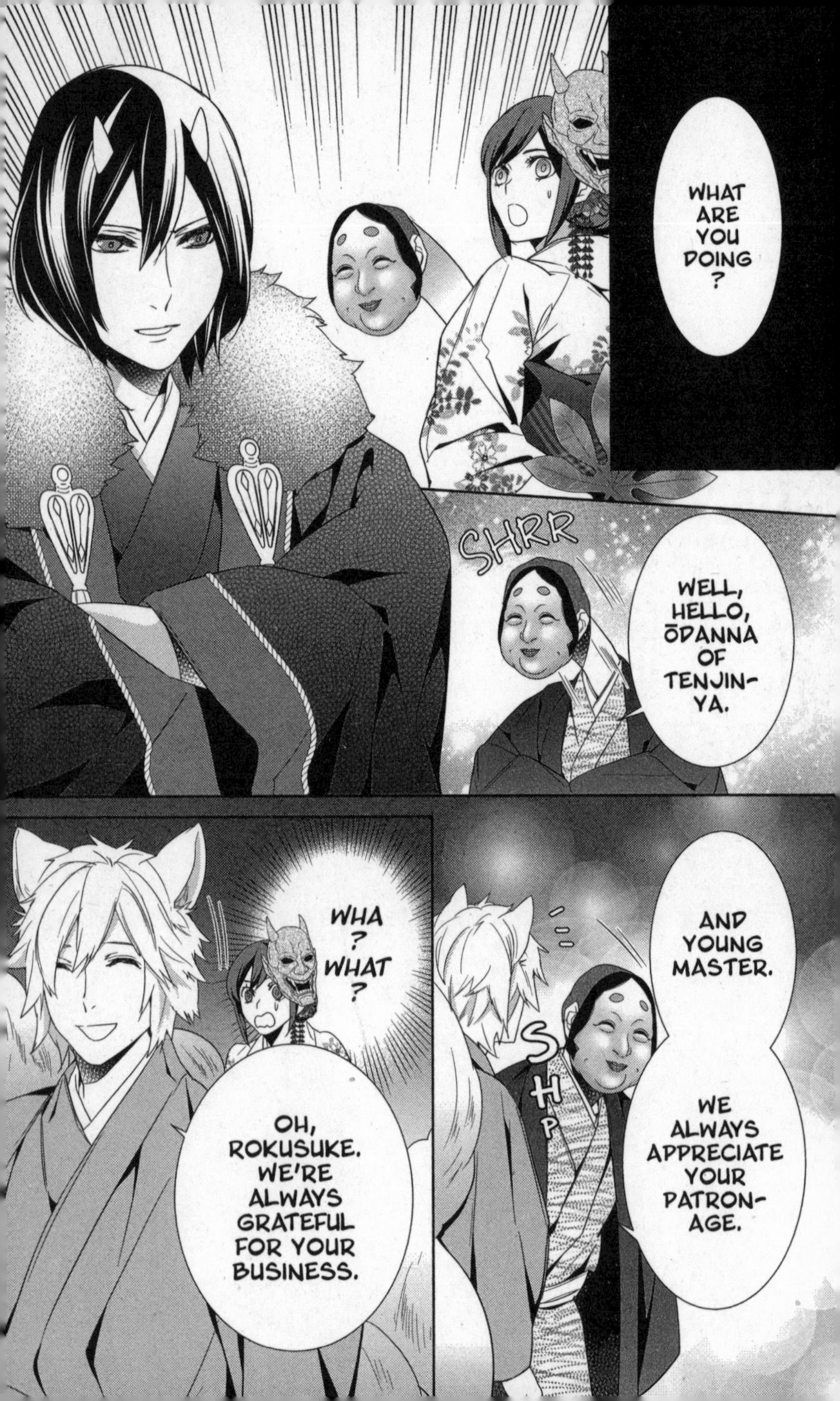
WHAT ARE YOU DOING?
SHRR
WELL, HELLO, ŌDANNA OF TENJIN-YA.
AND YOUNG MASTER.
SHP
WE ALWAYS APPRECIATE YOUR PATRON-AGE.
WHA? WHAT?
OH, ROKUSUKE. WE'RE ALWAYS GRATEFUL FOR YOUR BUSINESS.

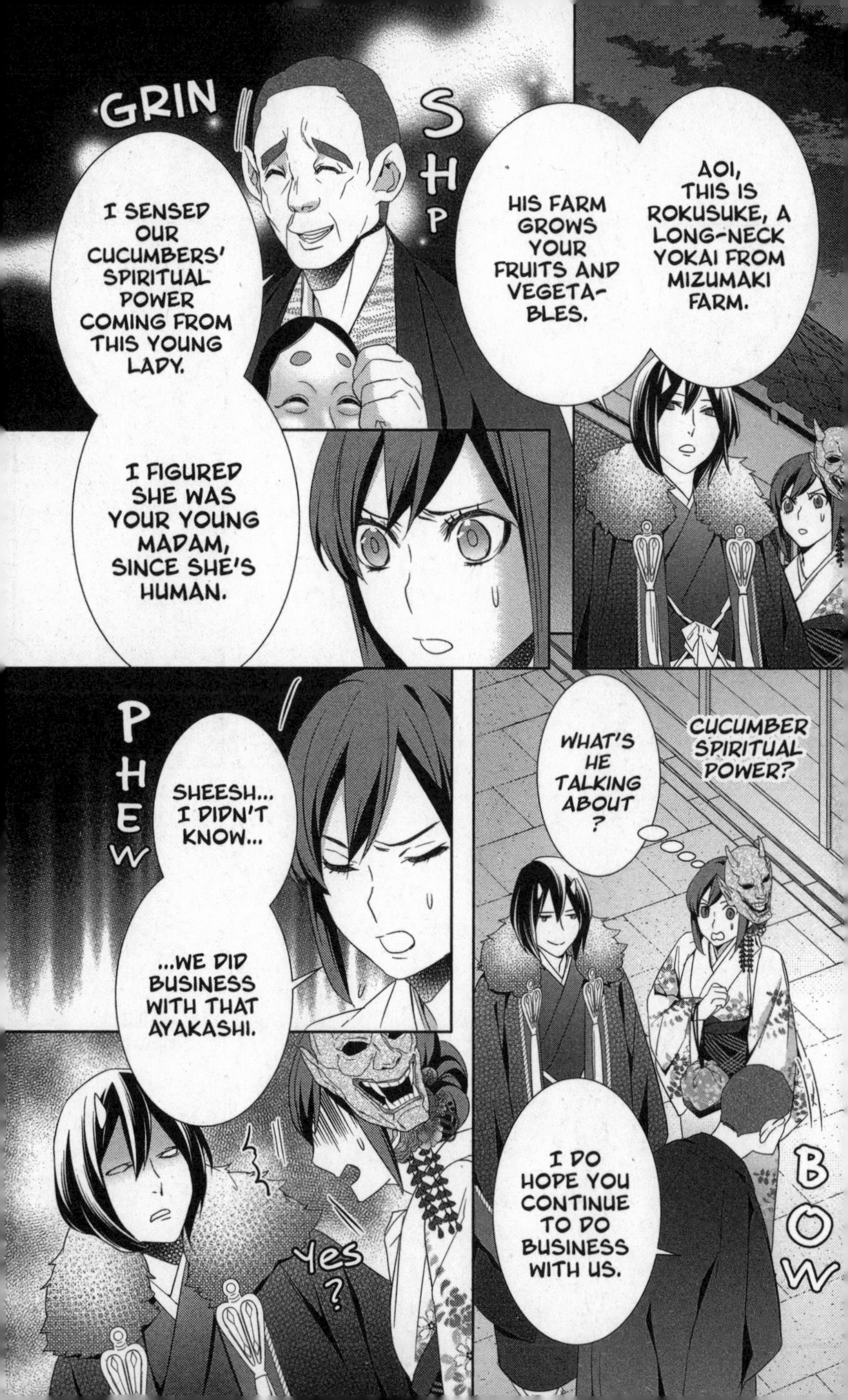
AOI, THIS IS ROKUSUKE, A LONG-NECK YOKAI FROM MIZUMAKI FARM.
HIS FARM GROWS YOUR FRUITS AND VEGETA-BLES.
SHP
GRIN
I SENSED OUR CUCUMBERS' SPIRITUAL POWER COMING FROM THIS YOUNG LADY.
I FIGURED SHE WAS YOUR YOUNG MADAM, SINCE SHE'S HUMAN.
CUCUMBER SPIRITUAL POWER?
WHAT'S HE TALKING ABOUT?
BOW
I DO HOPE YOU CONTINUE TO DO BUSINESS WITH US.
PHEW
SHEESH... I DIDN'T KNOW...
...WE DID BUSINESS WITH THAT AYAKASHI.
Yes?

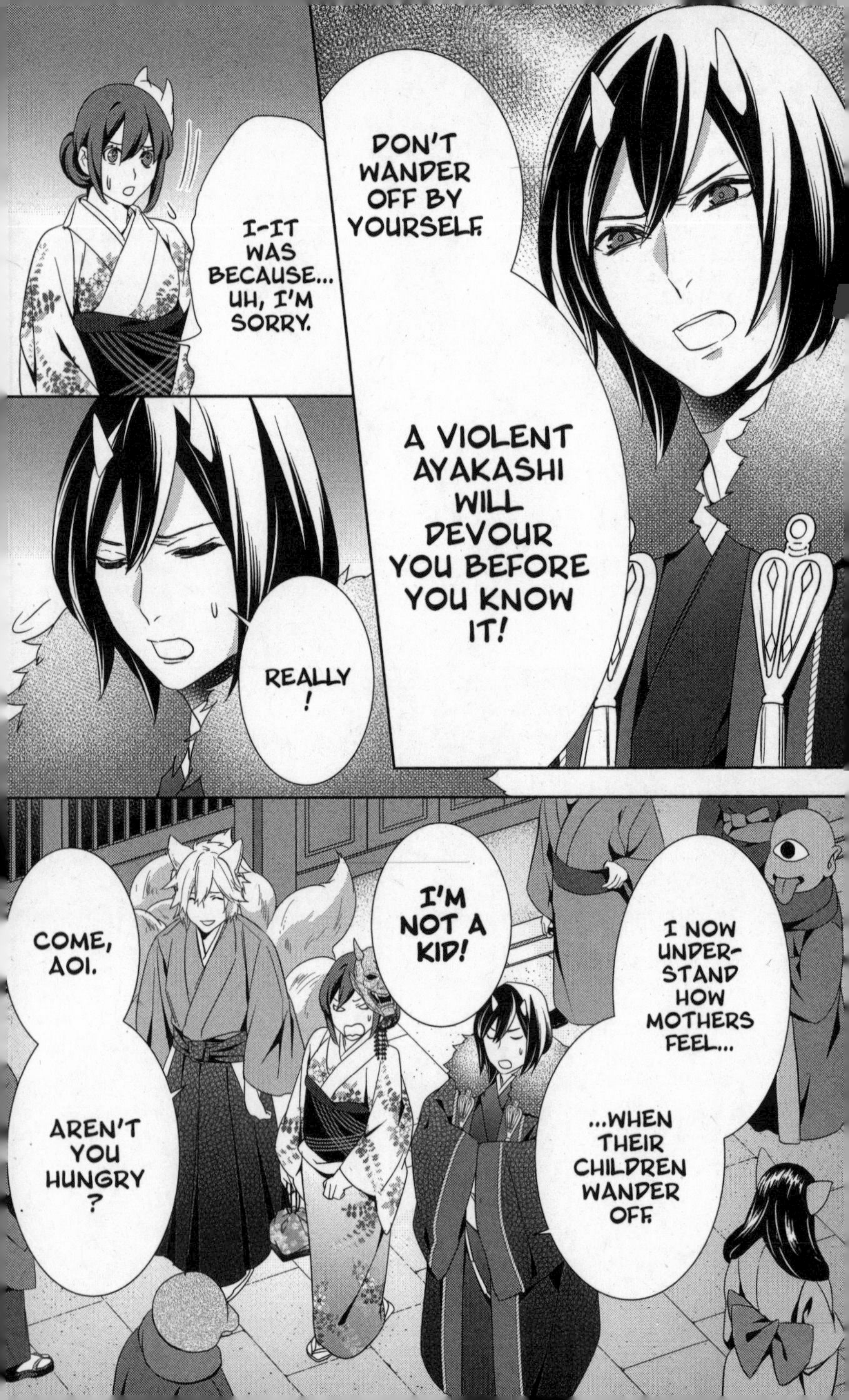
DON'T WANDER OFF BY YOURSELF.
A VIOLENT AYAKASHI WILL DEVOUR YOU BEFORE YOU KNOW IT!
I-IT WAS BECAUSE... UH, I'M SORRY.
REALLY!
I NOW UNDER-STAND HOW MOTHERS FEEL...
...WHEN THEIR CHILDREN WANDER OFF.
I'M NOT A KID!
COME, AOI.
AREN'T YOU HUNGRY?

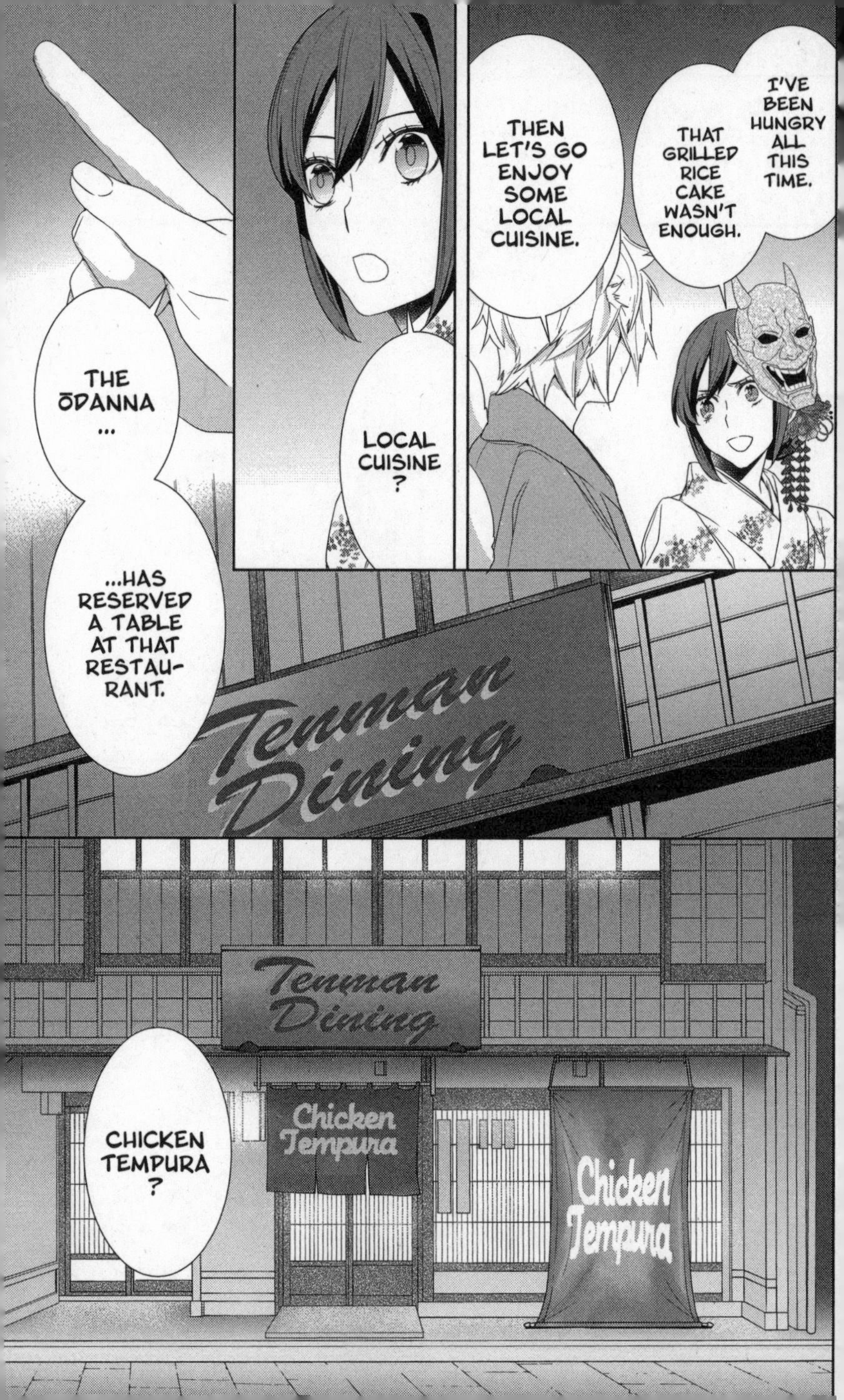
I'VE BEEN HUNGRY ALL THIS TIME.
THAT GRILLED RICE CAKE WASN'T ENOUGH.
THEN LET'S GO ENJOY SOME LOCAL CUISINE.
LOCAL CUISINE?
THE ŌDANNA...
...HAS RESERVED A TABLE AT THAT RESTAURANT.
Tenman Dining
Tenman Dining
Chicken Tempura
Chicken Tempura
CHICKEN TEMPURA?

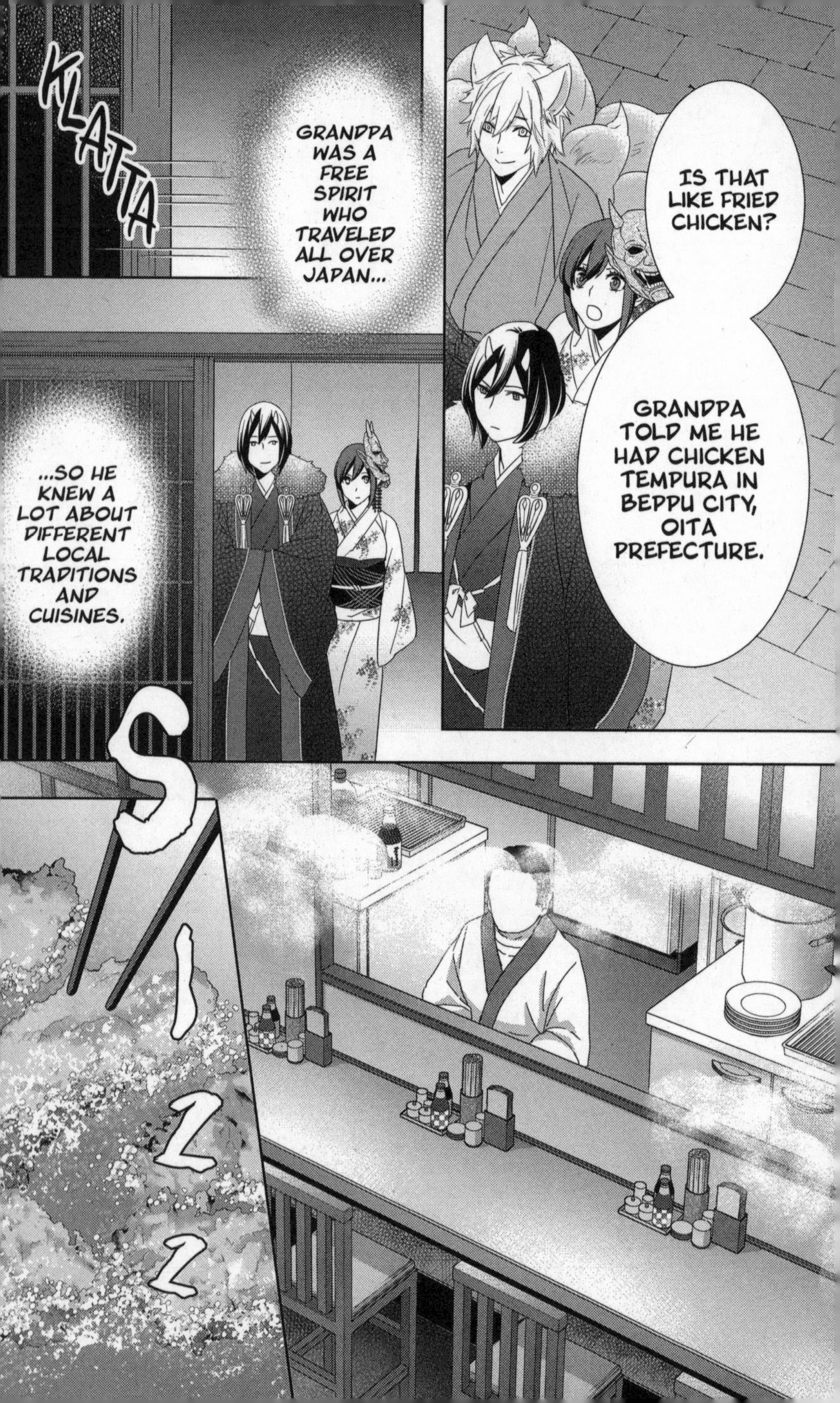
IS THAT LIKE FRIED CHICKEN?
GRANDPA TOLD ME HE HAD CHICKEN TEMPURA IN BEPPU CITY, OITA PREFECTURE.
KLATTA
GRANDPA WAS A FREE SPIRIT WHO TRAVELED ALL OVER JAPAN...
...SO HE KNEW A LOT ABOUT DIFFERENT LOCAL TRADITIONS AND CUISINES.
SIZZ

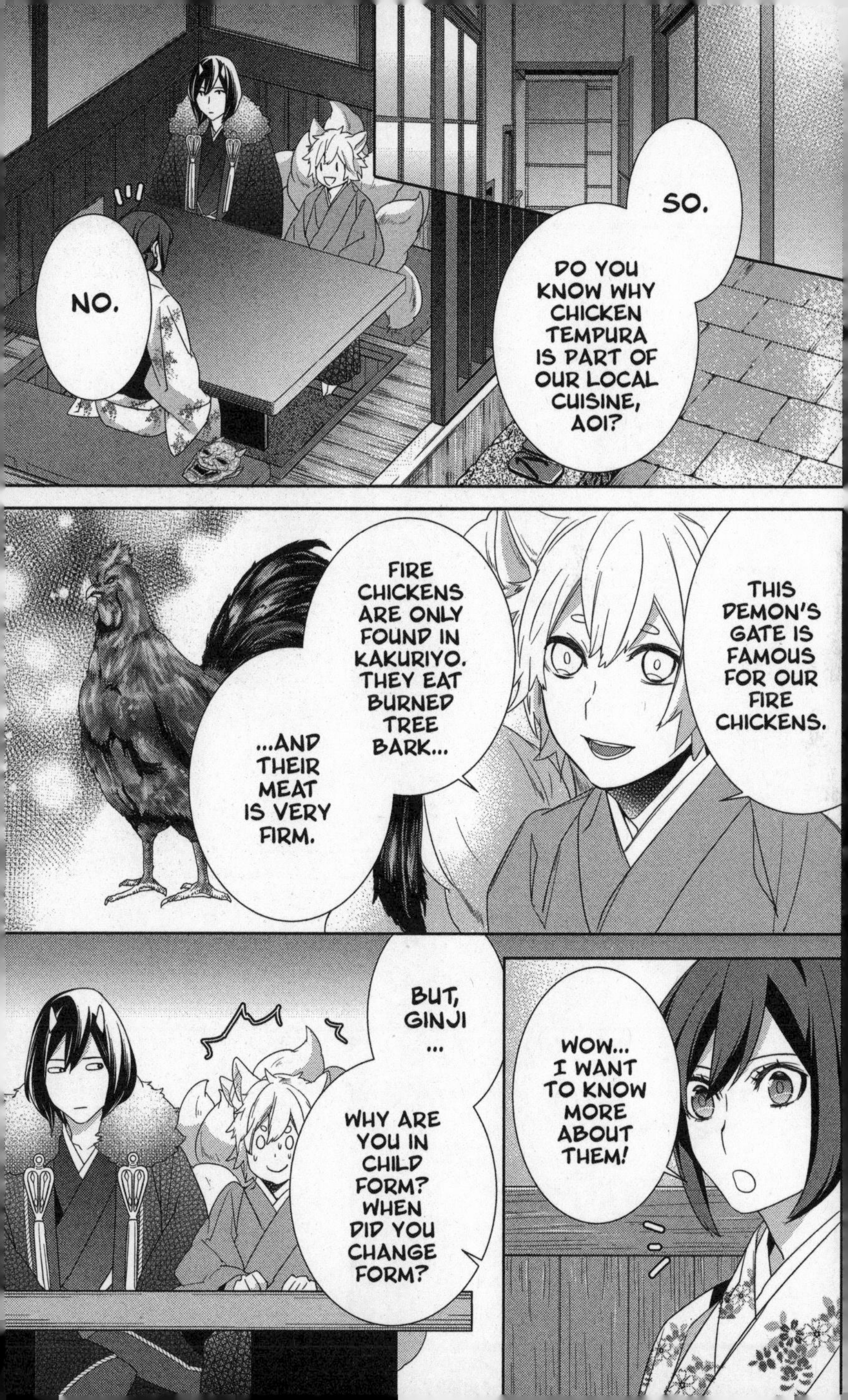
SO.
DO YOU KNOW WHY CHICKEN TEMPURA IS PART OF OUR LOCAL CUISINE, AOI?
NO.
THIS DEMON'S GATE IS FAMOUS FOR OUR FIRE CHICKENS.
FIRE CHICKENS ARE ONLY FOUND IN KAKURIYO. THEY EAT BURNED TREE BARK...
...AND THEIR MEAT IS VERY FIRM.
WOW... I WANT TO KNOW MORE ABOUT THEM!
BUT, GINJI...
WHY ARE YOU IN CHILD FORM? WHEN DID YOU CHANGE FORM?

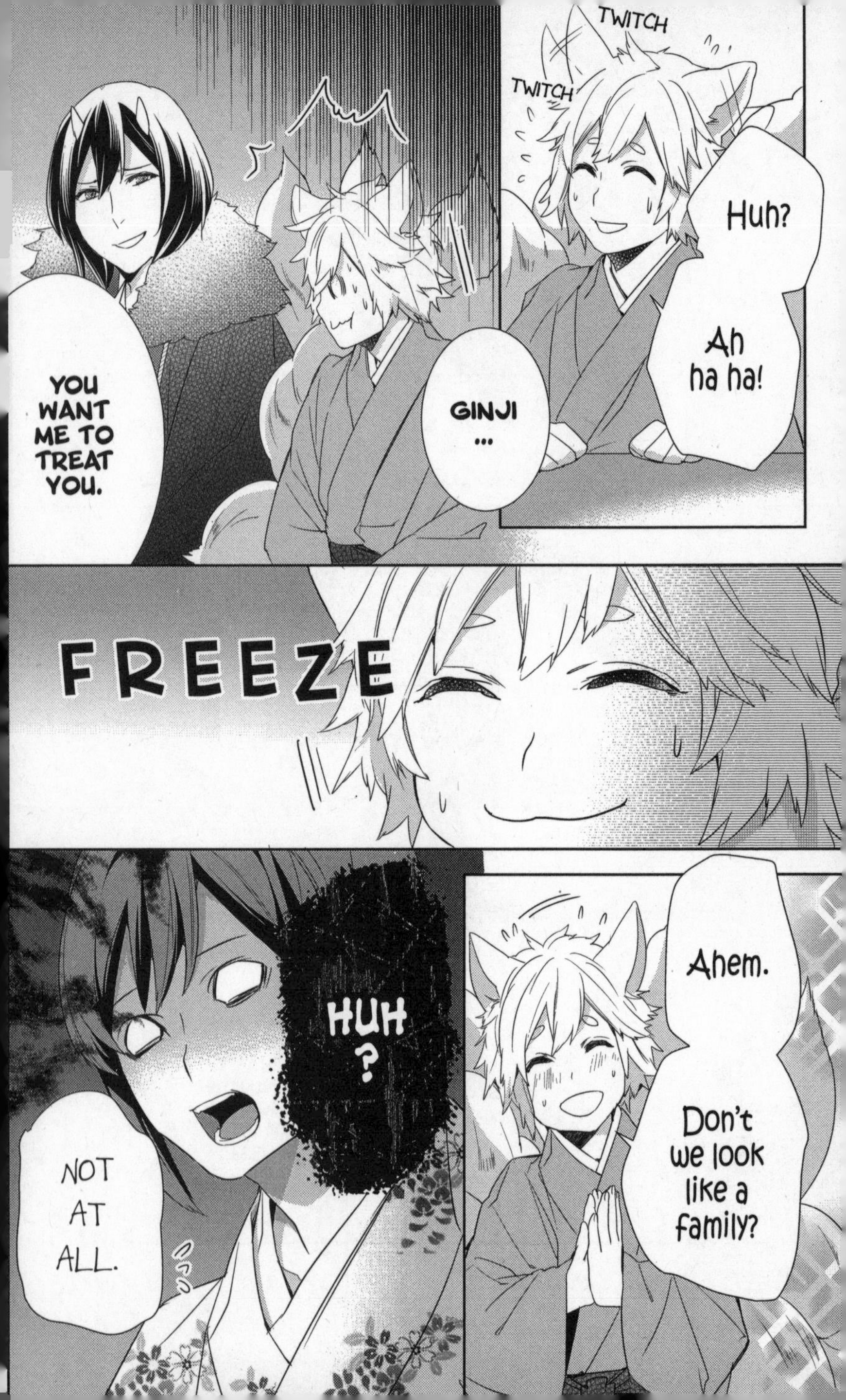
TWITCH
TWITCH
Huh?
Ah ha ha!
GINJI ...
YOU WANT ME TO TREAT YOU.
FREEZE
Ahem.
Don't we look like a family?
HUH ?
NOT AT ALL.

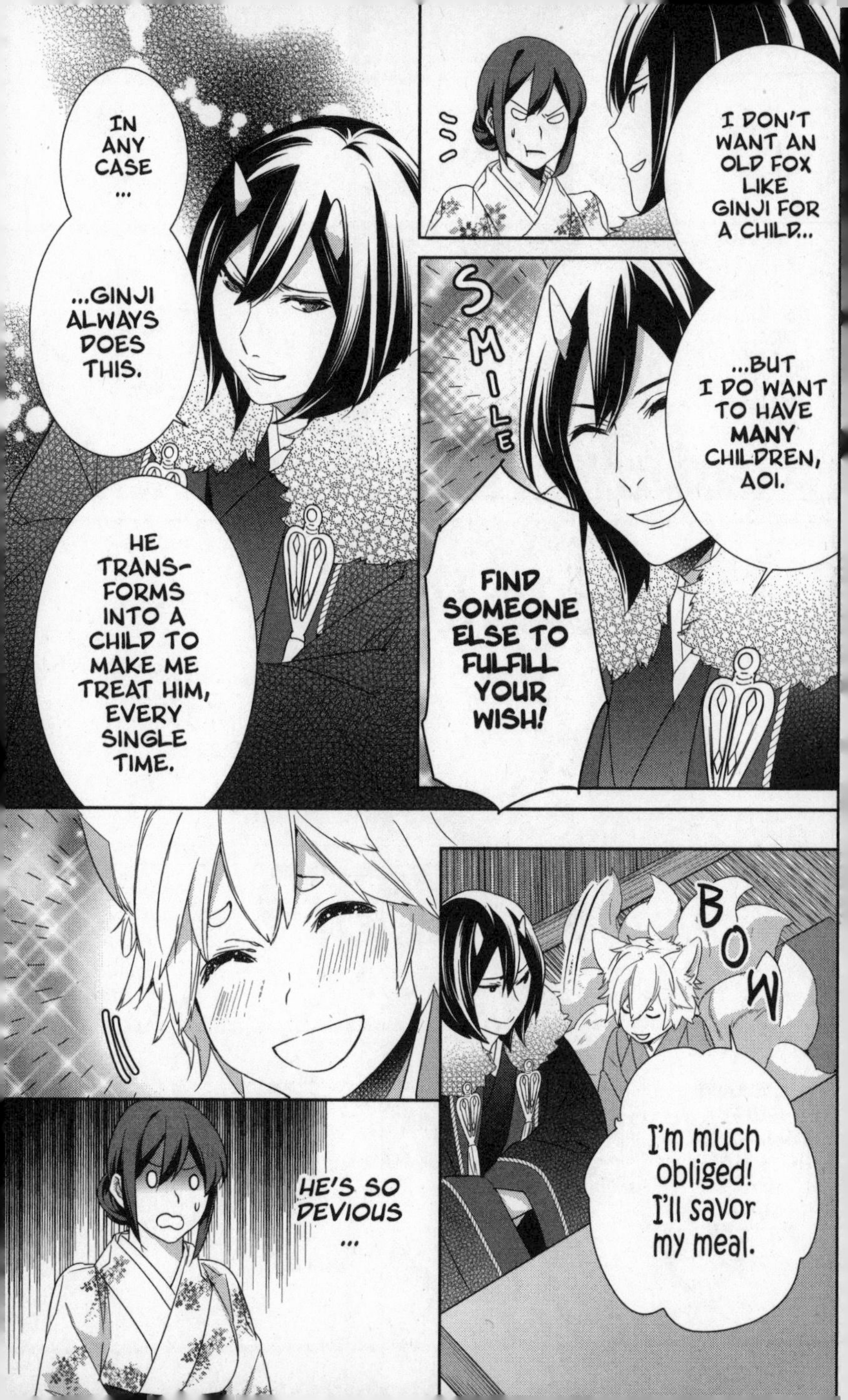
...
I DON'T WANT AN OLD FOX LIKE GINJI FOR A CHILD...
...BUT I DO WANT TO HAVE MANY CHILDREN, AOI.
SMILE
FIND SOMEONE ELSE TO FULFILL YOUR WISH!
IN ANY CASE...
...GINJI ALWAYS DOES THIS.
HE TRANSFORMS INTO A CHILD TO MAKE ME TREAT HIM, EVERY SINGLE TIME.
BOW
I'm much obliged! I'll savor my meal.
HE'S SO DEVIOUS...

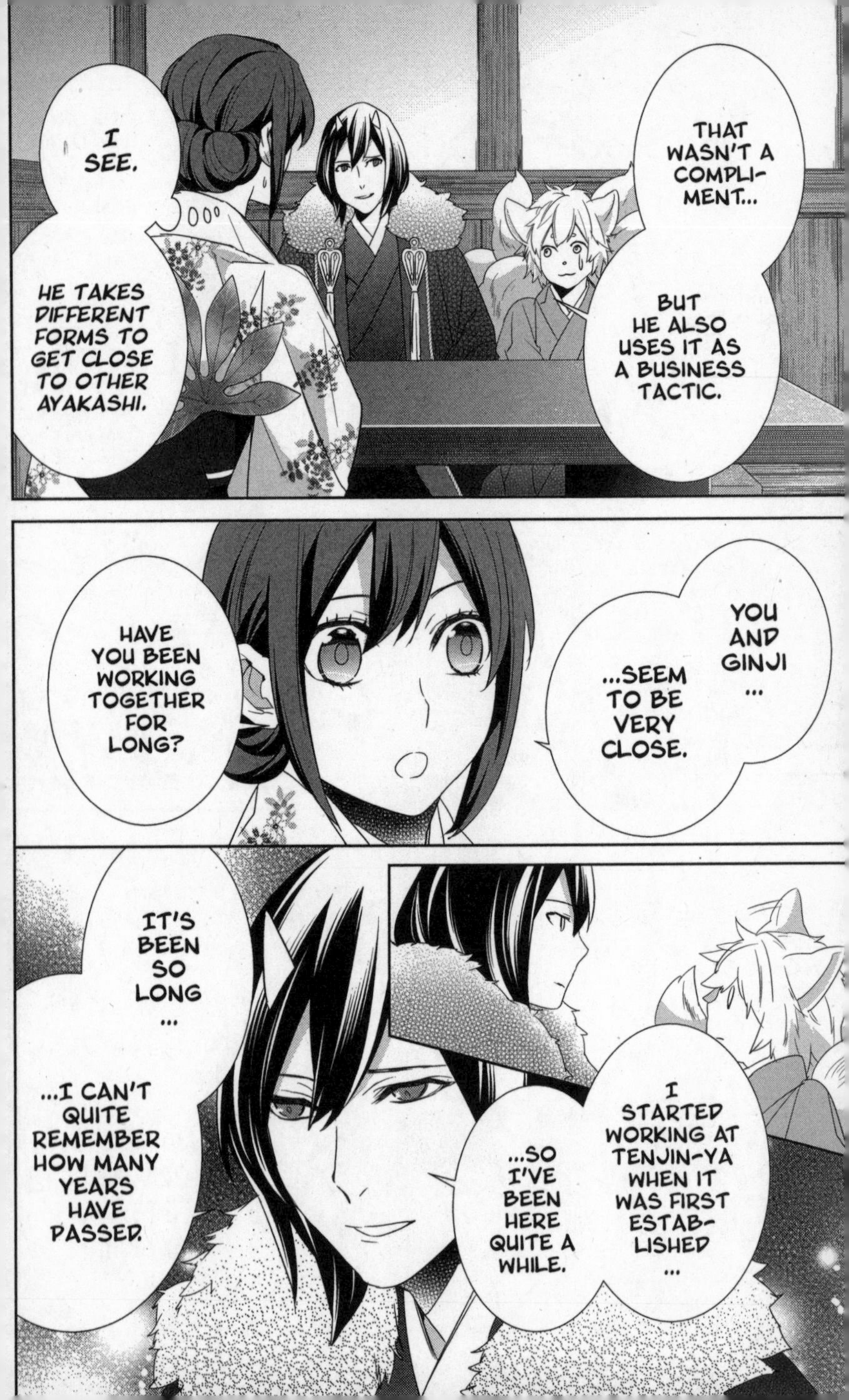
THAT WASN'T A COMPLIMENT...
I SEE.
BUT HE ALSO USES IT AS A BUSINESS TACTIC.
HE TAKES DIFFERENT FORMS TO GET CLOSE TO OTHER AYAKASHI.
YOU AND GINJI ...
...SEEM TO BE VERY CLOSE.
HAVE YOU BEEN WORKING TOGETHER FOR LONG?
I STARTED WORKING AT TENJIN-YA WHEN IT WAS FIRST ESTABLISHED ...
...SO I'VE BEEN HERE QUITE A WHILE.
IT'S BEEN SO LONG ...
...I CAN'T QUITE REMEMBER HOW MANY YEARS HAVE PASSED.

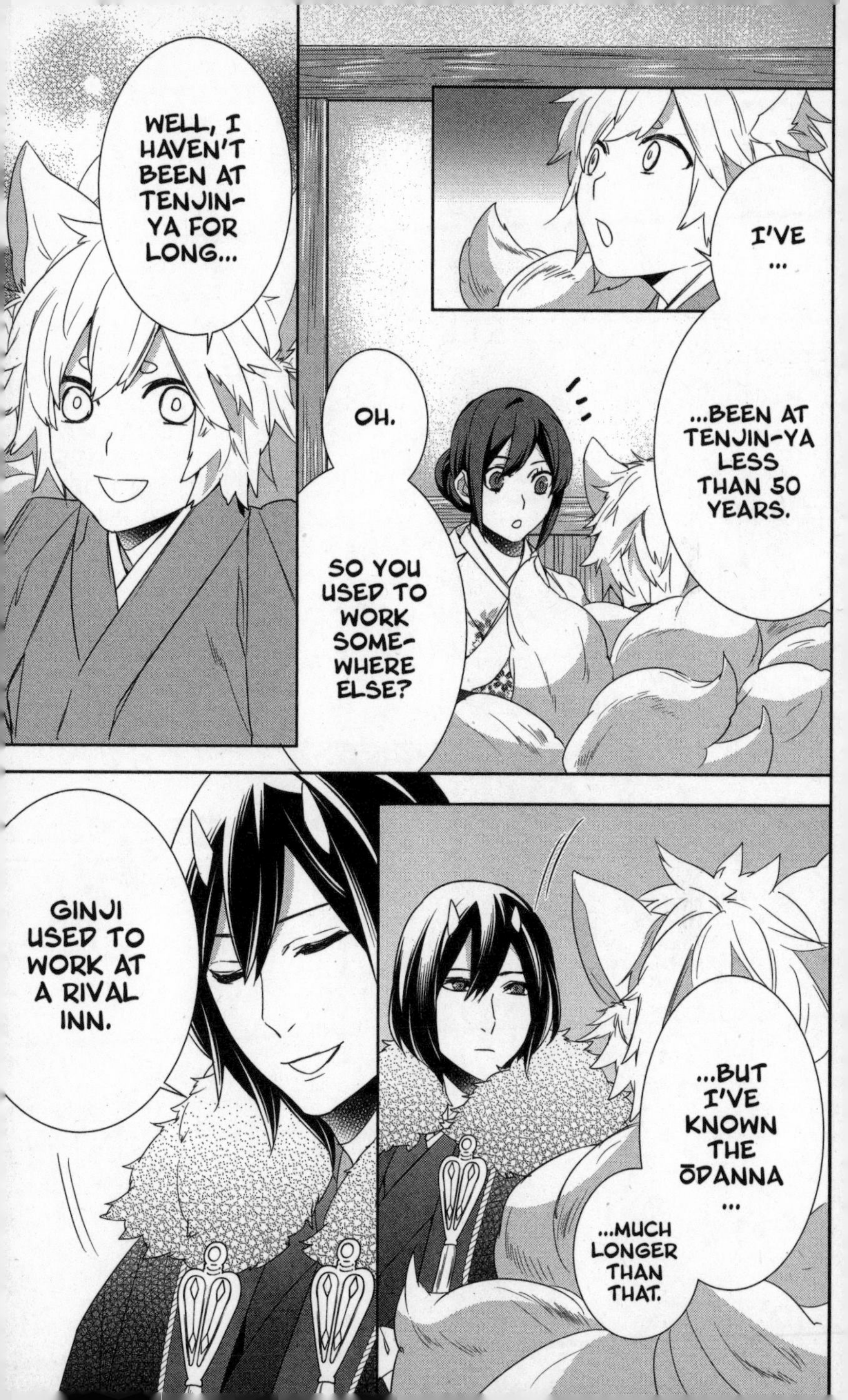
I'VE ...
...BEEN AT TENJIN-YA LESS THAN 50 YEARS.
OH.
SO YOU USED TO WORK SOME-WHERE ELSE?
WELL, I HAVEN'T BEEN AT TENJIN-YA FOR LONG...
...BUT I'VE KNOWN THE ŌDANNA ...
...MUCH LONGER THAN THAT.
GINJI USED TO WORK AT A RIVAL INN.

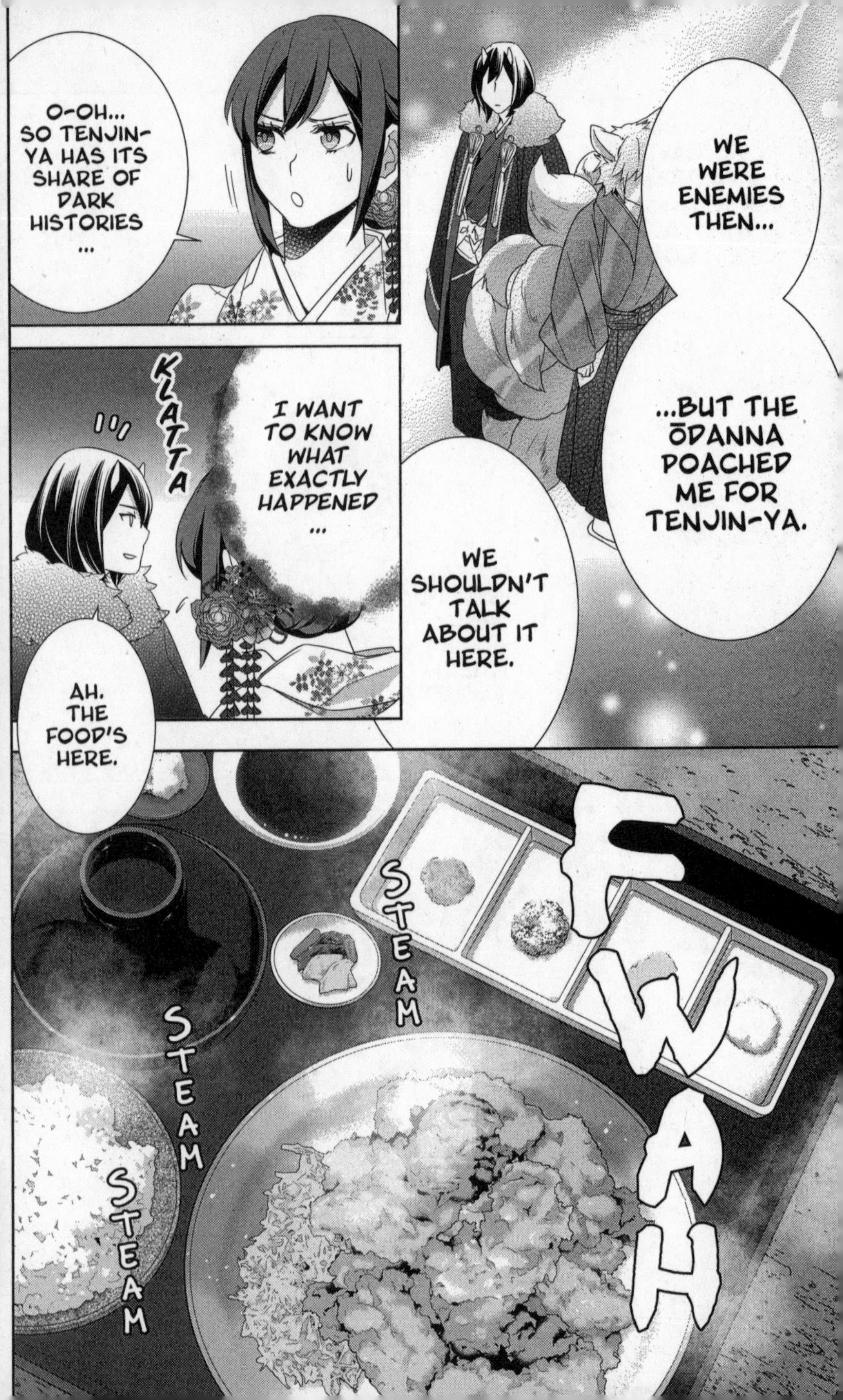
WE WERE ENEMIES THEN...
...BUT THE ŌDANNA POACHED ME FOR TENJIN-YA.
O-OH... SO TENJIN-YA HAS ITS SHARE OF DARK HISTORIES ...
I WANT TO KNOW WHAT EXACTLY HAPPENED ...
KLATTA
WE SHOULDN'T TALK ABOUT IT HERE.
AH. THE FOOD'S HERE.
FWAH
STEAM
STEAM
STEAM

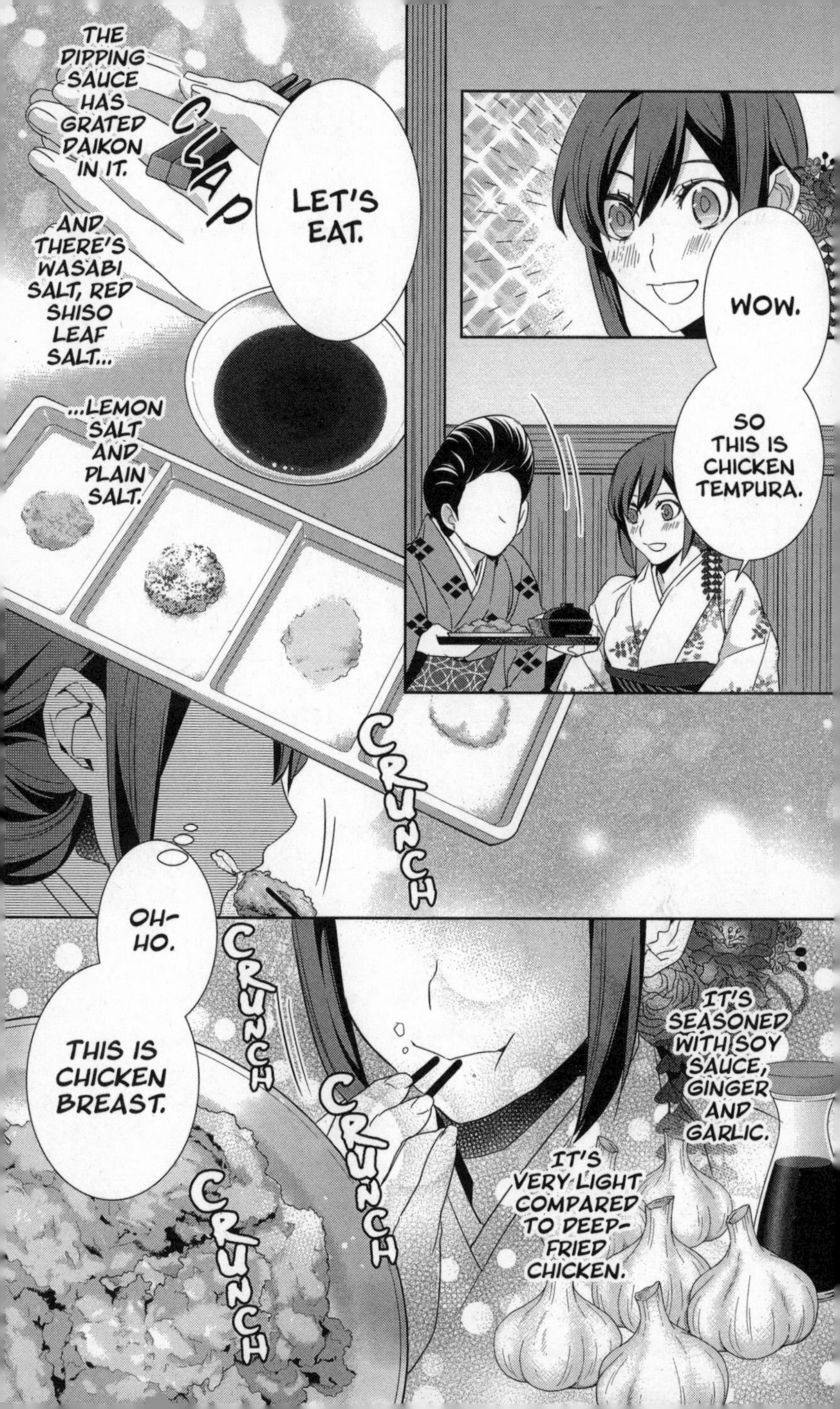
WOW.
SO THIS IS CHICKEN TEMPURA.
LET'S EAT.
CLAP
THE DIPPING SAUCE HAS GRATED DAIKON IN IT.
AND THERE'S WASABI SALT, RED SHISO LEAF SALT...
...LEMON SALT AND PLAIN SALT.
CRUNCH
IT'S SEASONED WITH SOY SAUCE, GINGER AND GARLIC.
IT'S VERY LIGHT COMPARED TO DEEP-FRIED CHICKEN.
CRUNCH
CRUNCH
CRUNCH
OH-HO.
THIS IS CHICKEN BREAST.

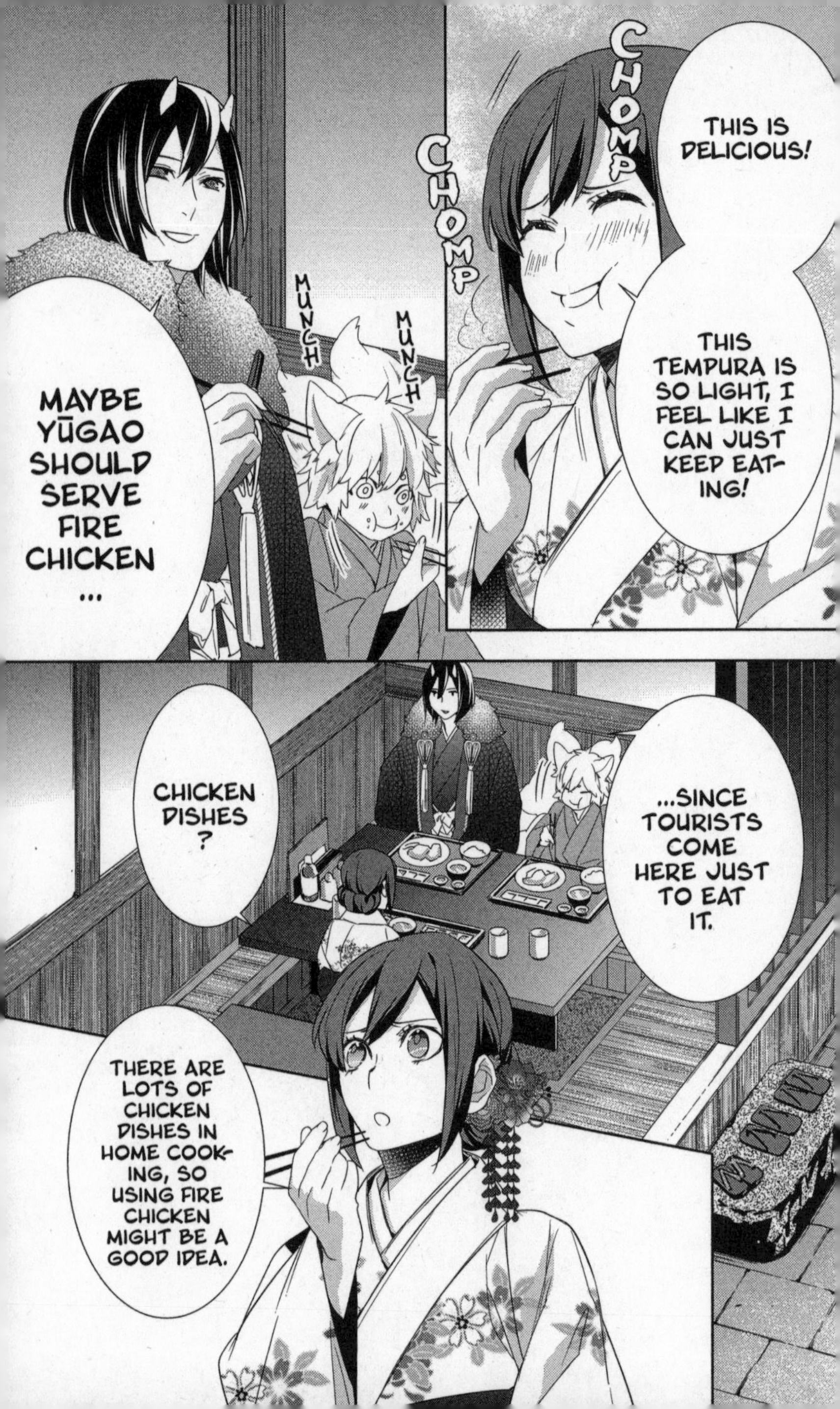
CHOMP
CHOMP
THIS IS DELICIOUS!
THIS TEMPURA IS SO LIGHT, I FEEL LIKE I CAN JUST KEEP EAT-ING!
MUNCH
MUNCH
MAYBE YŪGAO SHOULD SERVE FIRE CHICKEN ...
...SINCE TOURISTS COME HERE JUST TO EAT IT.
CHICKEN DISHES?
THERE ARE LOTS OF CHICKEN DISHES IN HOME COOK-ING, SO USING FIRE CHICKEN MIGHT BE A GOOD IDEA.

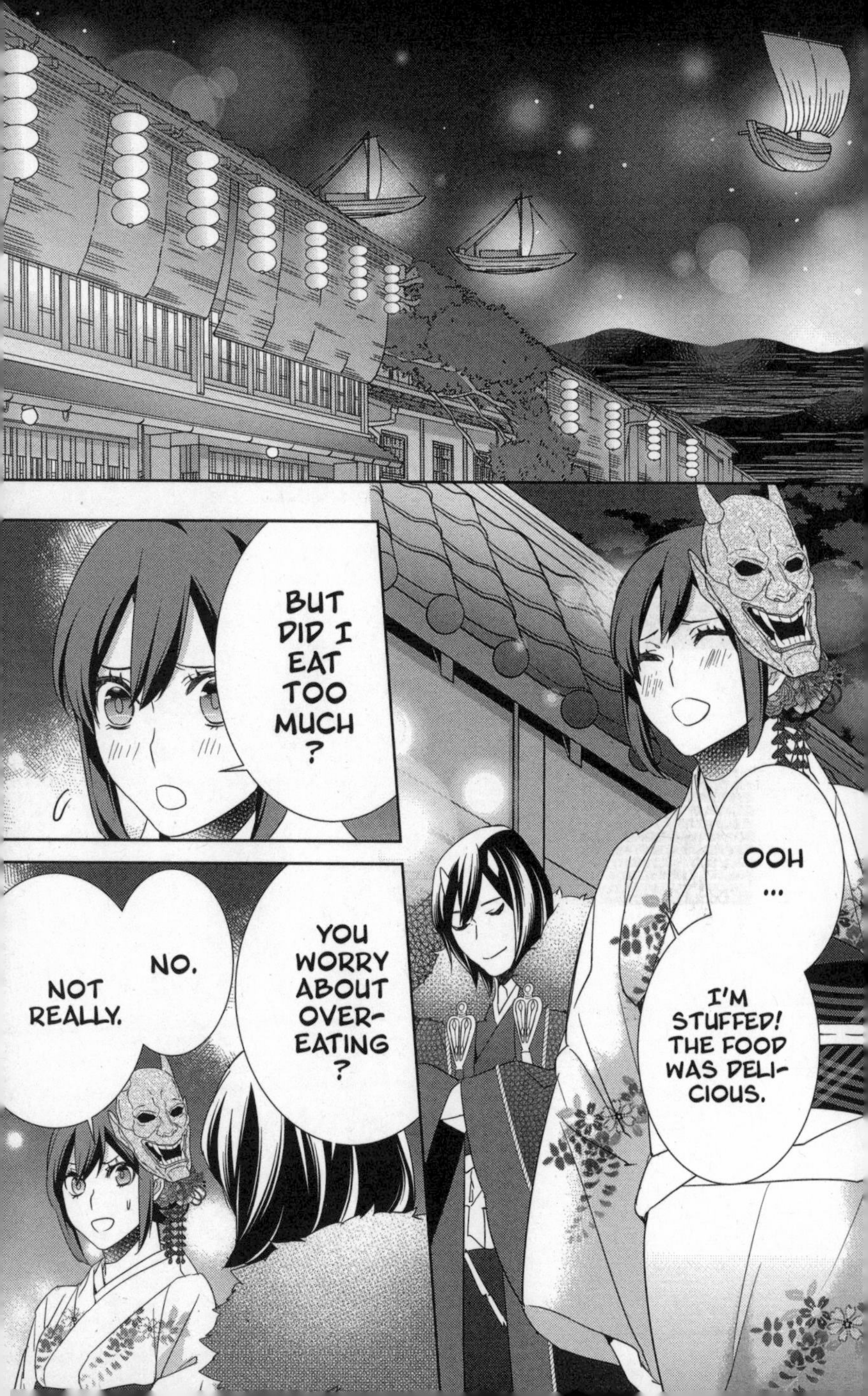
OOH ...
I'M STUFFED! THE FOOD WAS DELICIOUS.
BUT DID I EAT TOO MUCH?
YOU WORRY ABOUT OVER-EATING?
NO.
NOT REALLY.

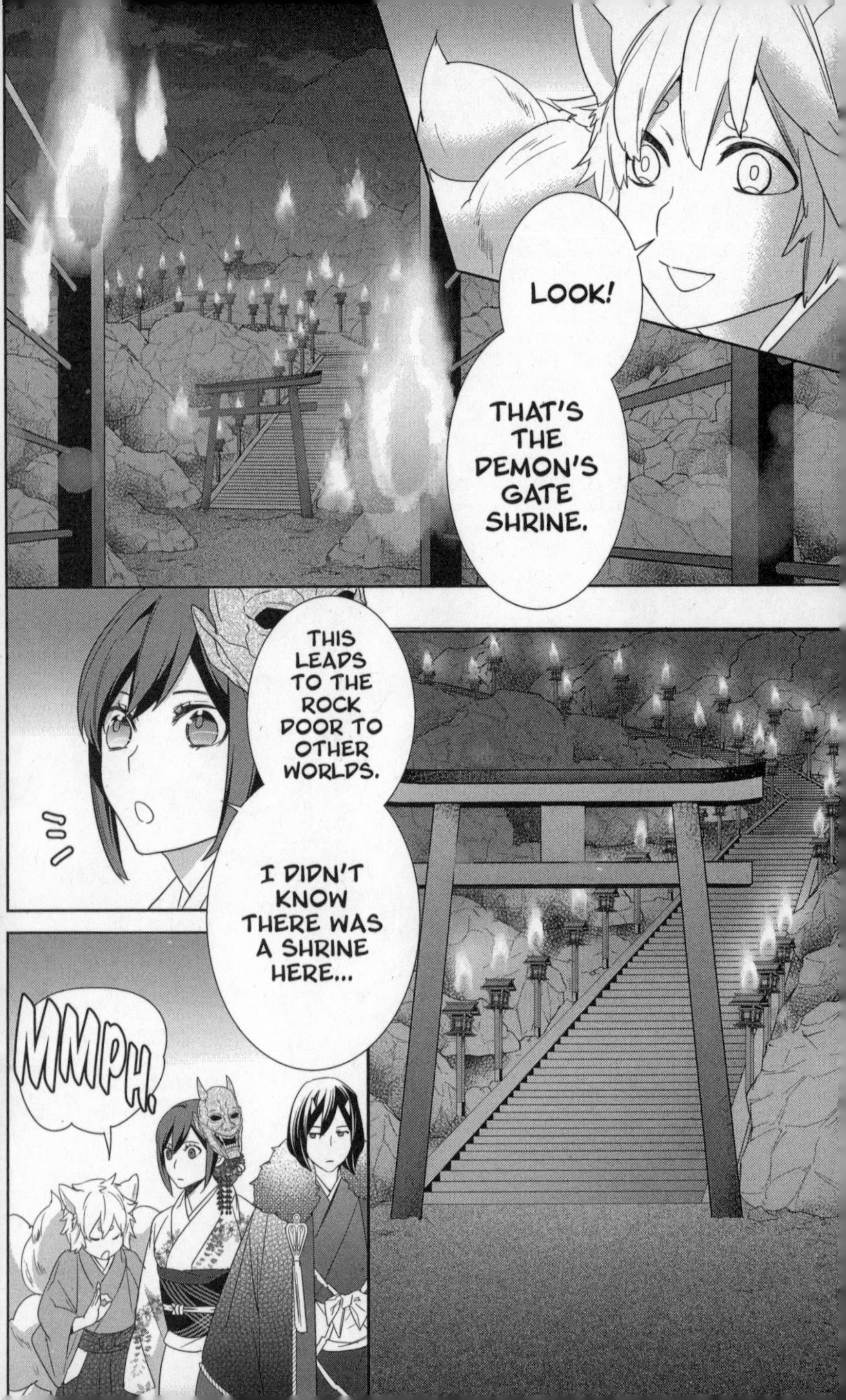
LOOK!
THAT'S THE DEMON'S GATE SHRINE.
THIS LEADS TO THE ROCK DOOR TO OTHER WORLDS.
I DIDN'T KNOW THERE WAS A SHRINE HERE...
MMPH.

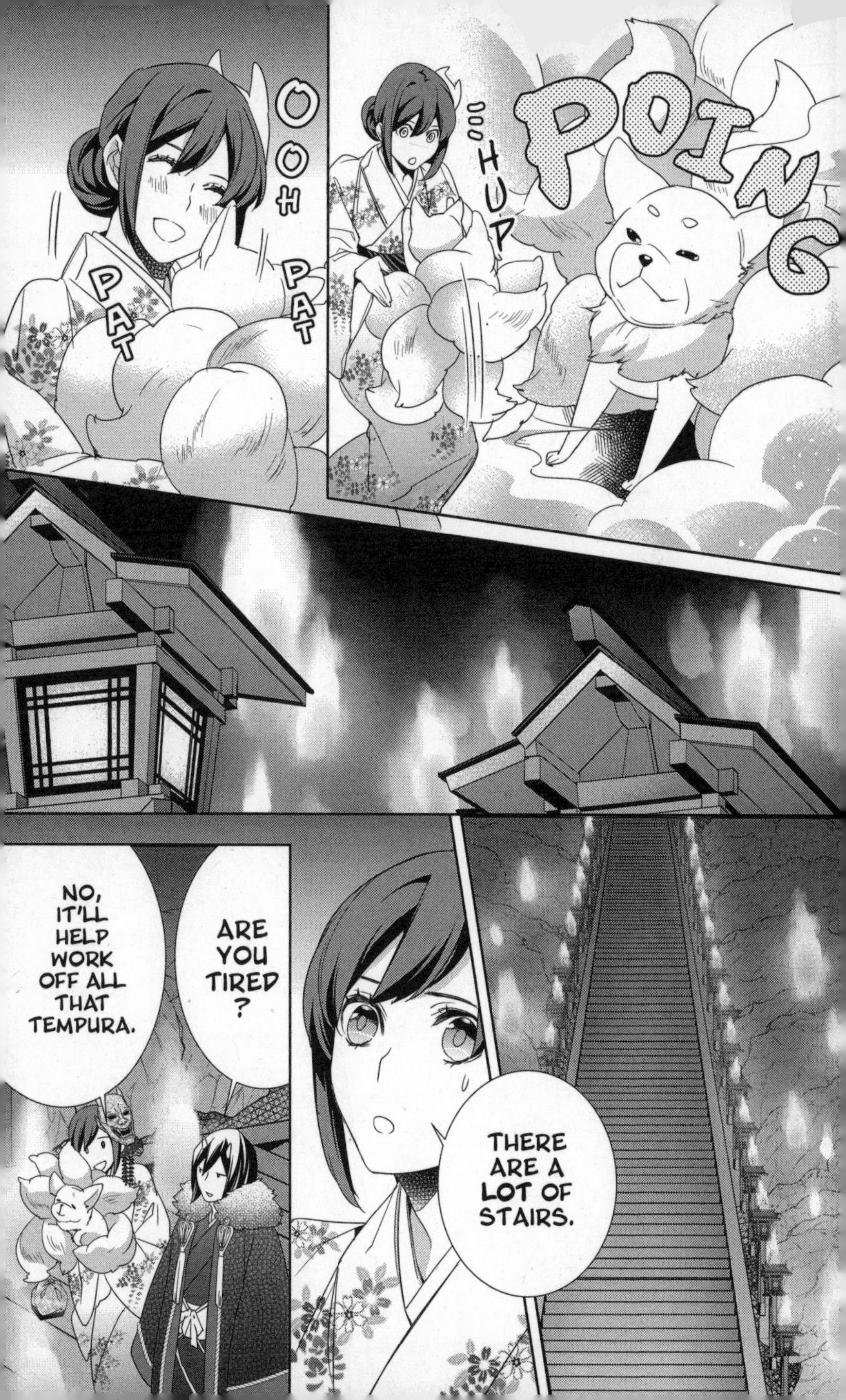
POING
...HUP
OOH
PAT PAT
THERE ARE A LOT OF STAIRS.
ARE YOU TIRED?
NO, IT'LL HELP WORK OFF ALL THAT TEMPURA.

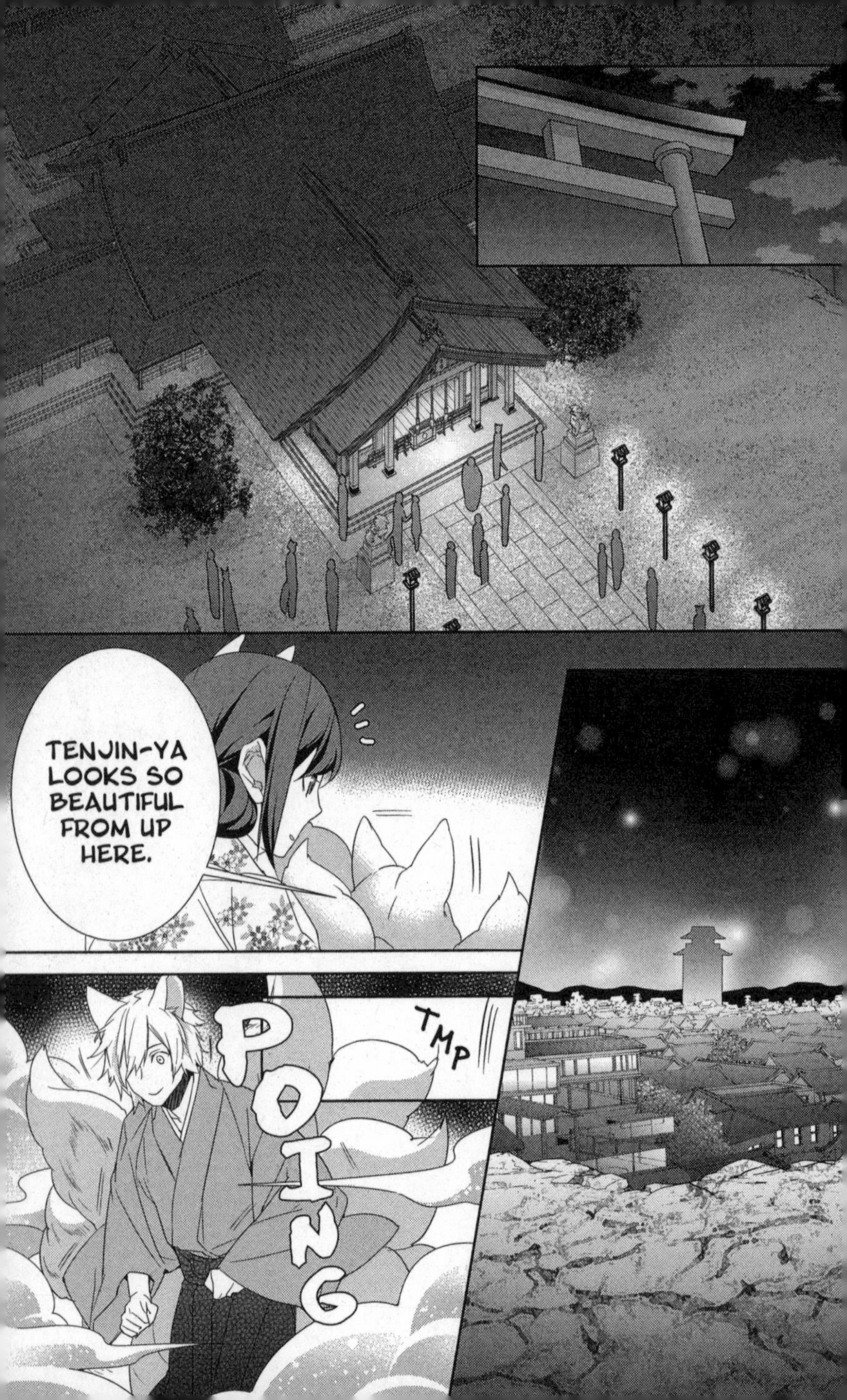
TENJIN-YA LOOKS SO BEAUTIFUL FROM UP HERE.
TMP
POING

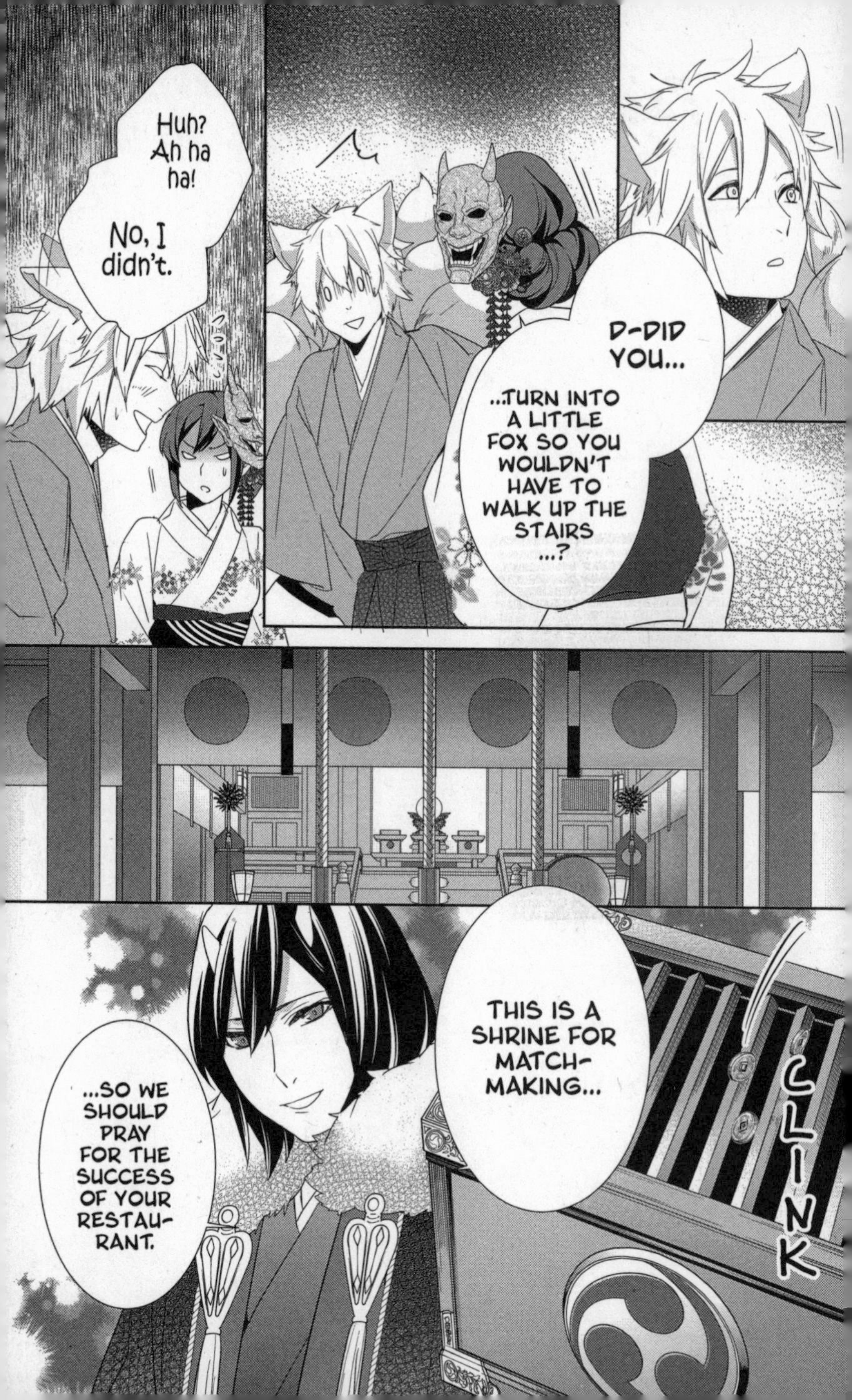

D-DID YOU...
...TURN INTO A LITTLE FOX SO YOU WOULDN'T HAVE TO WALK UP THE STAIRS ...?
Huh? Ah ha ha!
No, I didn't.
CLINK
THIS IS A SHRINE FOR MATCH-MAKING...
...SO WE SHOULD PRAY FOR THE SUCCESS OF YOUR RESTAU-RANT.

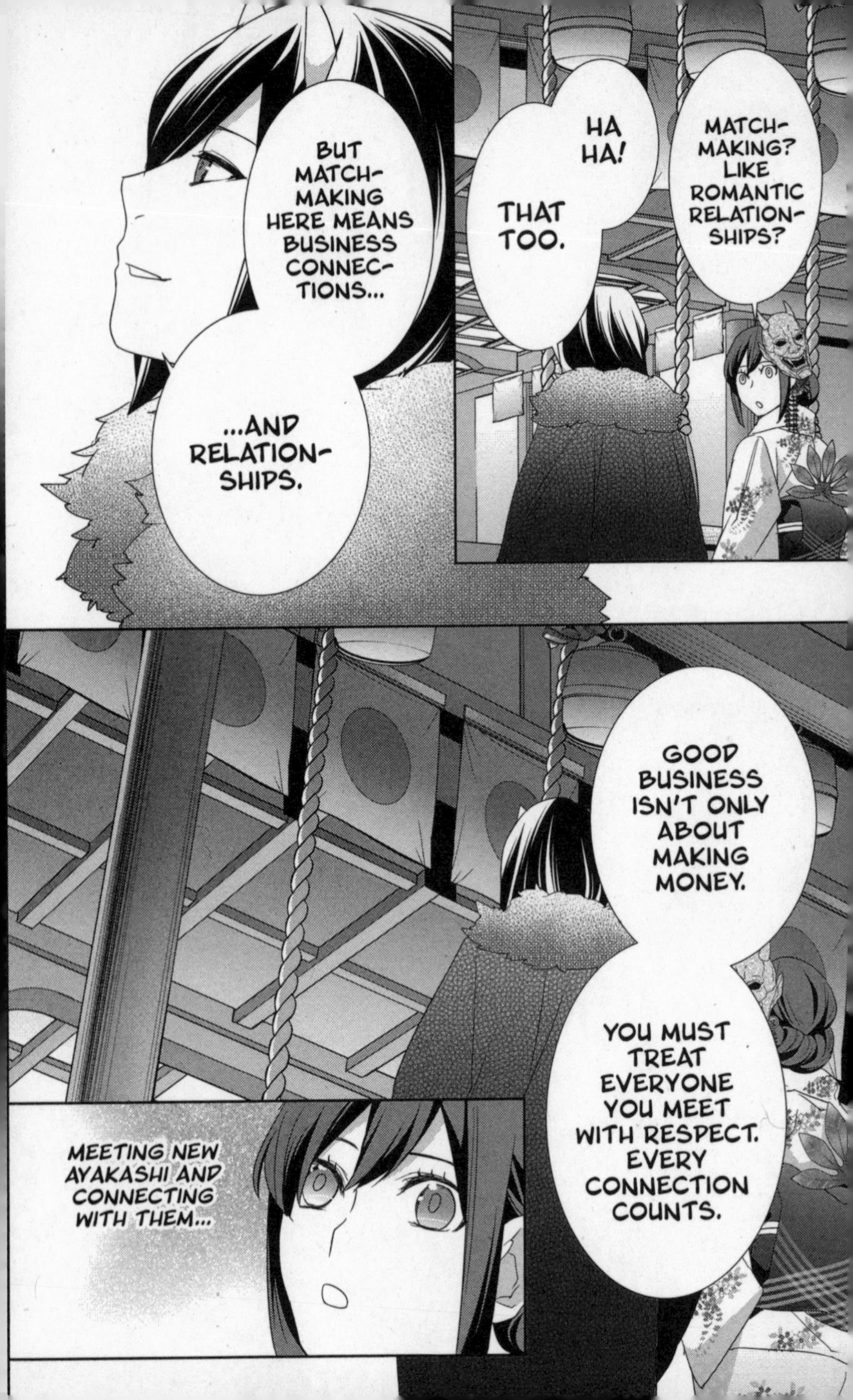
MATCH-MAKING? LIKE ROMANTIC RELATION-SHIPS?
HA HA!
THAT TOO.
BUT MATCH-MAKING HERE MEANS BUSINESS CONNEC-TIONS...
...AND RELATION-SHIPS.
GOOD BUSINESS ISN'T ONLY ABOUT MAKING MONEY.
YOU MUST TREAT EVERYONE YOU MEET WITH RESPECT. EVERY CONNECTION COUNTS.
MEETING NEW AYAKASHI AND CONNECTING WITH THEM...

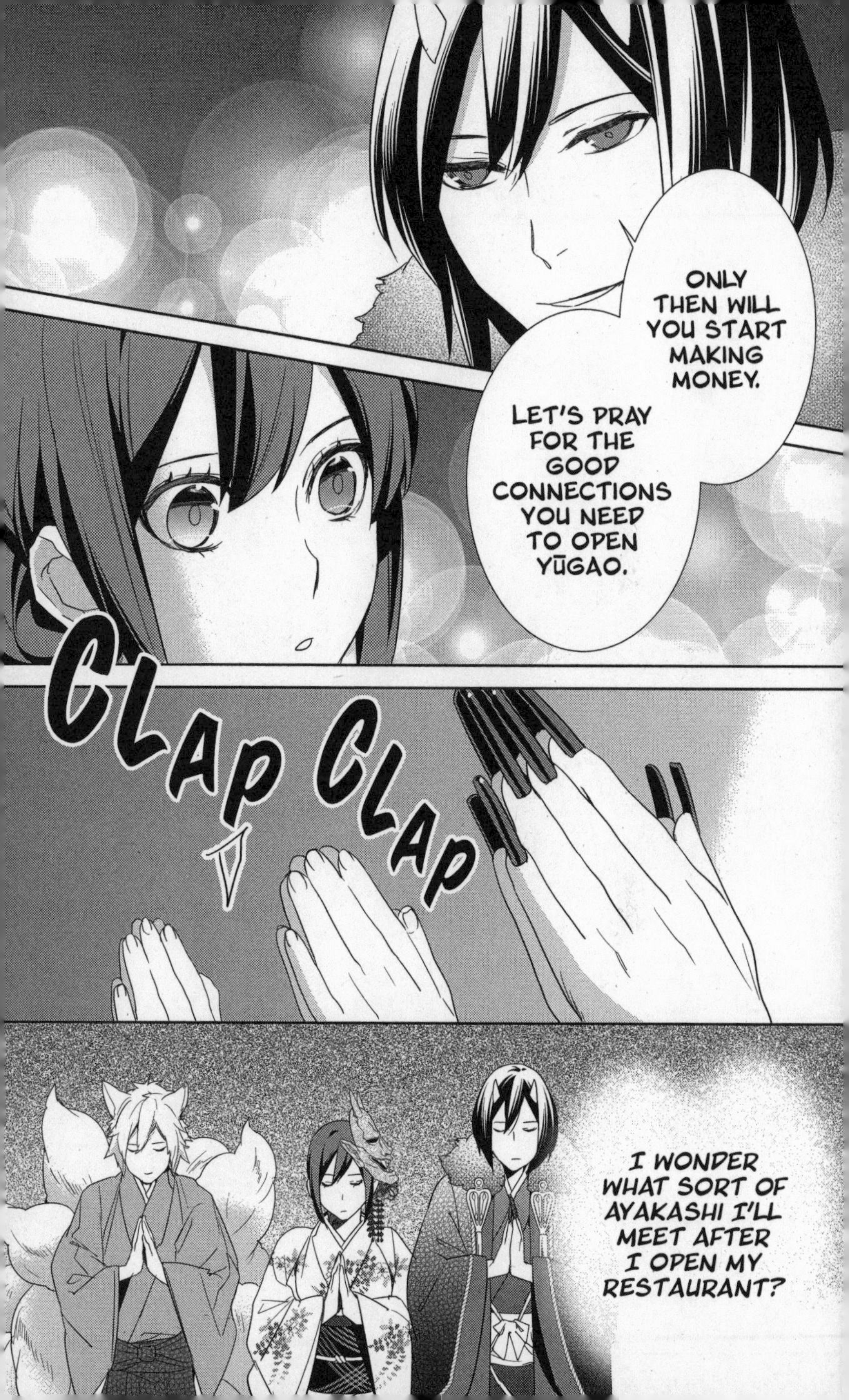
ONLY THEN WILL YOU START MAKING MONEY.
LET'S PRAY FOR THE GOOD CONNECTIONS YOU NEED TO OPEN YŪGAO.
CLAP CLAP
I WONDER WHAT SORT OF AYAKASHI I'LL MEET AFTER I OPEN MY RESTAURANT?

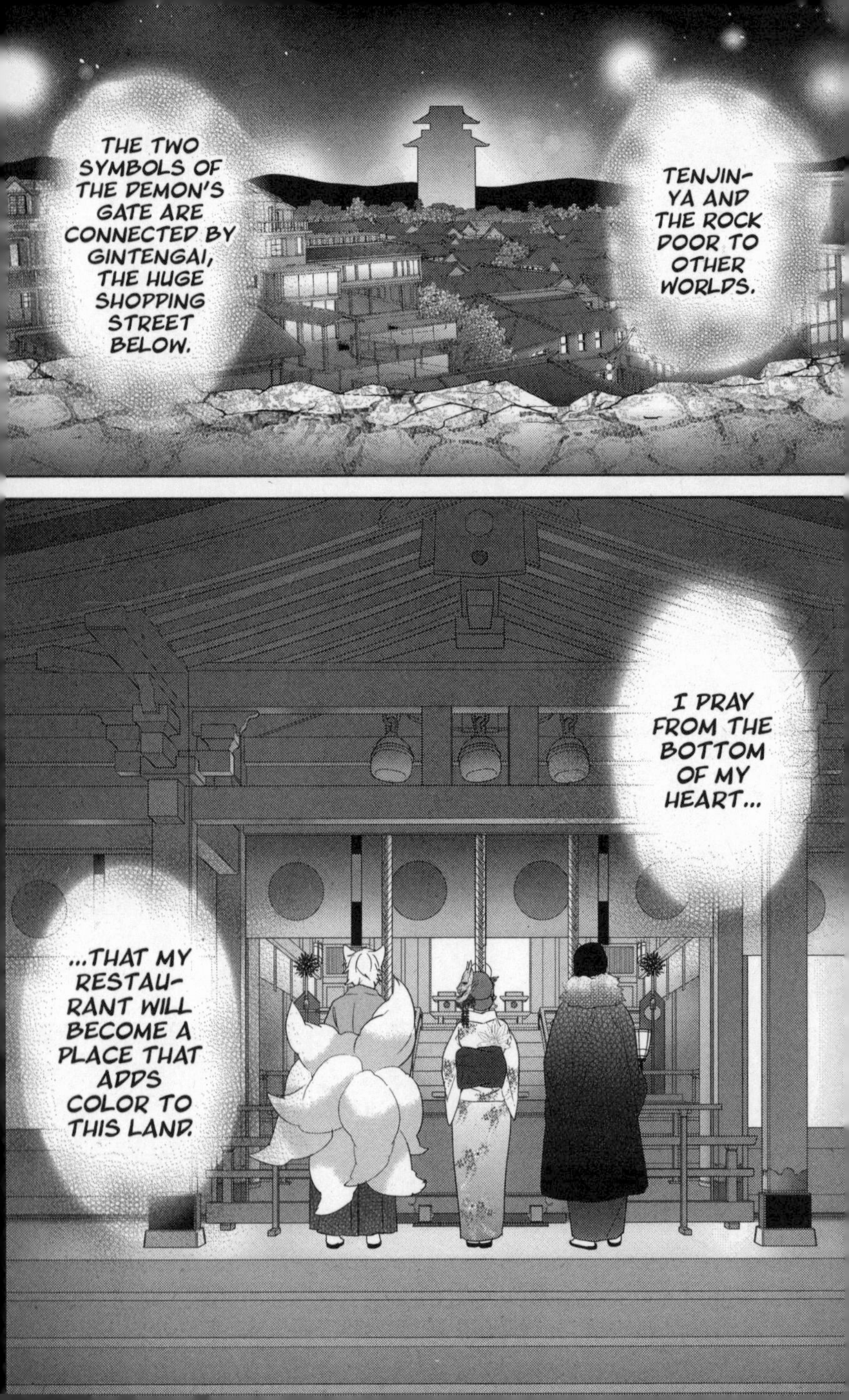
TENJIN-YA AND THE ROCK DOOR TO OTHER WORLDS.
THE TWO SYMBOLS OF THE DEMON'S GATE ARE CONNECTED BY GINTENGAI, THE HUGE SHOPPING STREET BELOW.
I PRAY FROM THE BOTTOM OF MY HEART...
...THAT MY RESTAU-RANT WILL BECOME A PLACE THAT ADDS COLOR TO THIS LAND.

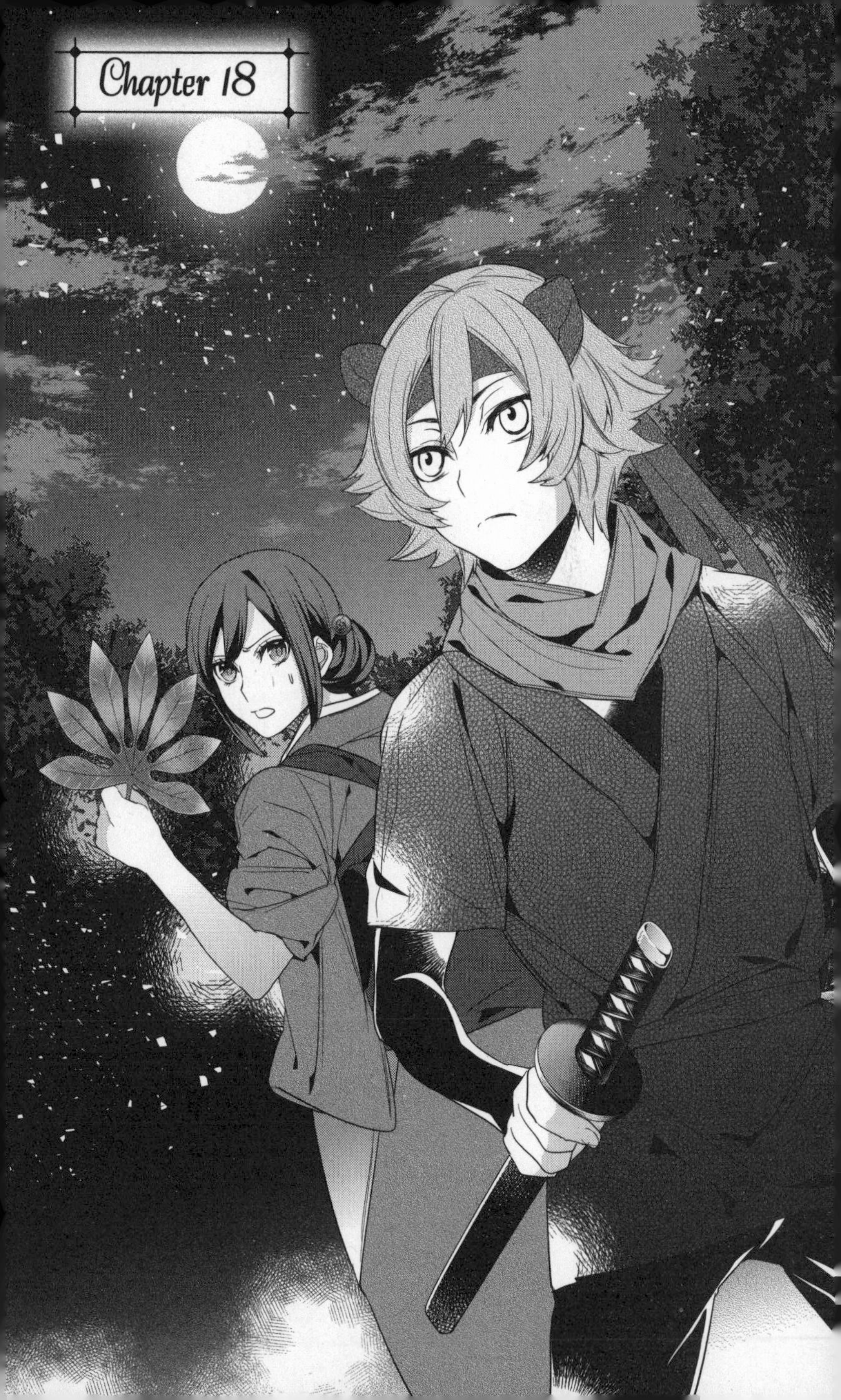
Chapter 18

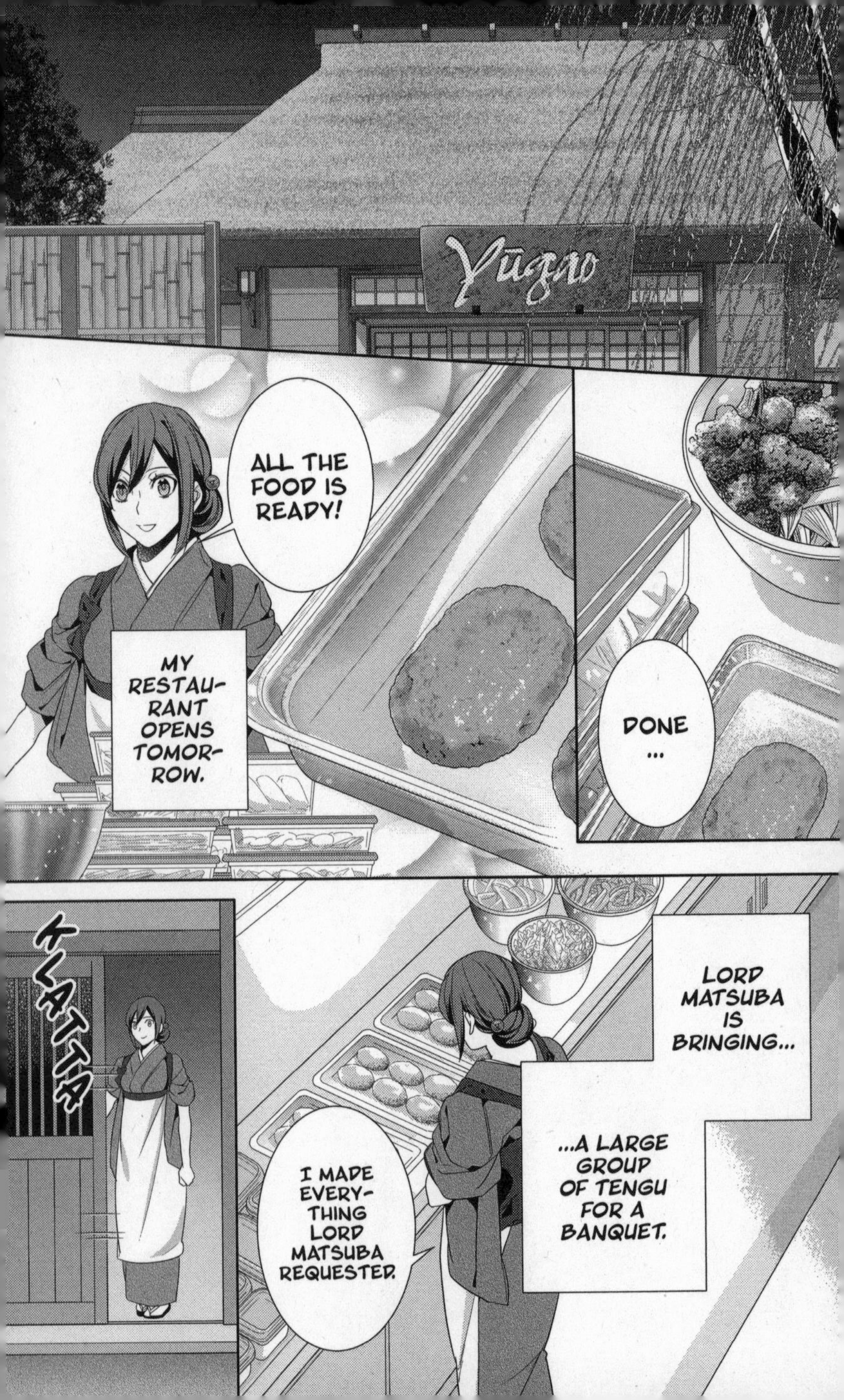
Yūgao
DONE ...
ALL THE FOOD IS READY!
MY RESTAURANT OPENS TOMORROW.
LORD MATSUBA IS BRINGING...
...A LARGE GROUP OF TENGU FOR A BANQUET.
I MADE EVERYTHING LORD MATSUBA REQUESTED.
KATTA

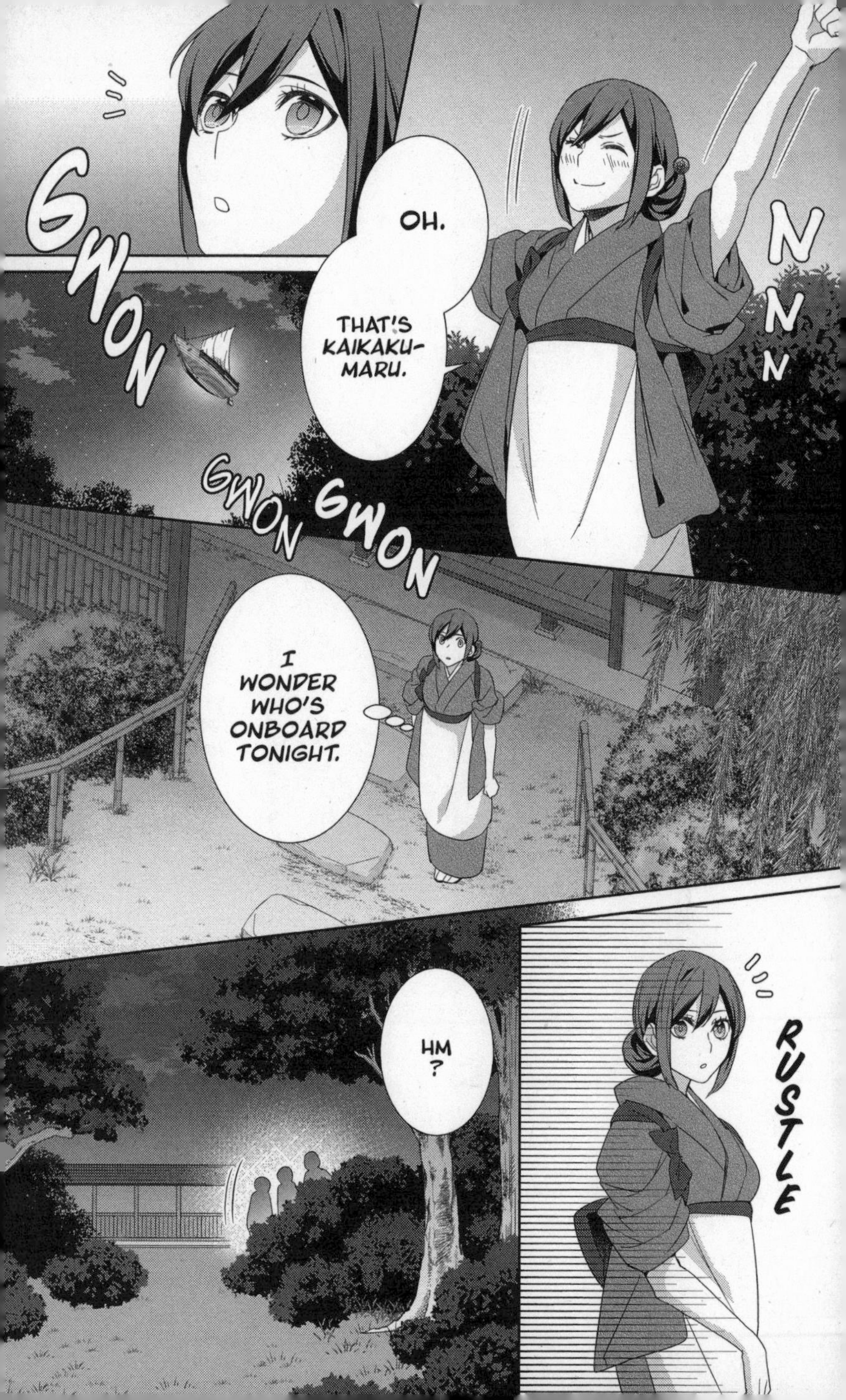
NNNN
GWON
OH.
THAT'S KAIKAKU-MARU.
GWON GWON
I WONDER WHO'S ONBOARD TONIGHT.
RUSTLE
HM?

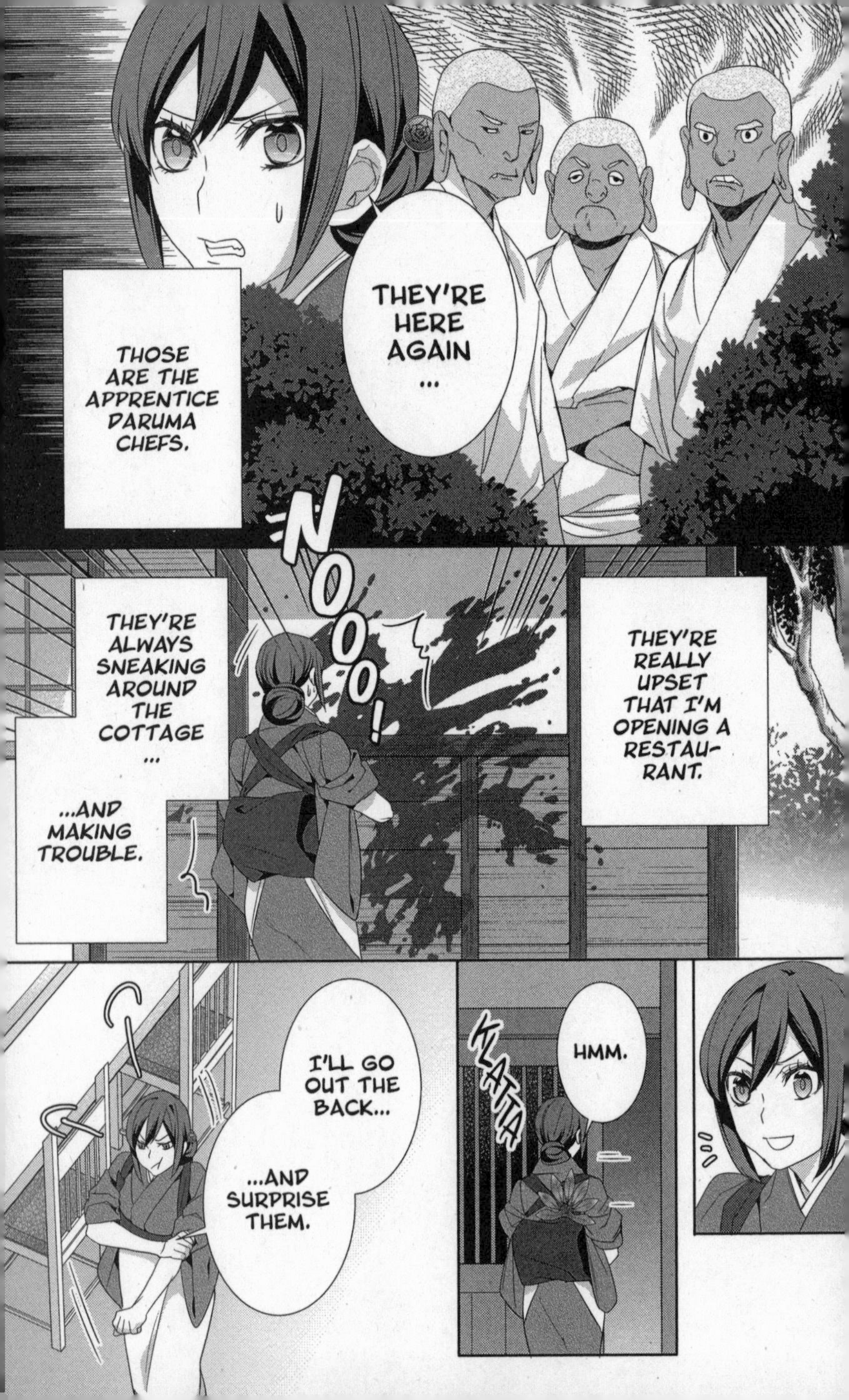
THEY'RE HERE AGAIN ...
THOSE ARE THE APPRENTICE DARUMA CHEFS.
NOOOO!
THEY'RE REALLY UPSET THAT I'M OPENING A RESTAURANT.
THEY'RE ALWAYS SNEAKING AROUND THE COTTAGE ...
...AND MAKING TROUBLE.
HMM.
KLATA
I'LL GO OUT THE BACK...
...AND SURPRISE THEM.

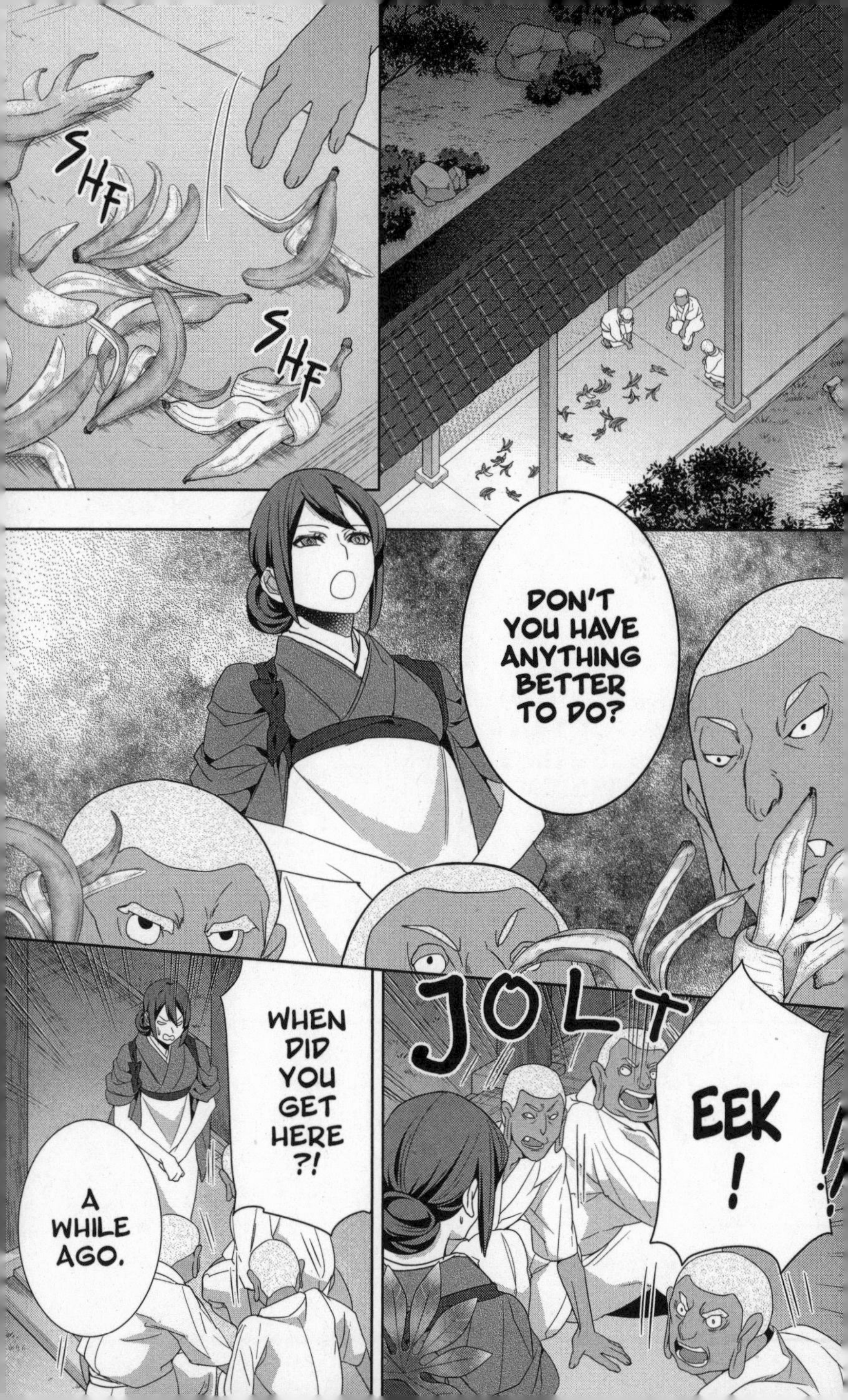
SHF
SHF
DON'T YOU HAVE ANYTHING BETTER TO DO?
JOLT
EEK!
!!
WHEN DID YOU GET HERE?!
A WHILE AGO.

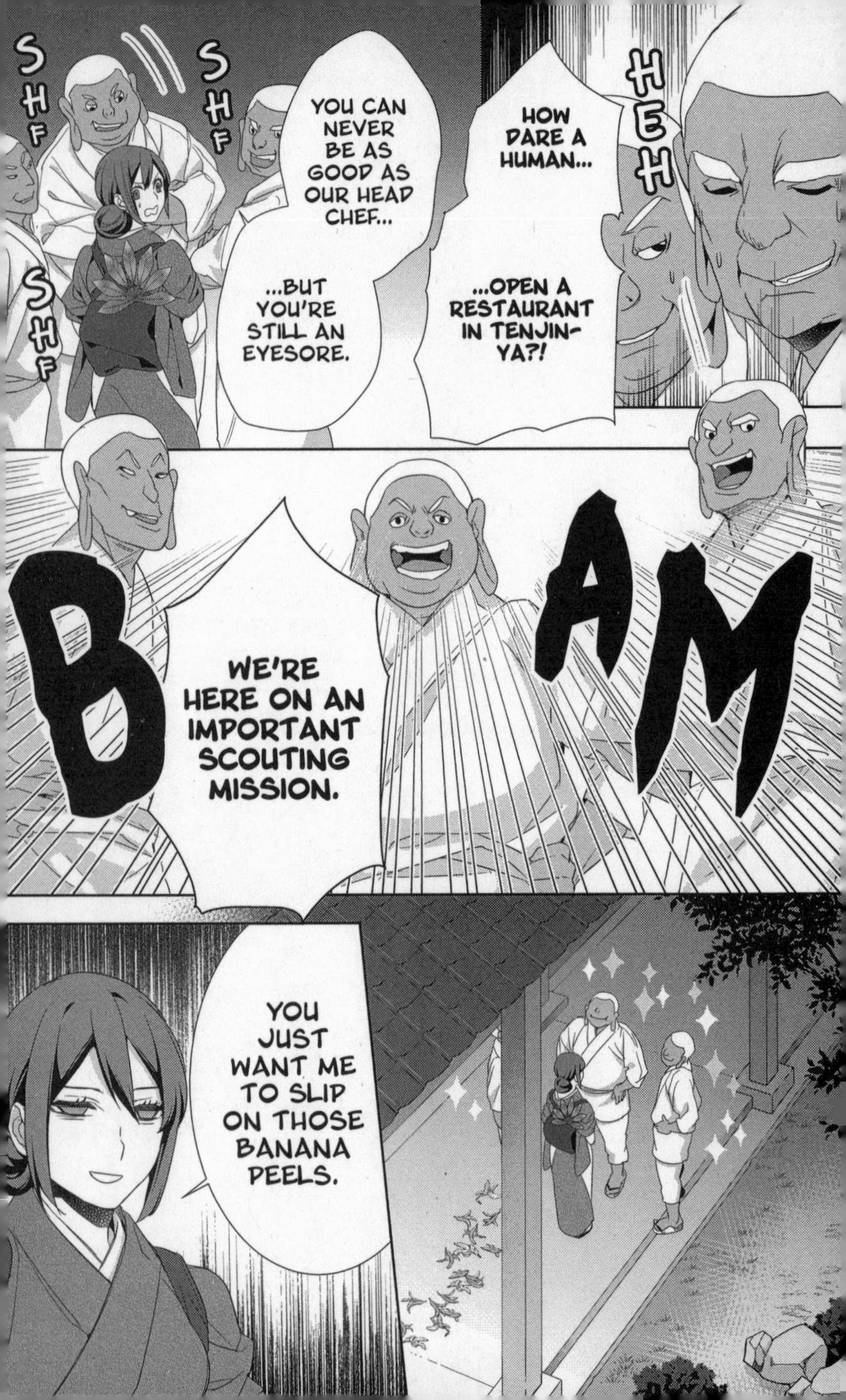
HEH
HOW DARE A HUMAN...
...OPEN A RESTAURANT IN TENJIN-YA?!
SHF
SHF
SHF
YOU CAN NEVER BE AS GOOD AS OUR HEAD CHEF...
...BUT YOU'RE STILL AN EYESORE.
BAM
WE'RE HERE ON AN IMPORTANT SCOUTING MISSION.
YOU JUST WANT ME TO SLIP ON THOSE BANANA PEELS.

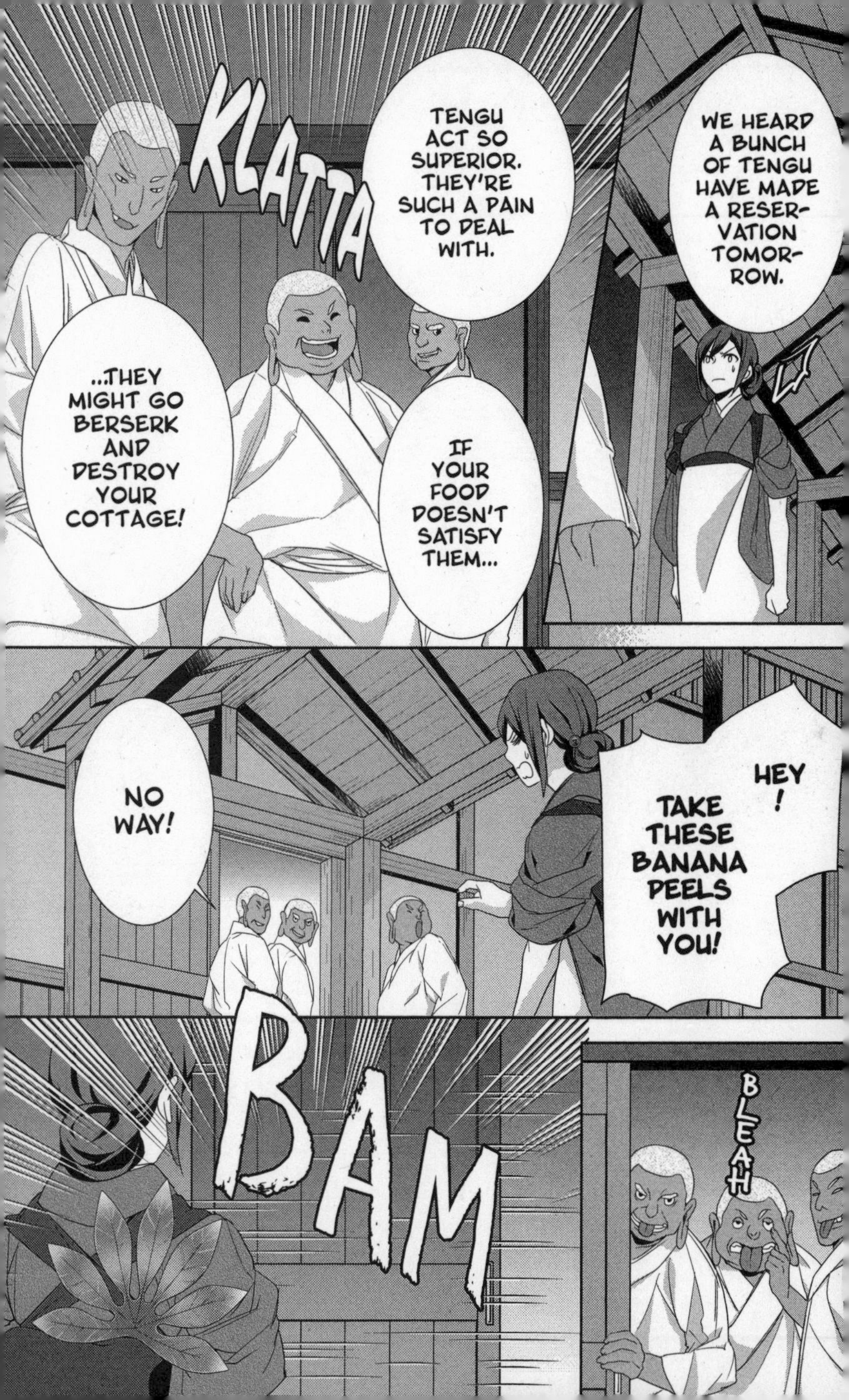
WE HEARD A BUNCH OF TENGU HAVE MADE A RESER-VATION TOMOR-ROW.
KLATTA
TENGU ACT SO SUPERIOR. THEY'RE SUCH A PAIN TO DEAL WITH.
IF YOUR FOOD DOESN'T SATISFY THEM...
...THEY MIGHT GO BERSERK AND DESTROY YOUR COTTAGE!
HEY!
TAKE THESE BANANA PEELS WITH YOU!
NO WAY!
BLEAH
BAM

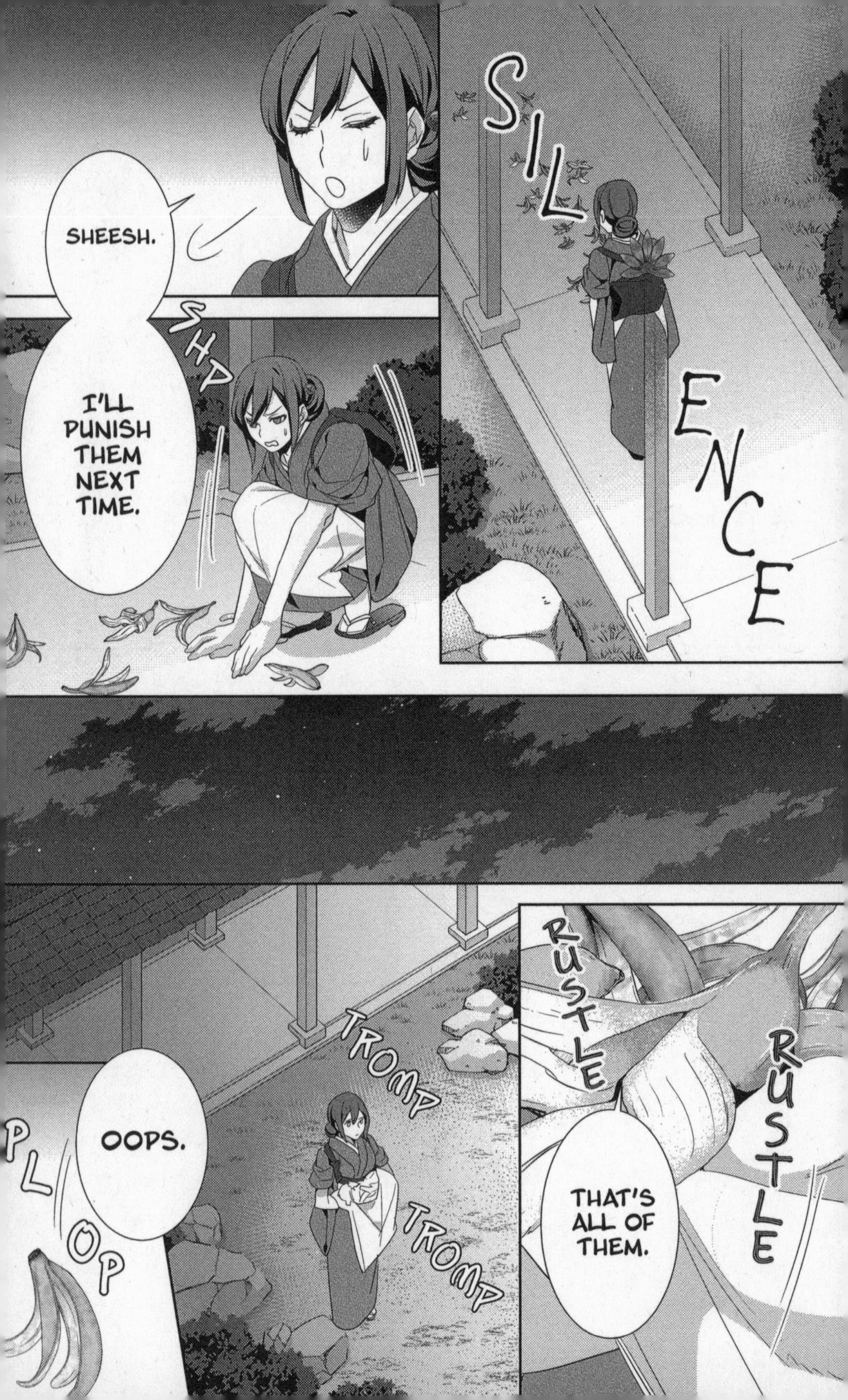
SILENCE
SHEESH.
I'LL PUNISH THEM NEXT TIME.
SHP
RUSTLE
RUSTLE
THAT'S ALL OF THEM.
TROMP
TROMP
OOPS.
PLOP

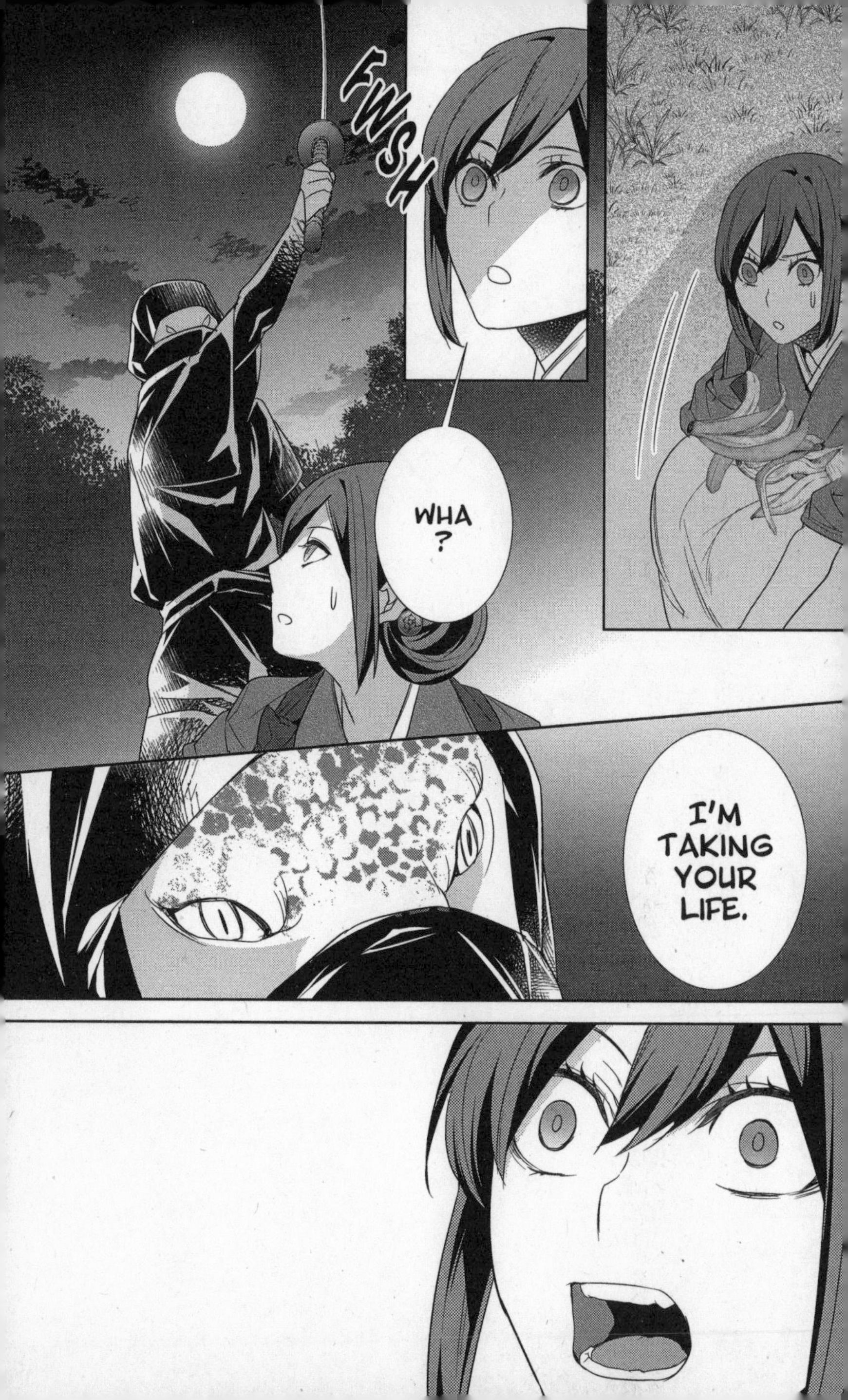
FWSH
WHA?
I'M TAKING YOUR LIFE.

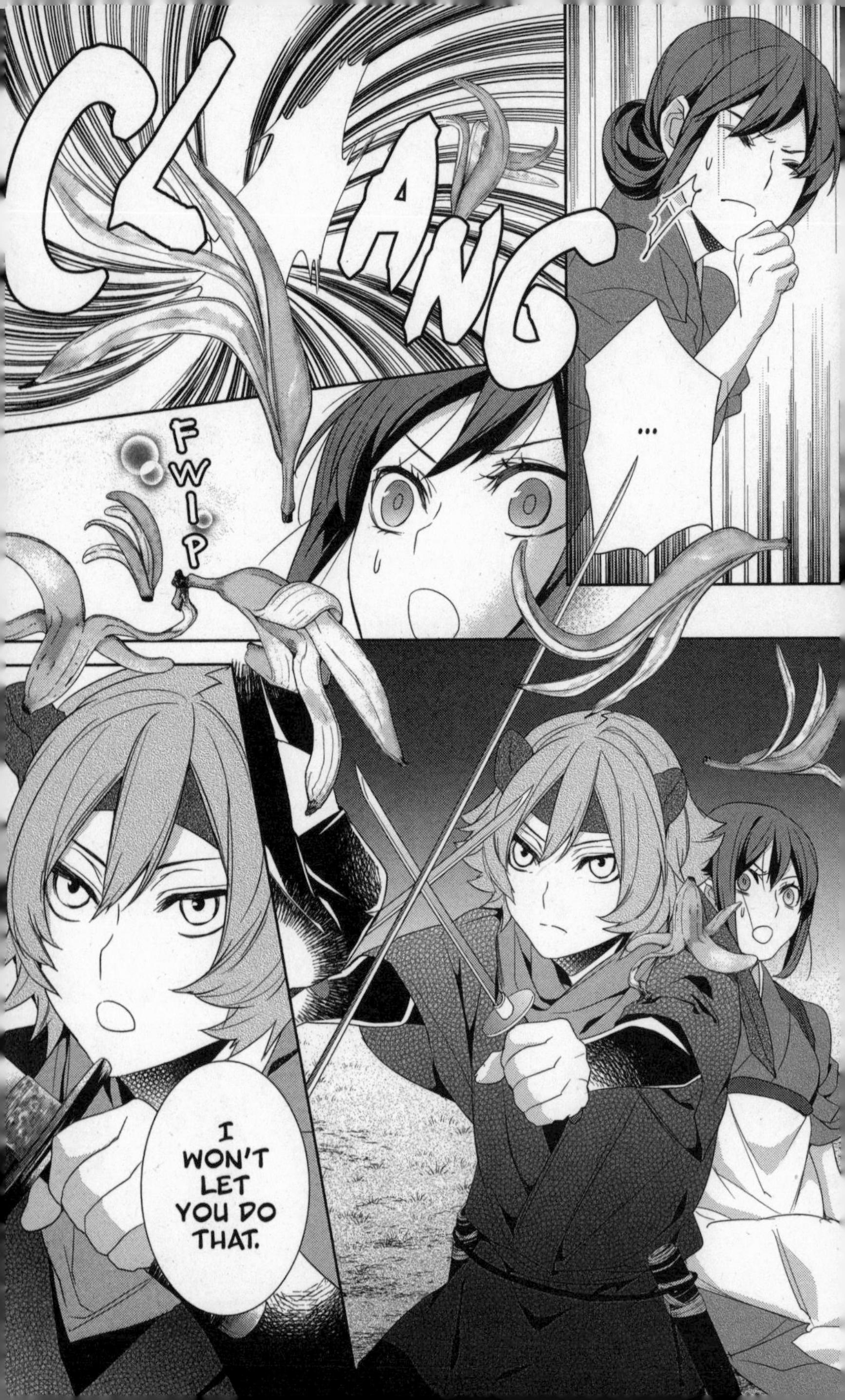
...
CLANG
FWIP
I WON'T LET YOU DO THAT.

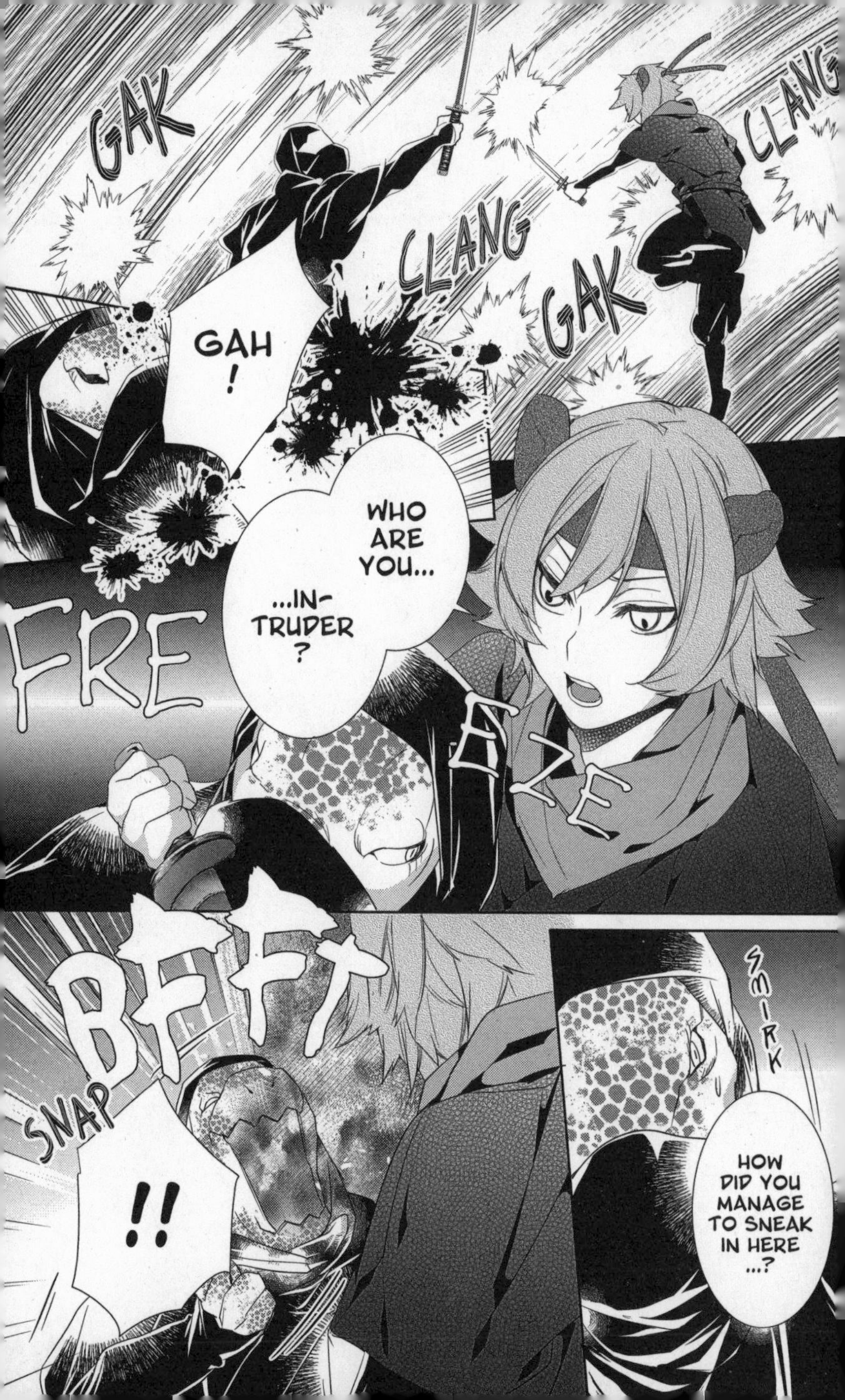
CLANG
GAK
CLANG
GAK
GAH!
WHO ARE YOU...
...IN-TRUDER?
FREEZE
SMIRK
HOW DID YOU MANAGE TO SNEAK IN HERE ...?
BFFT
SNAP
!!

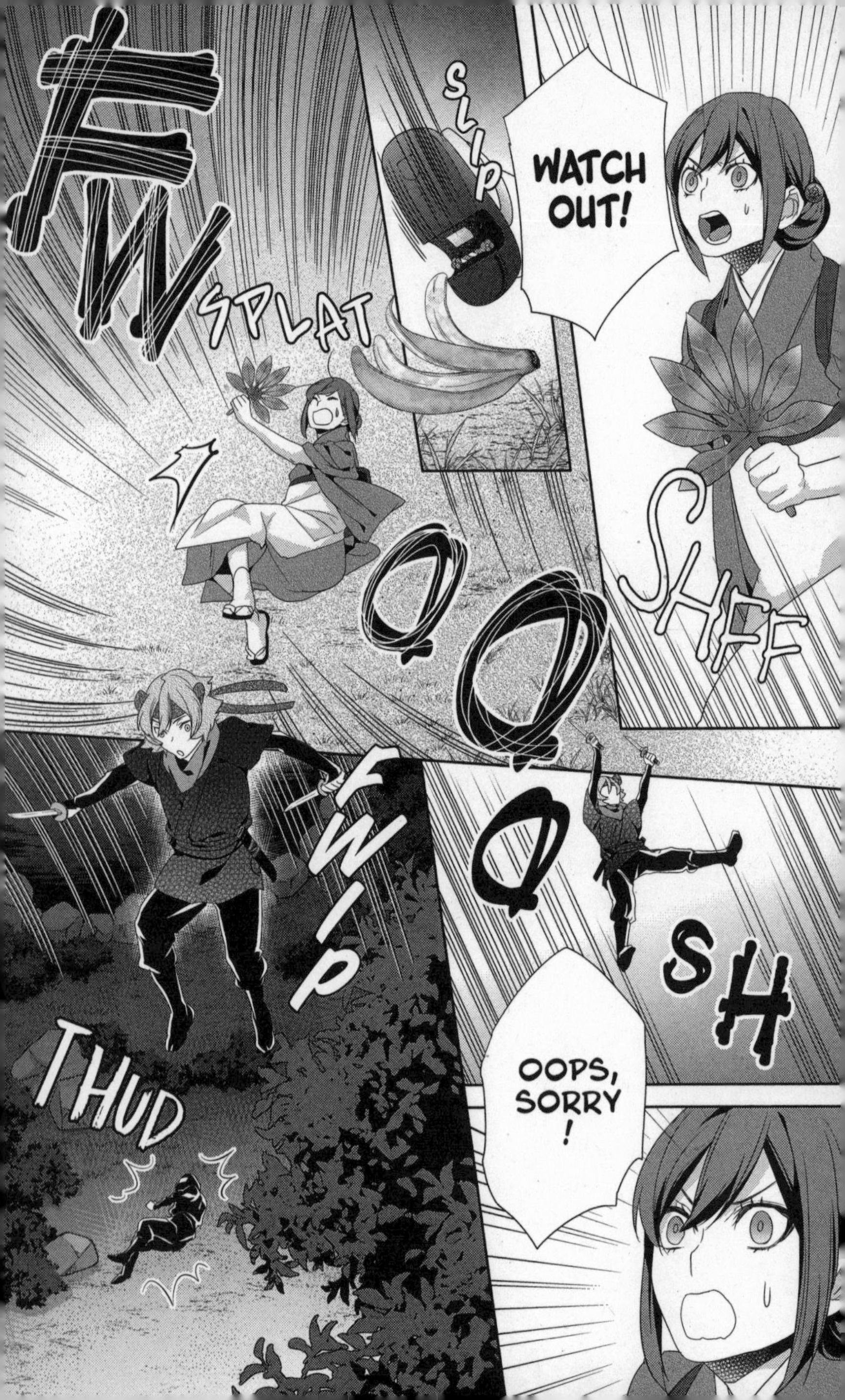
WATCH OUT!
SHFF
SLIP
ドン
SPLAT
OOPS, SORRY!
SH
FWIP
THUD

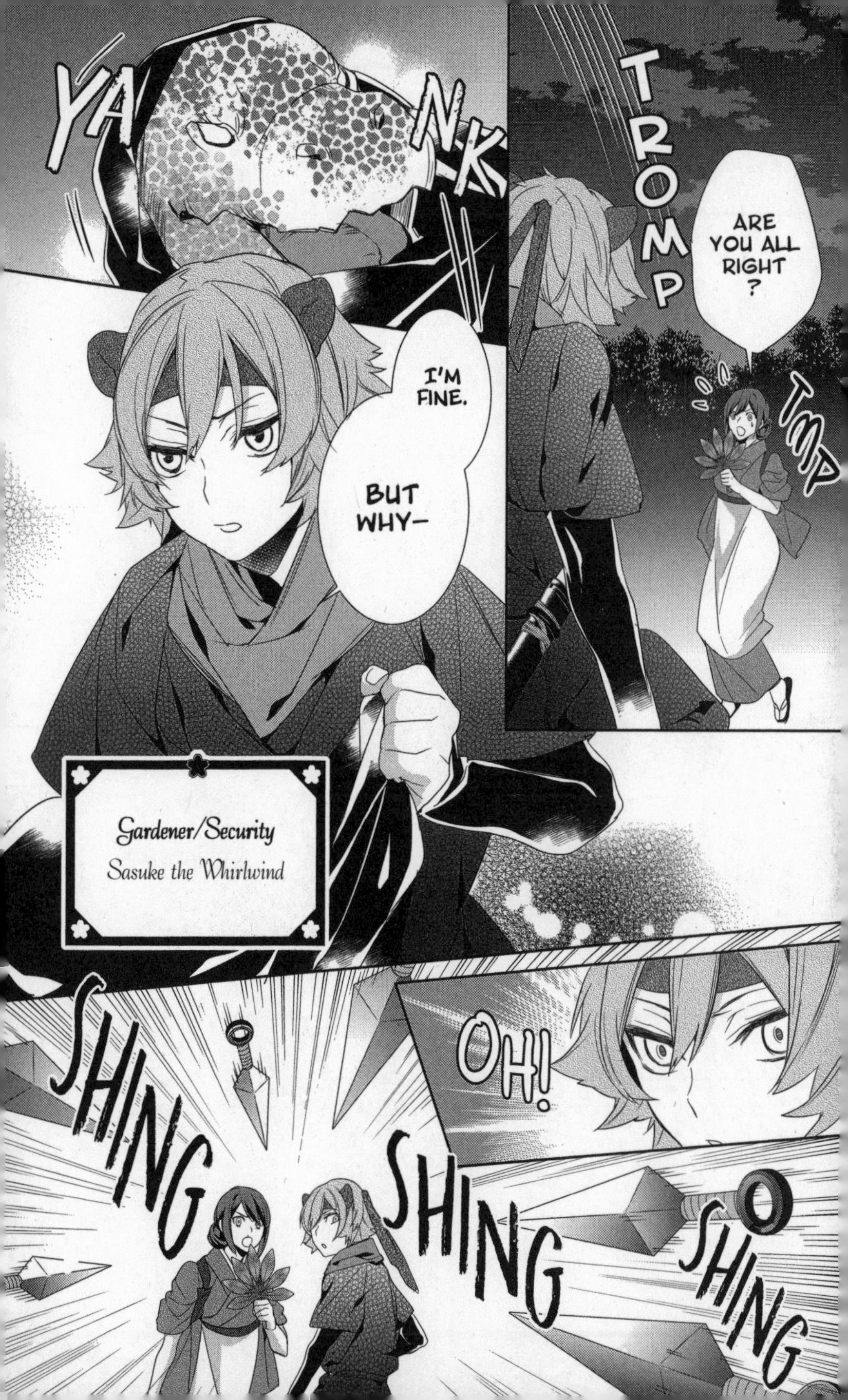
TROMP
ARE YOU ALL RIGHT?
TMP
YANK
I'M FINE.
BUT WHY–
Gardener/Security
Sasuke the Whirlwind
OH!
SHING
SHING
SHING

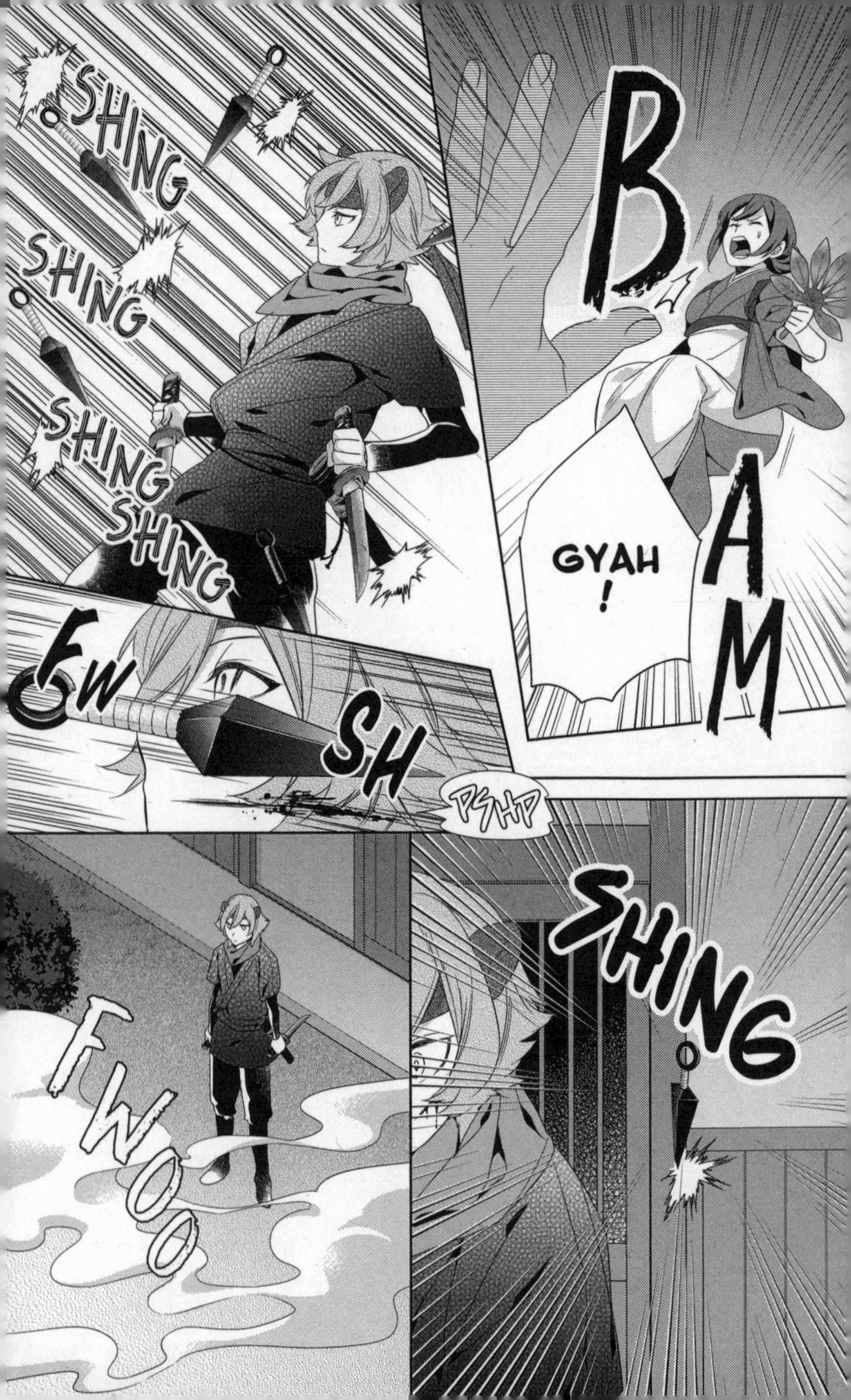
BAM
GYAH!
SHING
SHING
SHING
SHING
FWSH
PSHP
SHING
FWOOO

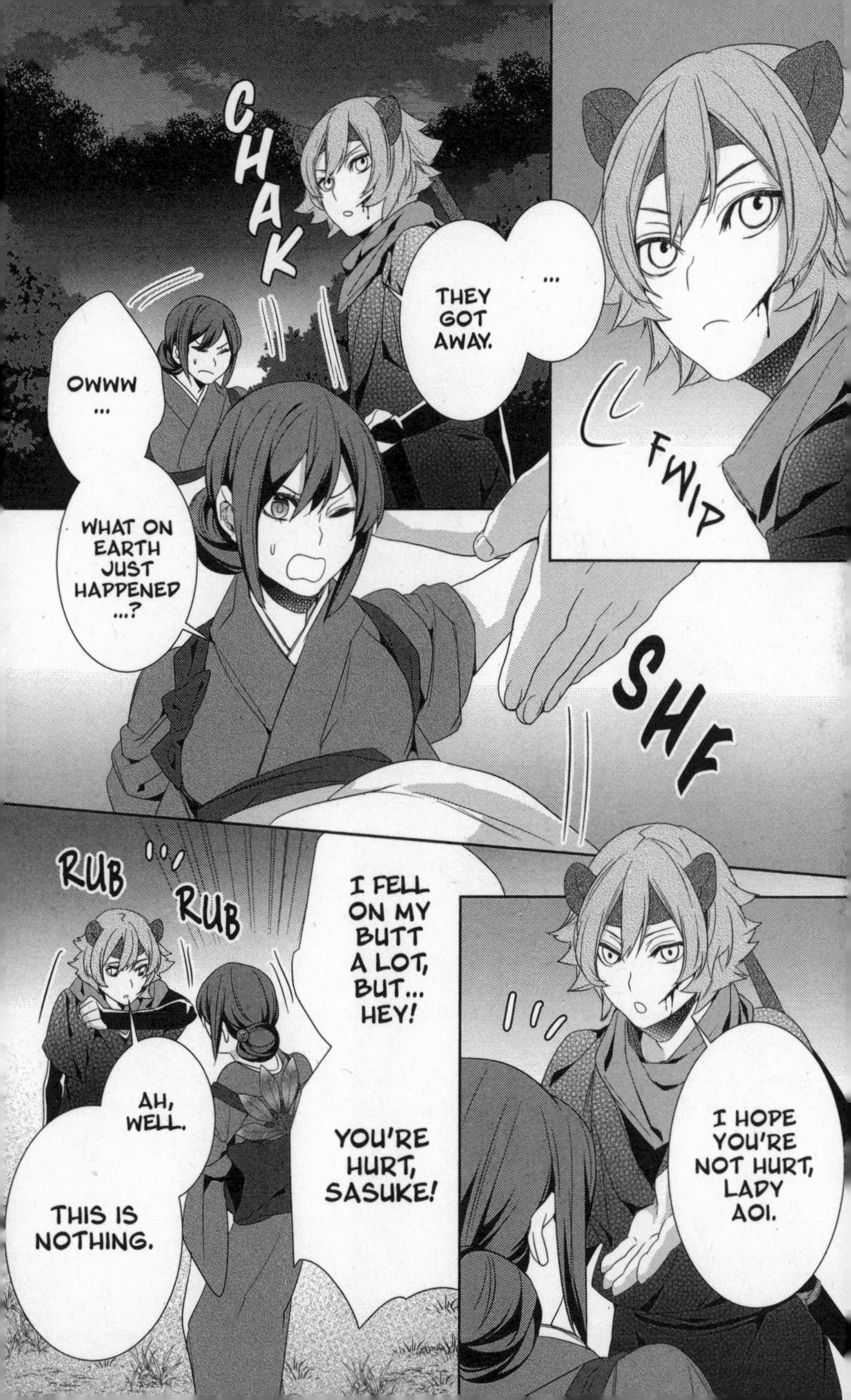
...
FWIP
CHAK
THEY GOT AWAY.
OWWW ...
WHAT ON EARTH JUST HAPPENED ...?
SHF
I HOPE YOU'RE NOT HURT, LADY AOI.
I FELL ON MY BUTT A LOT, BUT... HEY!
YOU'RE HURT, SASUKE!
RUB RUB
AH, WELL.
THIS IS NOTHING.

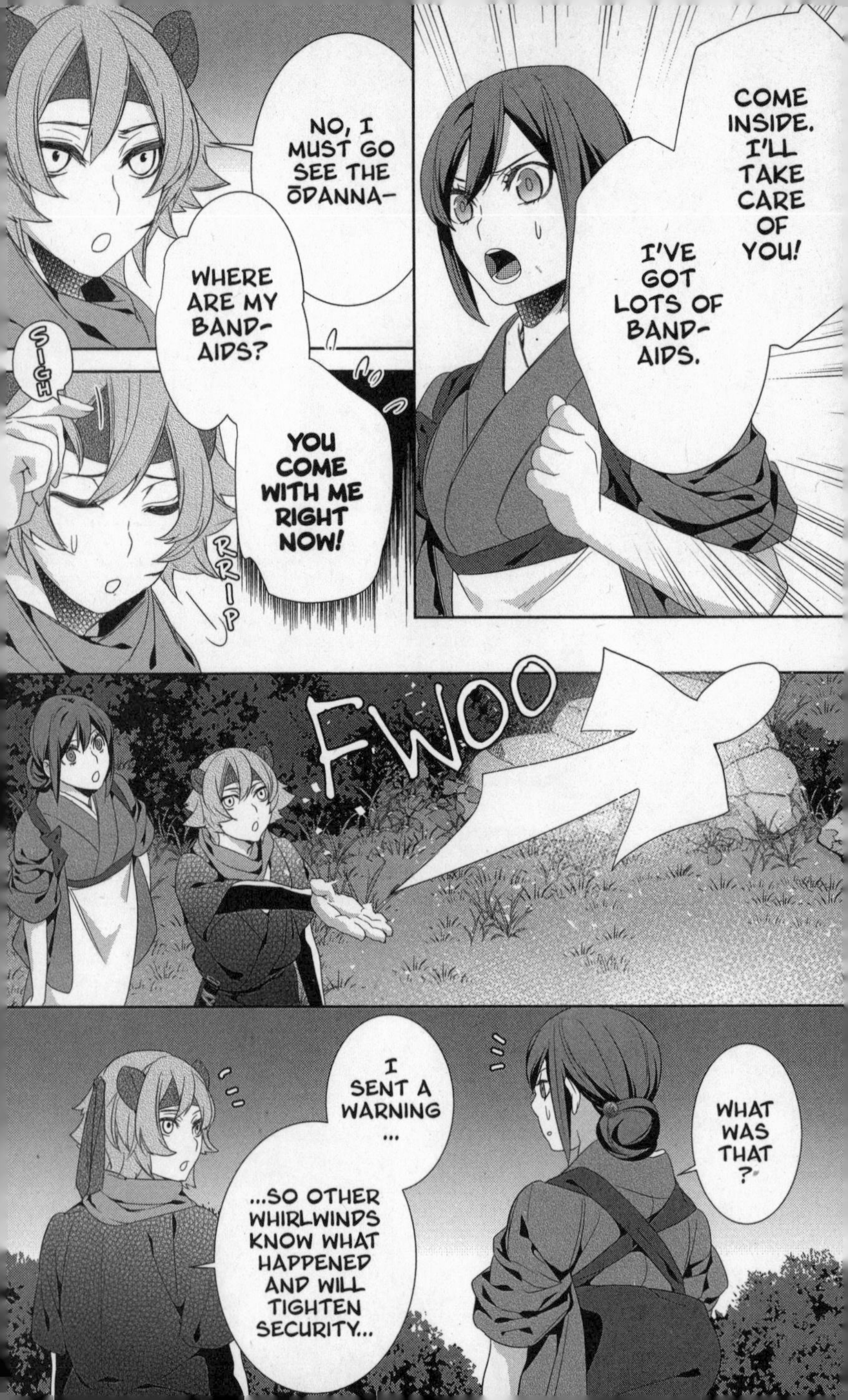
COME INSIDE. I'LL TAKE CARE OF YOU!
I'VE GOT LOTS OF BAND-AIDS.
NO, I MUST GO SEE THE ŌDANNA–
WHERE ARE MY BAND-AIDS?
SIGH
YOU COME WITH ME RIGHT NOW!
RRIP
FWOO
WHAT WAS THAT?
I SENT A WARNING...
...SO OTHER WHIRLWINDS KNOW WHAT HAPPENED AND WILL TIGHTEN SECURITY...

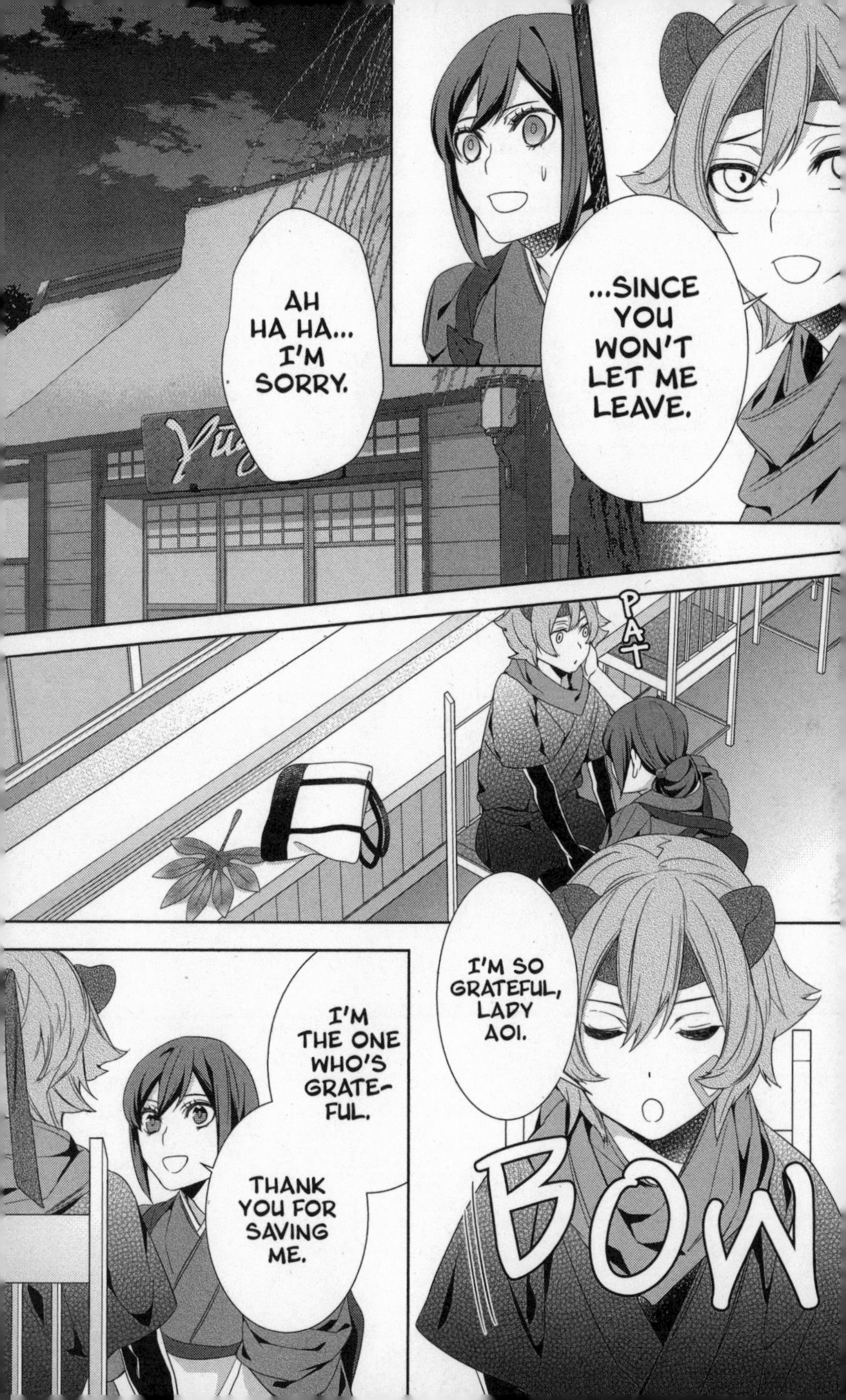
...SINCE YOU WON'T LET ME LEAVE.
AH HA HA... I'M SORRY.
PAT
I'M SO GRATEFUL, LADY AOI.
BOW
I'M THE ONE WHO'S GRATE-FUL.
THANK YOU FOR SAVING ME.

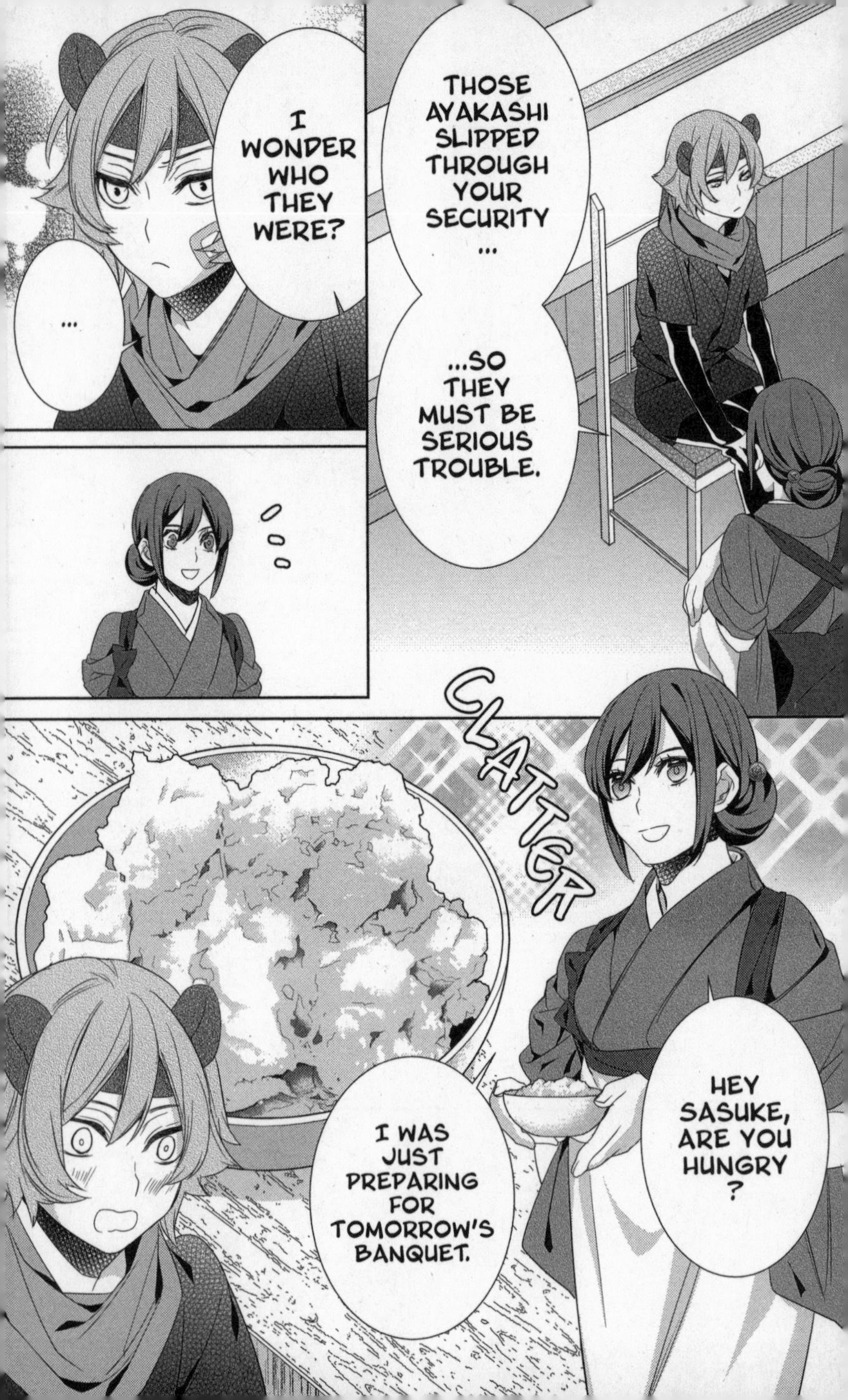
THOSE AYAKASHI SLIPPED THROUGH YOUR SECURITY ...
...SO THEY MUST BE SERIOUS TROUBLE.
I WONDER WHO THEY WERE?
...
CLATTER
HEY SASUKE, ARE YOU HUNGRY ?
I WAS JUST PREPARING FOR TOMORROW'S BANQUET.

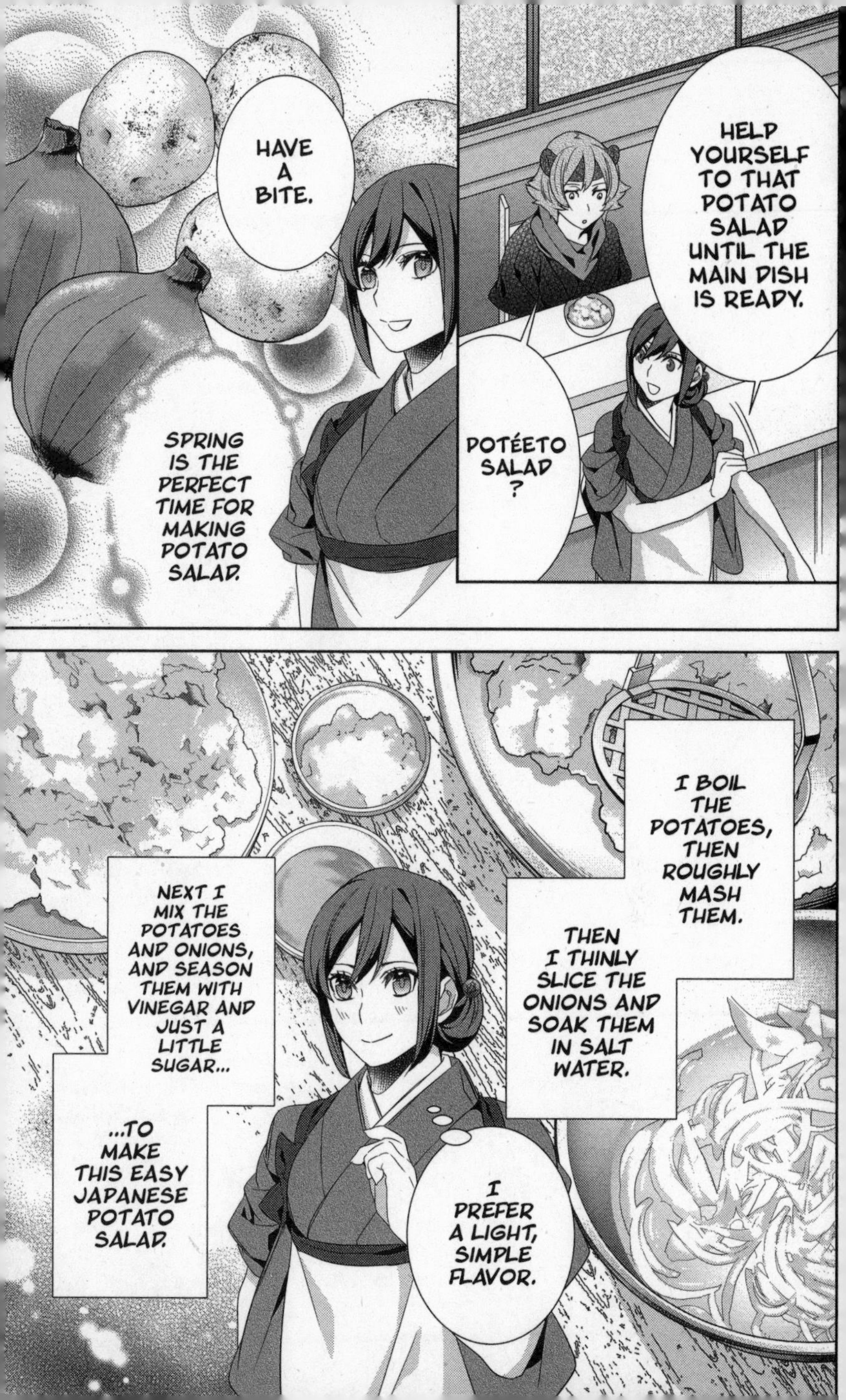

HELP YOURSELF TO THAT POTATO SALAD UNTIL THE MAIN DISH IS READY.
POTÉETO SALAD?
HAVE A BITE.
SPRING IS THE PERFECT TIME FOR MAKING POTATO SALAD.
I BOIL THE POTATOES, THEN ROUGHLY MASH THEM.
THEN I THINLY SLICE THE ONIONS AND SOAK THEM IN SALT WATER.
NEXT I MIX THE POTATOES AND ONIONS, AND SEASON THEM WITH VINEGAR AND JUST A LITTLE SUGAR...
...TO MAKE THIS EASY JAPANESE POTATO SALAD.
I PREFER A LIGHT, SIMPLE FLAVOR.

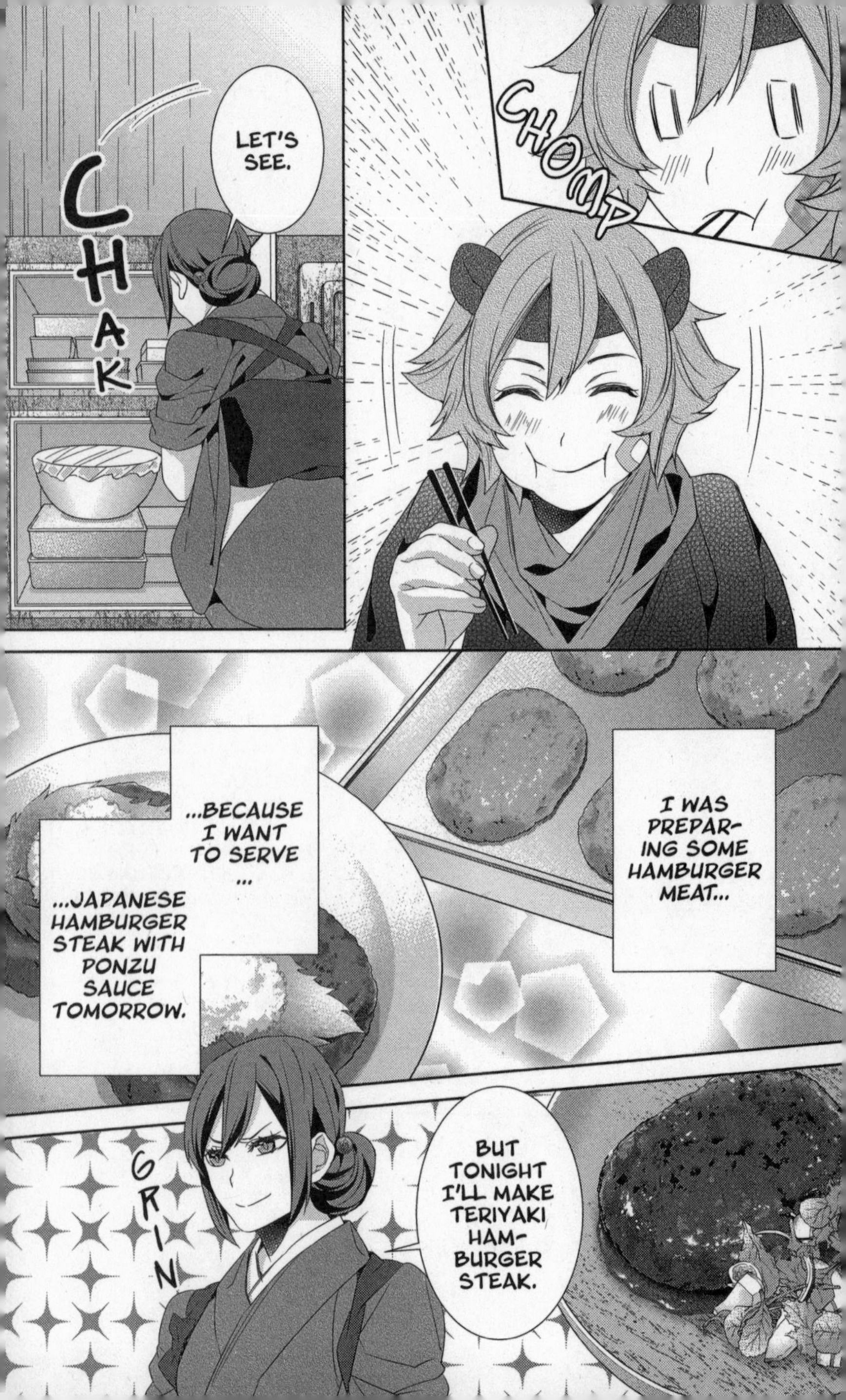
CHOMP
LET'S SEE.
CHAK
I WAS PREPARING SOME HAMBURGER MEAT...
...BECAUSE I WANT TO SERVE...
...JAPANESE HAMBURGER STEAK WITH PONZU SAUCE TOMORROW.
BUT TONIGHT I'LL MAKE TERIYAKI HAMBURGER STEAK.
GRIN

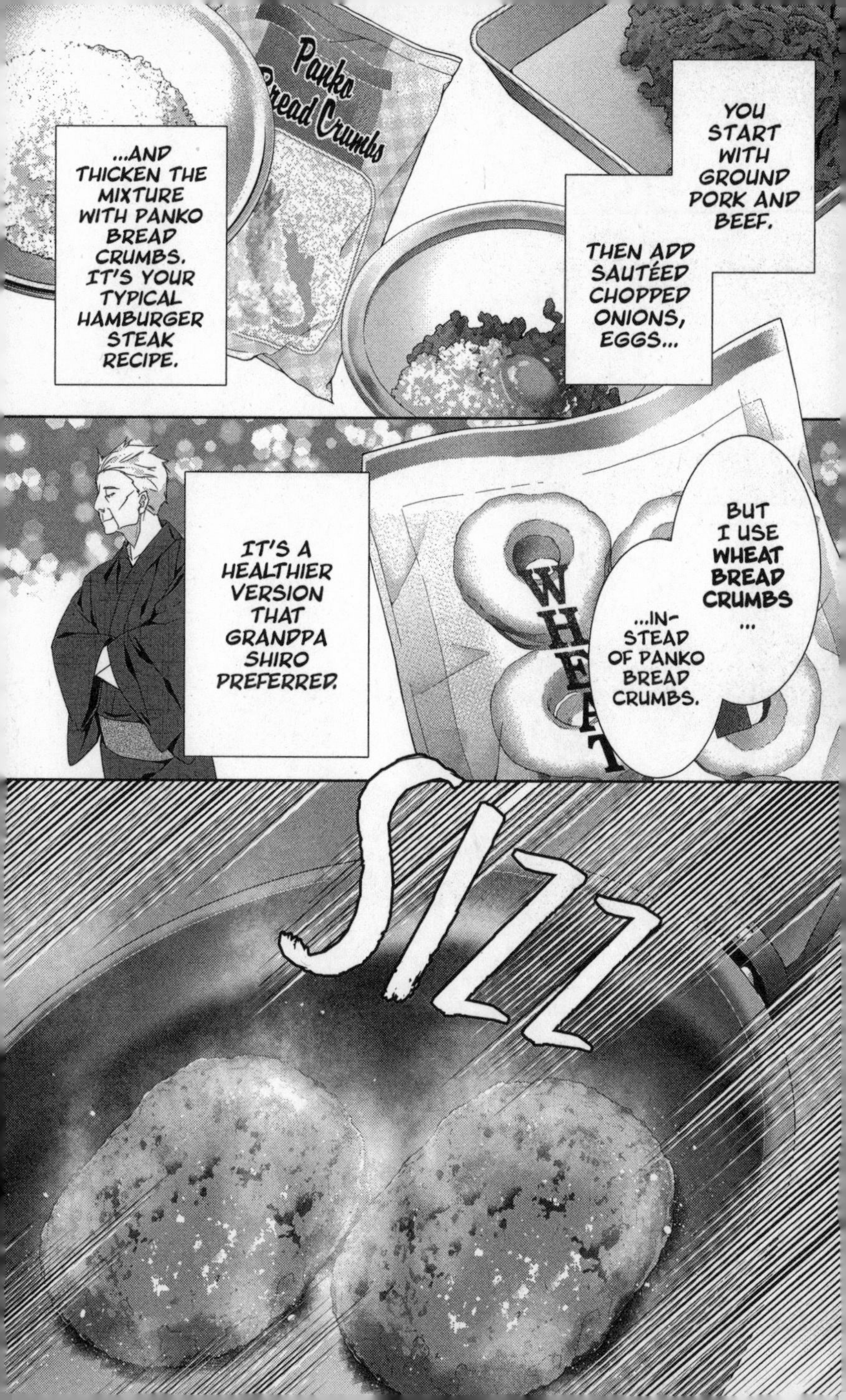
YOU START WITH GROUND PORK AND BEEF.
THEN ADD SAUTÉED CHOPPED ONIONS, EGGS...
Panko Bread Crumbs
...AND THICKEN THE MIXTURE WITH PANKO BREAD CRUMBS. IT'S YOUR TYPICAL HAMBURGER STEAK RECIPE.
BUT I USE WHEAT BREAD CRUMBS...
...IN-STEAD OF PANKO BREAD CRUMBS.
WHEAT
IT'S A HEALTHIER VERSION THAT GRANDPA SHIRO PREFERRED.
SIZZ

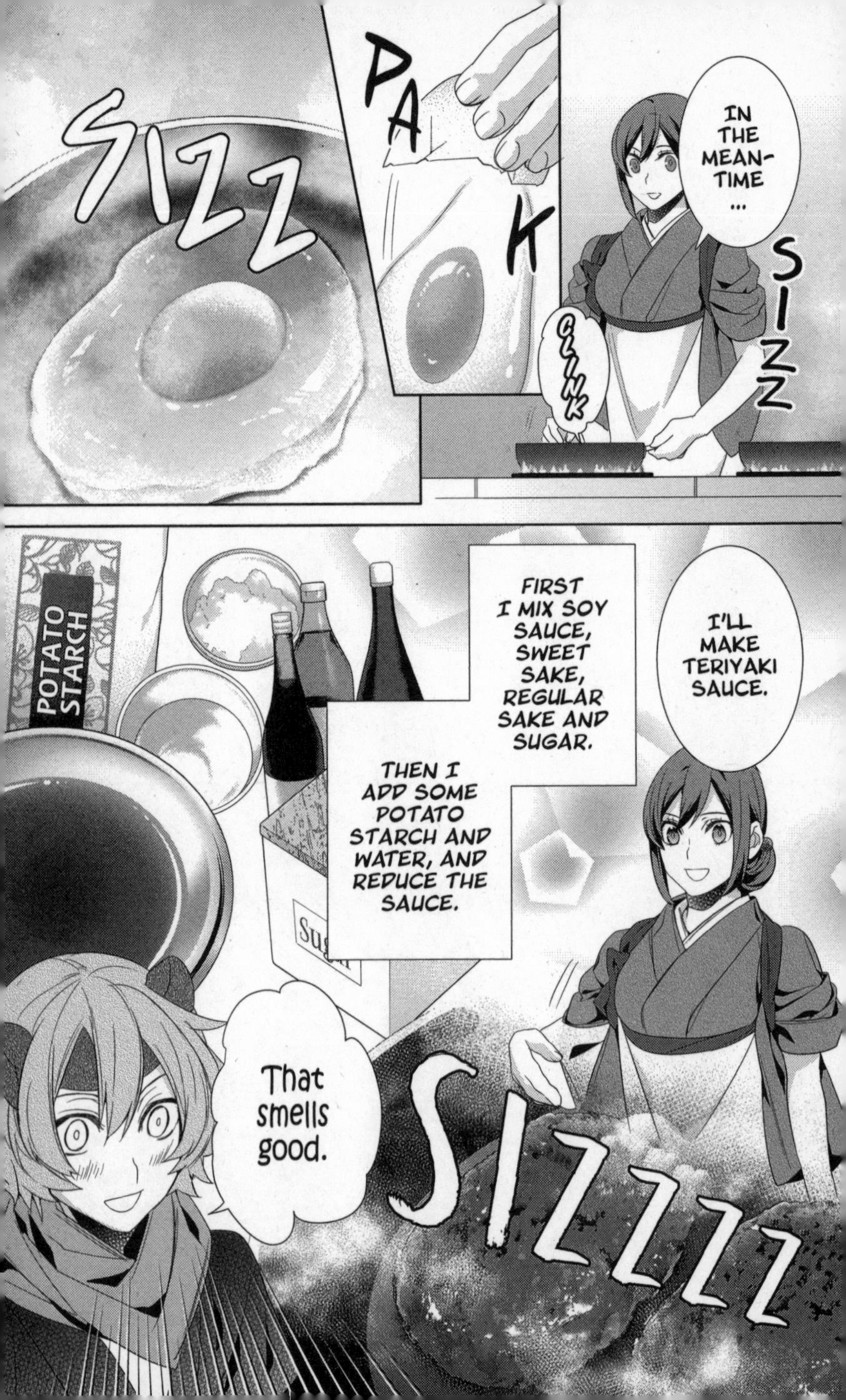
IN THE MEAN-TIME...
SIZZ
CLINK
PAK
SIZZ
I'LL MAKE TERIYAKI SAUCE.
FIRST I MIX SOY SAUCE, SWEET SAKE, REGULAR SAKE AND SUGAR.
THEN I ADD SOME POTATO STARCH AND WATER, AND REDUCE THE SAUCE.
POTATO STARCH
That smells good.
SIZZZZZ

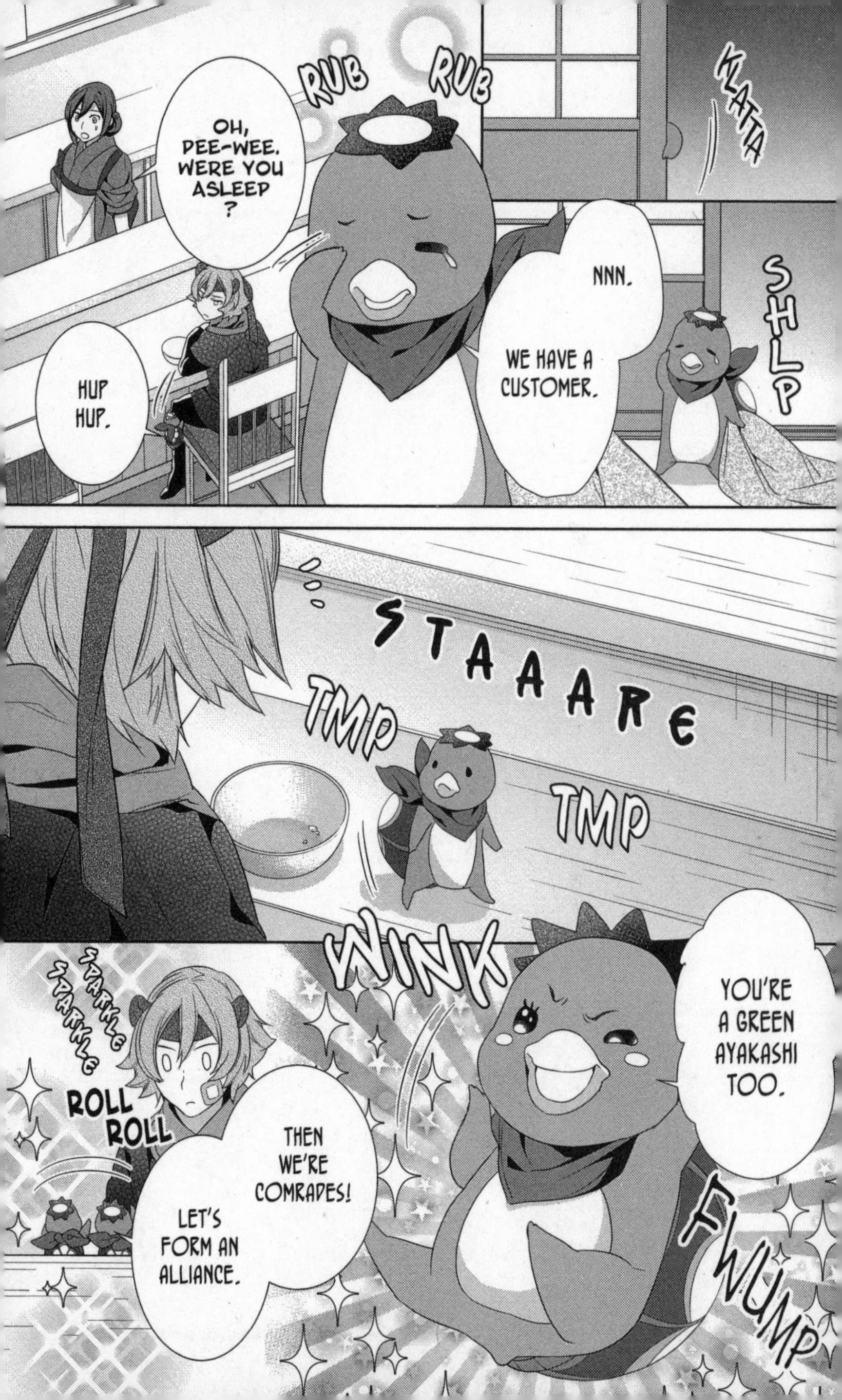
KLATTA
RUB RUB
NNN.
WE HAVE A CUSTOMER.
SHLP
OH, PEE-WEE. WERE YOU ASLEEP?
HUP HUP.
STAAAARE
TMP
TMP
WINK
YOU'RE A GREEN AYAKASHI TOO.
FWUMP
THEN WE'RE COMRADES!
LET'S FORM AN ALLIANCE.
SPARKLE SPARKLE
ROLL ROLL

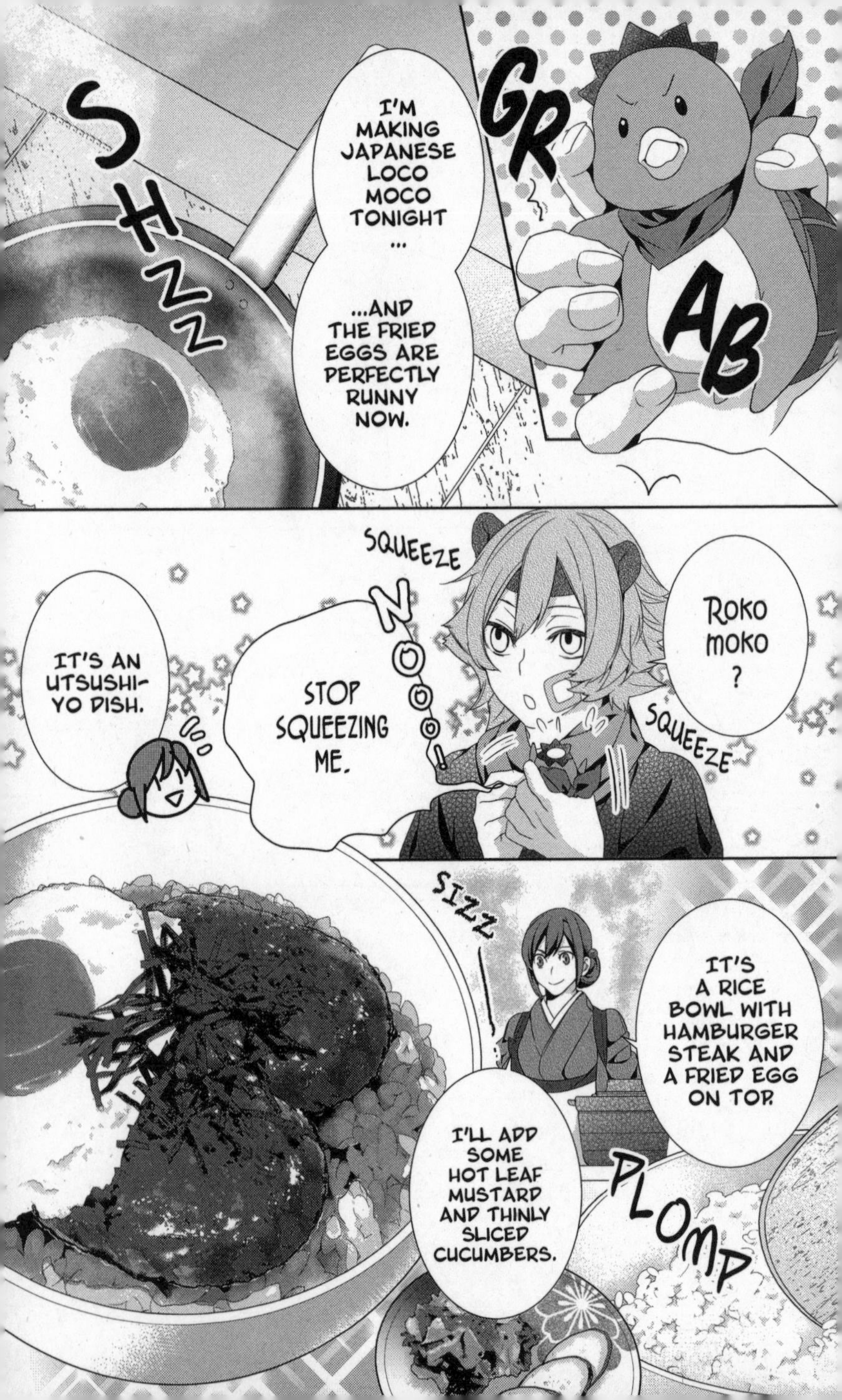
GRAB
I'M MAKING JAPANESE LOCO MOCO TONIGHT...
...AND THE FRIED EGGS ARE PERFECTLY RUNNY NOW.
SHZZ
ROKO MOKO?
SQUEEZE
SQUEEZE
NOOOO!
STOP SQUEEZING ME.
IT'S AN UTSUSHI-YO DISH.
SIZZ
IT'S A RICE BOWL WITH HAMBURGER STEAK AND A FRIED EGG ON TOP.
I'LL ADD SOME HOT LEAF MUSTARD AND THINLY SLICED CUCUMBERS.
PLOMP

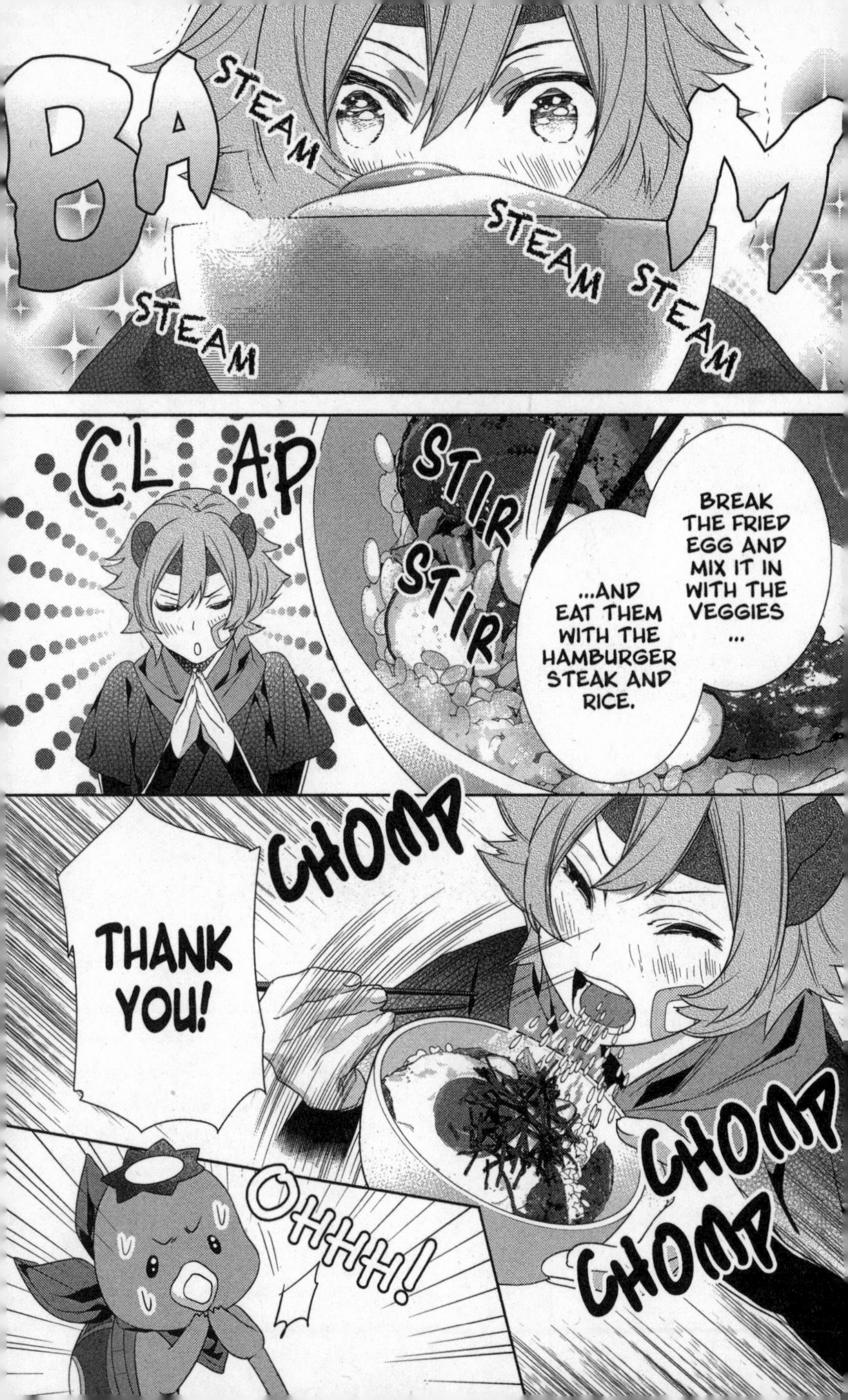
BAM
STEAM
STEAM STEAM
STEAM
STEAM
BREAK THE FRIED EGG AND MIX IT IN WITH THE VEGGIES ...
...AND EAT THEM WITH THE HAMBURGER STEAK AND RICE.
STIR STIR
CLAP
CHOMP
THANK YOU!
CHOMP CHOMP
OHHHH!

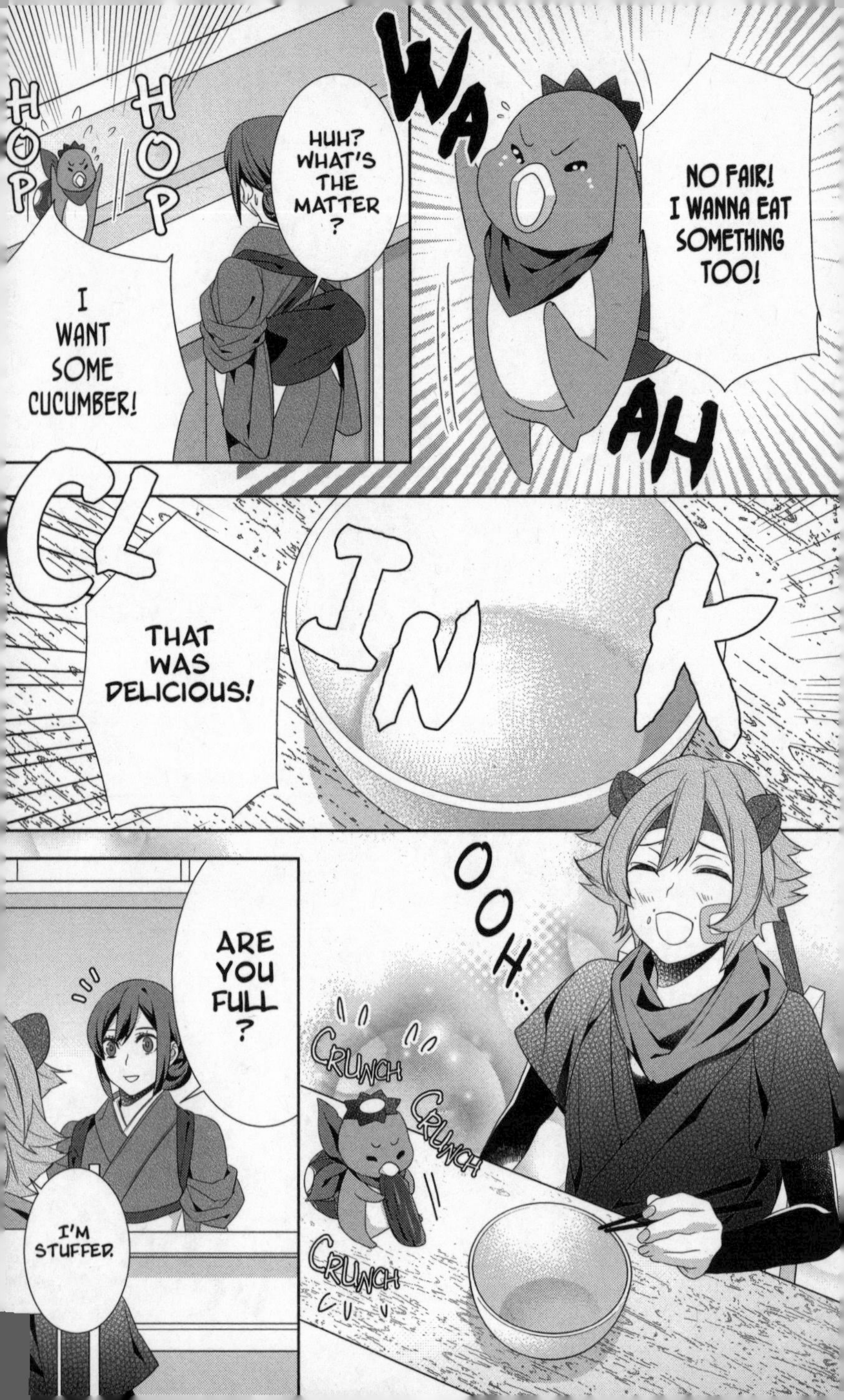
WA
AH
NO FAIR! I WANNA EAT SOMETHING TOO!
HOP
HOP
HUH? WHAT'S THE MATTER?
I WANT SOME CUCUMBER!
CLINK
THAT WAS DELICIOUS!
OOOH...
CRUNCH
CRUNCH
CRUNCH
ARE YOU FULL?
I'M STUFFED.

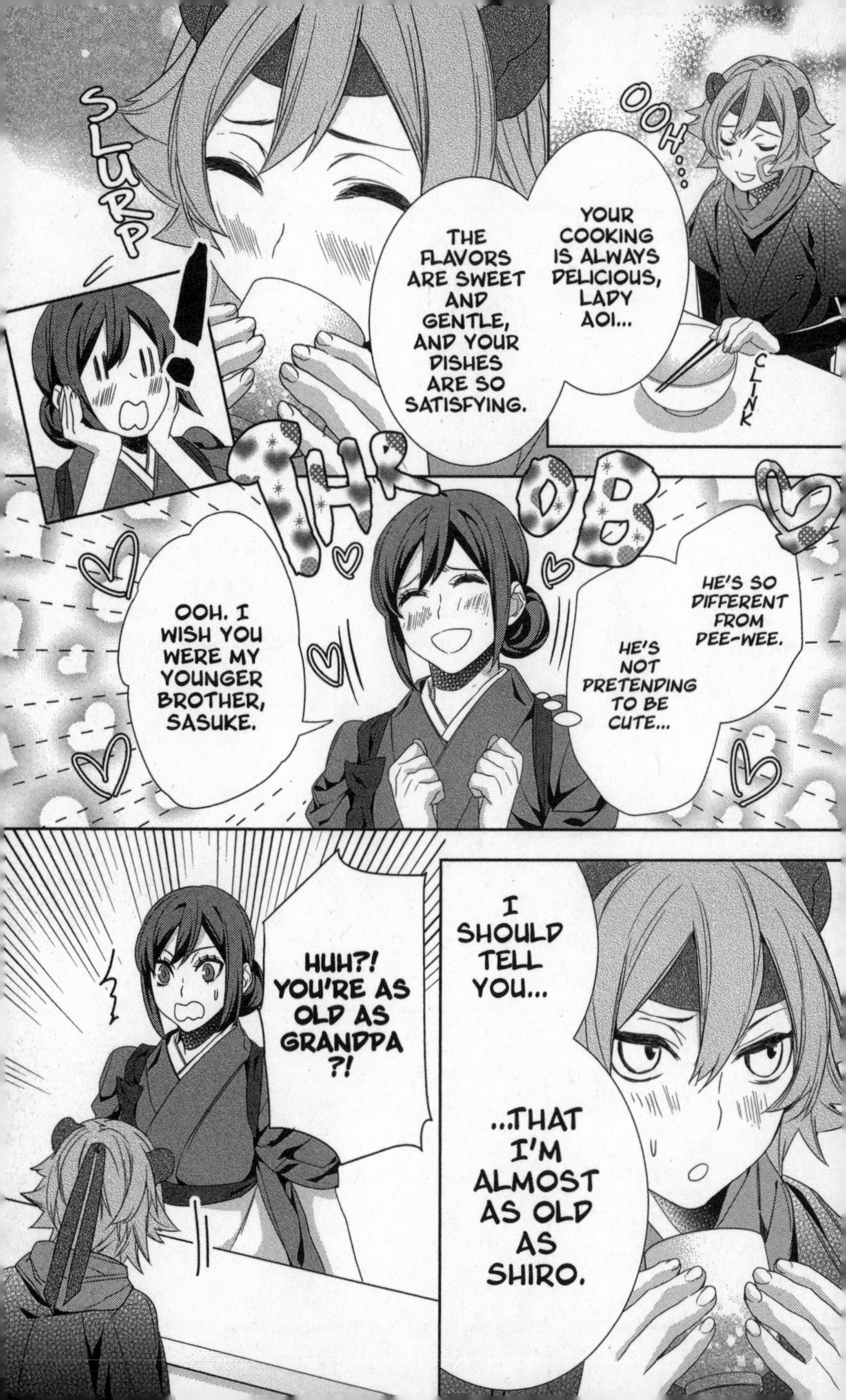
OOH...
YOUR COOKING IS ALWAYS DELICIOUS, LADY AOI...
THE FLAVORS ARE SWEET AND GENTLE, AND YOUR DISHES ARE SO SATISFYING.
CLINK
SLURP
THROB
HE'S SO DIFFERENT FROM PEE-WEE.
HE'S NOT PRETENDING TO BE CUTE...
OOH. I WISH YOU WERE MY YOUNGER BROTHER, SASUKE.
I SHOULD TELL YOU...
...THAT I'M ALMOST AS OLD AS SHIRO.
HUH?! YOU'RE AS OLD AS GRANDPA?!

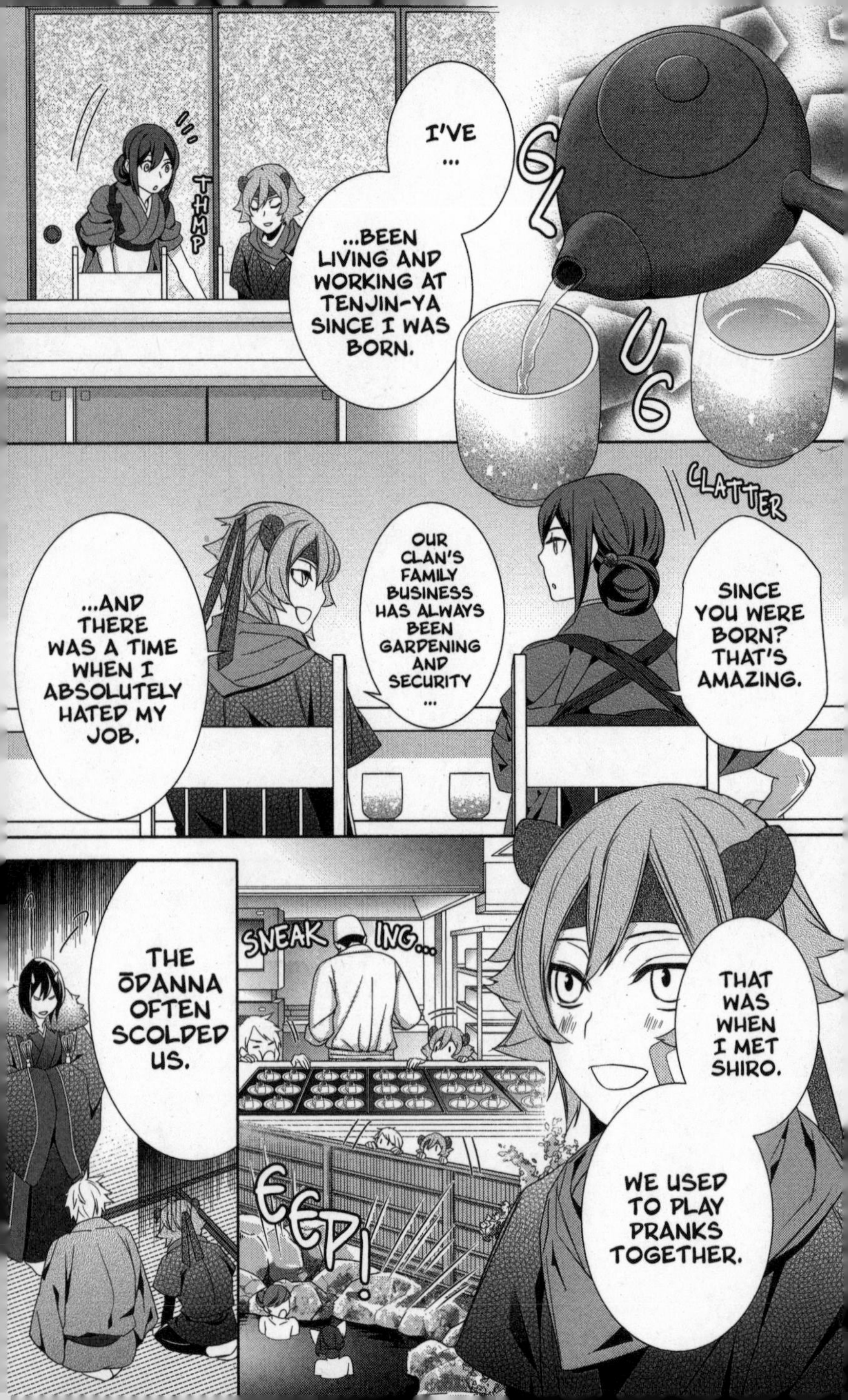

GLUG
I'VE ...
...BEEN LIVING AND WORKING AT TENJIN-YA SINCE I WAS BORN.
THMP
CLATTER
SINCE YOU WERE BORN? THAT'S AMAZING.
OUR CLAN'S FAMILY BUSINESS HAS ALWAYS BEEN GARDENING AND SECURITY ...
...AND THERE WAS A TIME WHEN I ABSOLUTELY HATED MY JOB.
THAT WAS WHEN I MET SHIRO.
WE USED TO PLAY PRANKS TOGETHER.
SNEAK ING...
EEP!
THE ŌDANNA OFTEN SCOLDED US.

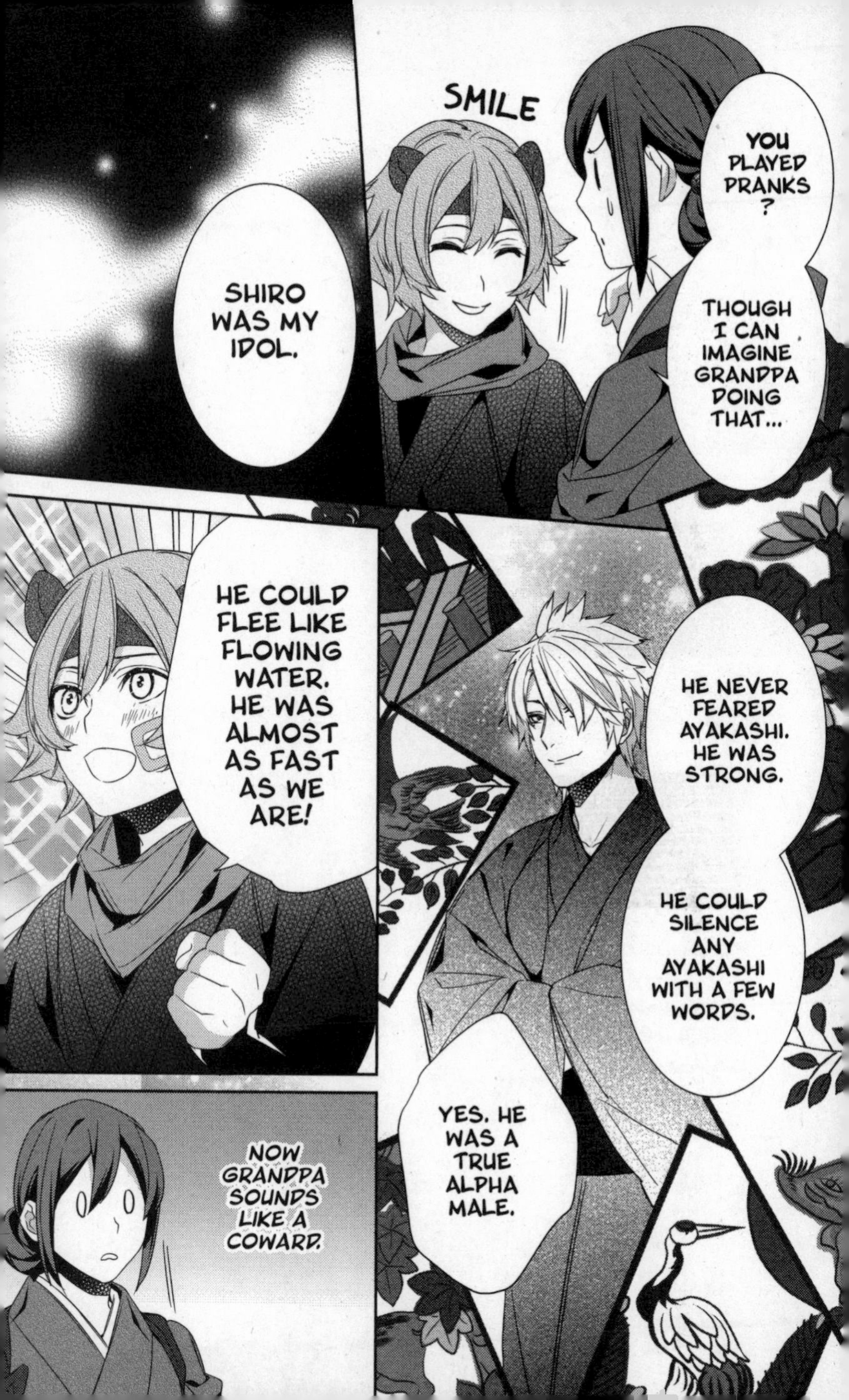
YOU PLAYED PRANKS?
SMILE
THOUGH I CAN IMAGINE GRANDPA DOING THAT...
SHIRO WAS MY IDOL.
HE NEVER FEARED AYAKASHI. HE WAS STRONG.
HE COULD SILENCE ANY AYAKASHI WITH A FEW WORDS.
YES. HE WAS A TRUE ALPHA MALE.
HE COULD FLEE LIKE FLOWING WATER. HE WAS ALMOST AS FAST AS WE ARE!
NOW GRANDPA SOUNDS LIKE A COWARD.

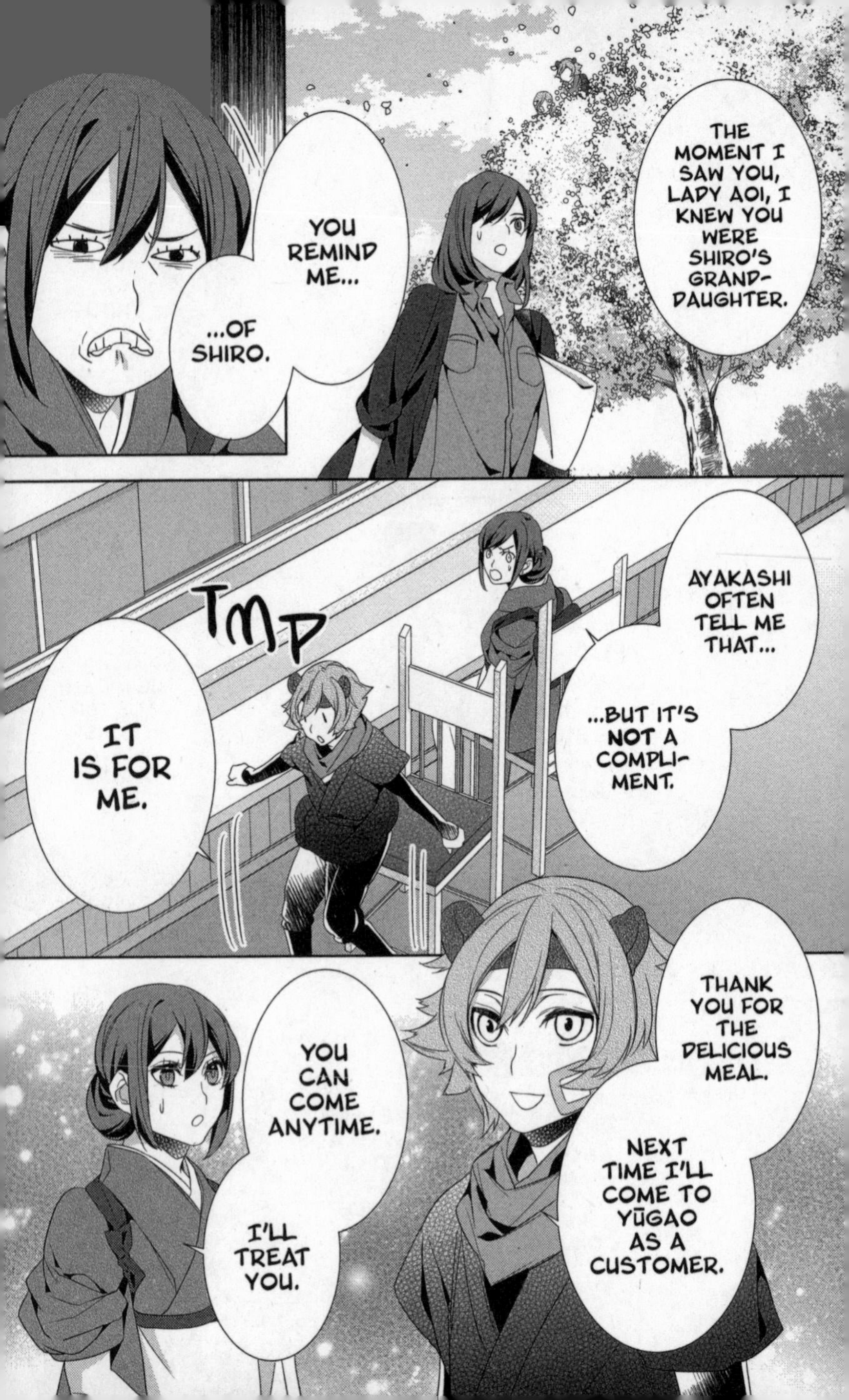
THE MOMENT I SAW YOU, LADY AOI, I KNEW YOU WERE SHIRO'S GRAND-DAUGHTER.
YOU REMIND ME...
...OF SHIRO.
AYAKASHI OFTEN TELL ME THAT...
...BUT IT'S NOT A COMPLI-MENT.
TMP
IT IS FOR ME.
THANK YOU FOR THE DELICIOUS MEAL.
NEXT TIME I'LL COME TO YŪGAO AS A CUSTOMER.
YOU CAN COME ANYTIME.
I'LL TREAT YOU.

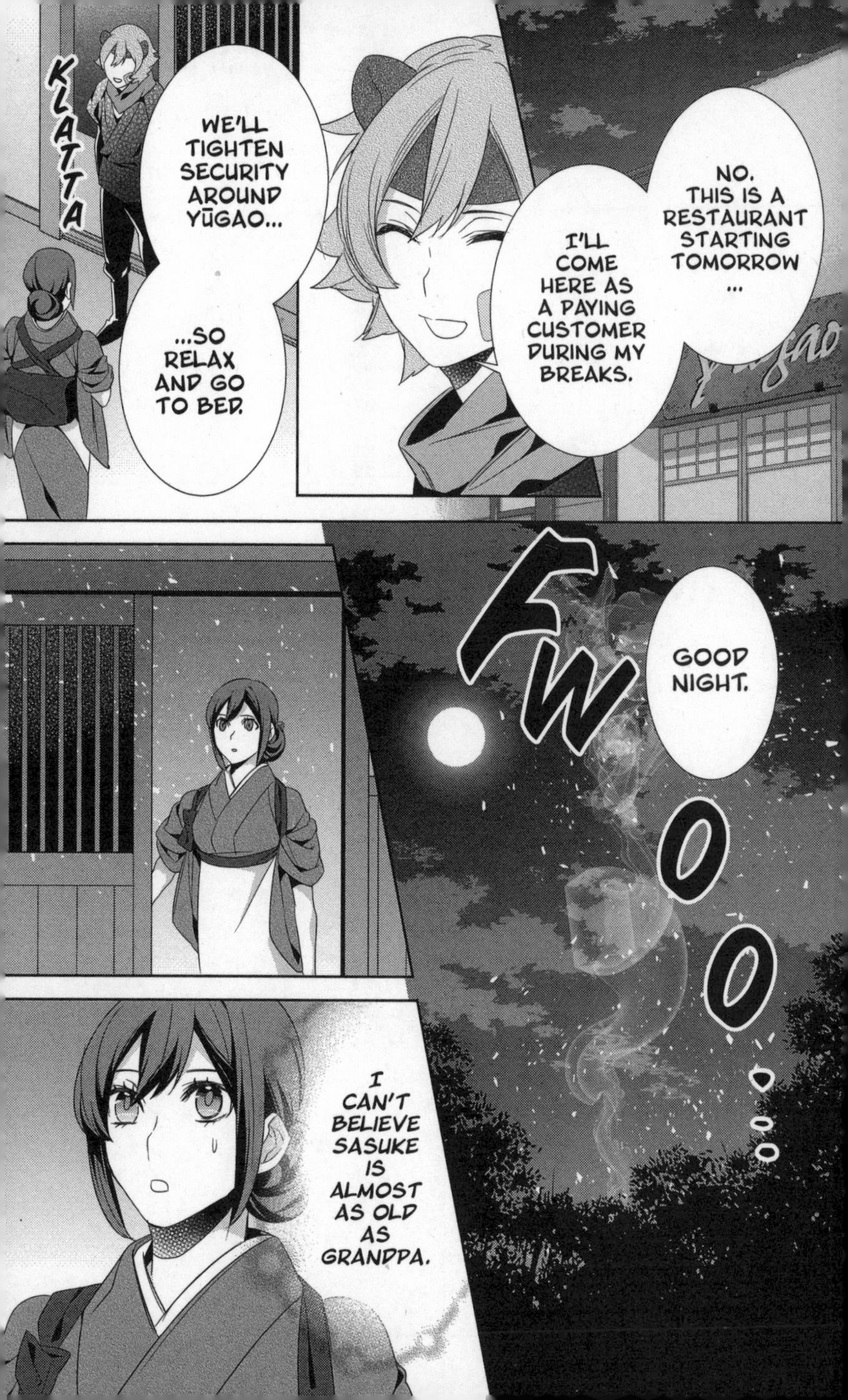
NO. THIS IS A RESTAURANT STARTING TOMORROW...
I'LL COME HERE AS A PAYING CUSTOMER DURING MY BREAKS.
KLATTA
WE'LL TIGHTEN SECURITY AROUND YŪGAO...
...SO RELAX AND GO TO BED.
GOOD NIGHT.
FWOOO...
I CAN'T BELIEVE SASUKE IS ALMOST AS OLD AS GRANDPA.

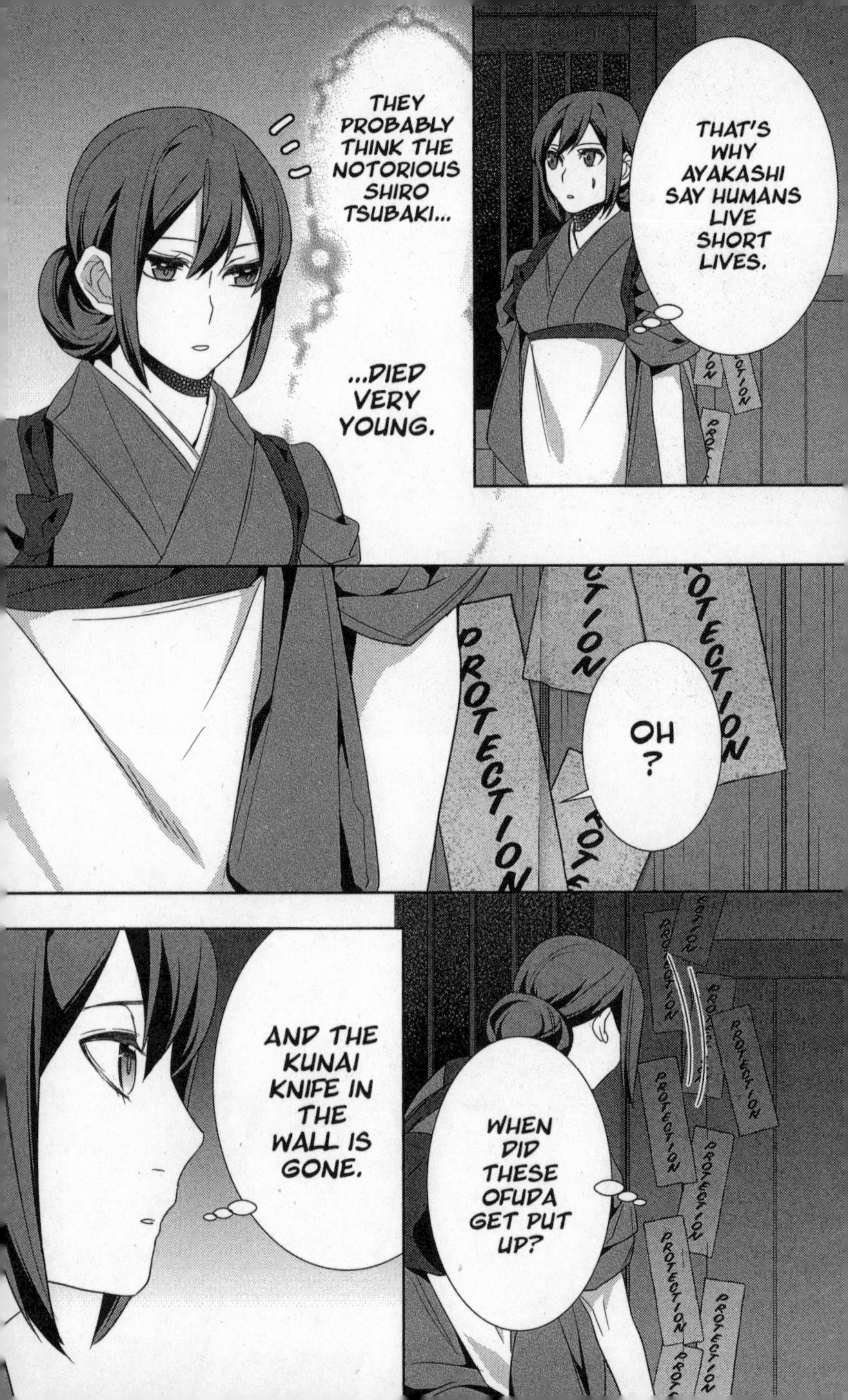
THAT'S WHY AYAKASHI SAY HUMANS LIVE SHORT LIVES.
THEY PROBABLY THINK THE NOTORIOUS SHIRO TSUBAKI...
...DIED VERY YOUNG.
PROTECTION
PROTECTION
OH?
WHEN DID THESE OFUDA GET PUT UP?
AND THE KUNAI KNIFE IN THE WALL IS GONE.

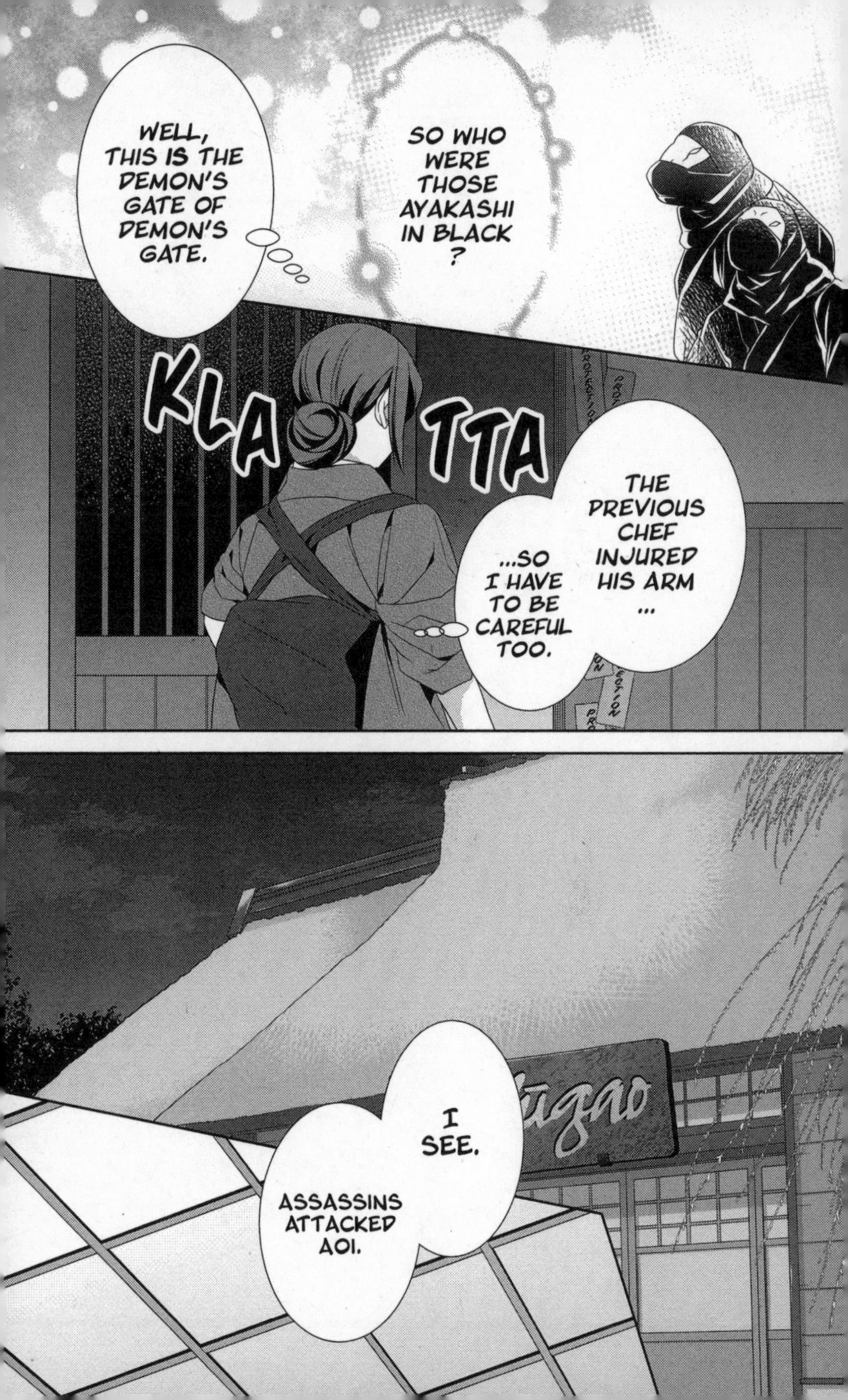
WELL, THIS IS THE DEMON'S GATE OF DEMON'S GATE.
SO WHO WERE THOSE AYAKASHI IN BLACK?
KLATTA
THE PREVIOUS CHEF INJURED HIS ARM...
...SO I HAVE TO BE CAREFUL TOO.
I SEE.
ASSASSINS ATTACKED AOI.

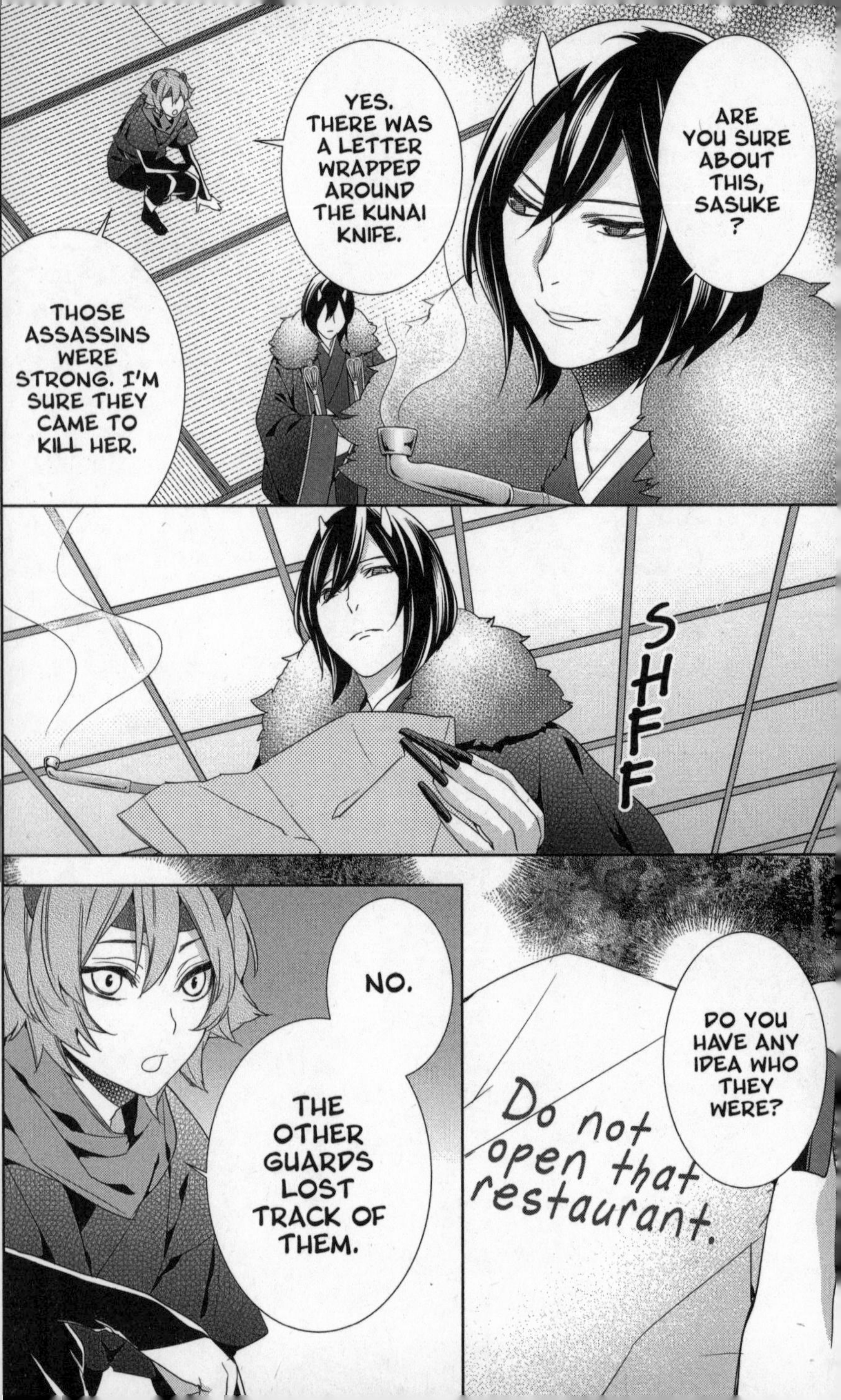
ARE YOU SURE ABOUT THIS, SASUKE?
YES. THERE WAS A LETTER WRAPPED AROUND THE KUNAI KNIFE.
THOSE ASSASSINS WERE STRONG. I'M SURE THEY CAME TO KILL HER.
SHFF
DO YOU HAVE ANY IDEA WHO THEY WERE?
Do not open that restaurant.
NO.
THE OTHER GUARDS LOST TRACK OF THEM.

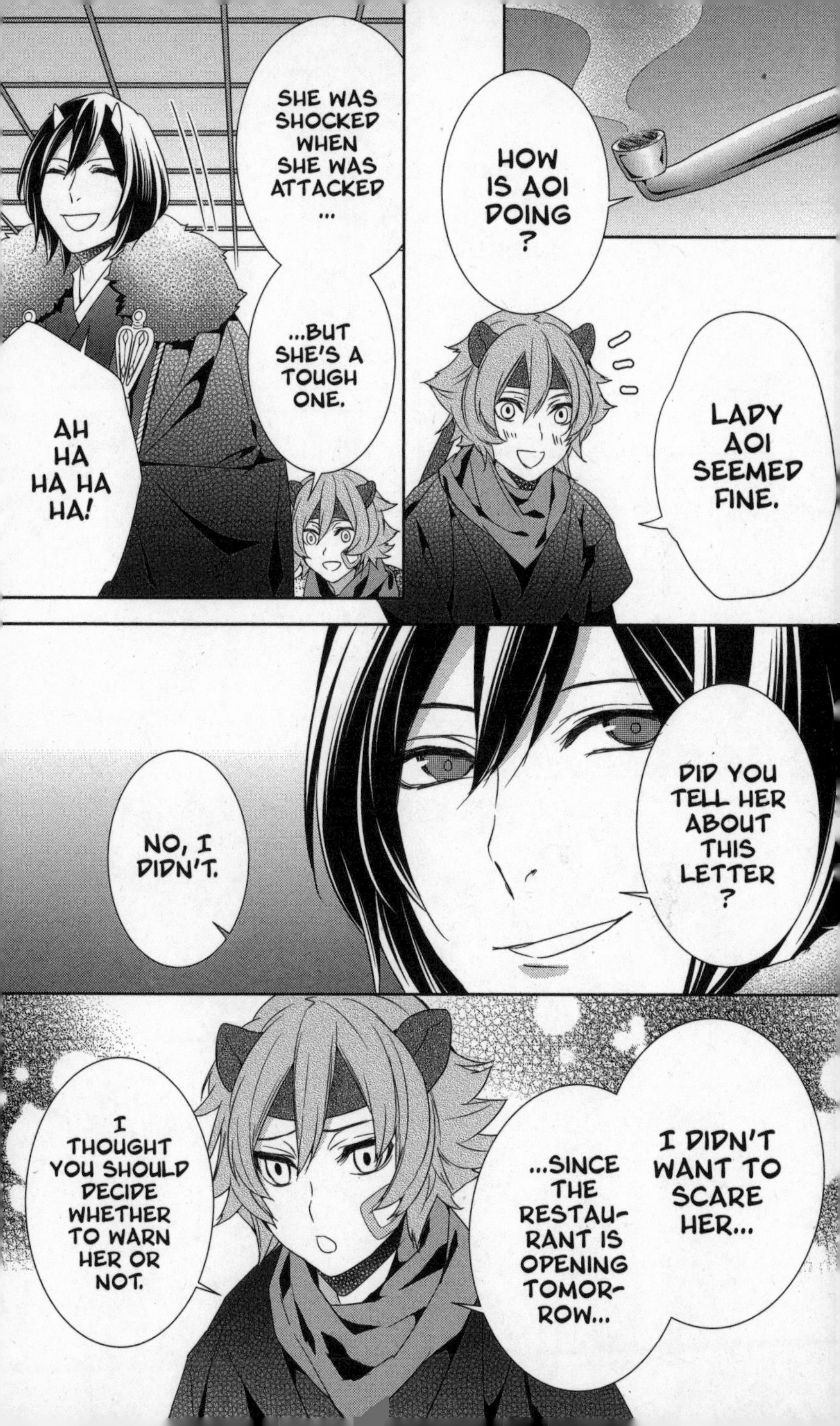
HOW IS AOI DOING?
LADY AOI SEEMED FINE.
SHE WAS SHOCKED WHEN SHE WAS ATTACKED...
...BUT SHE'S A TOUGH ONE.
AH HA HA HA HA!
DID YOU TELL HER ABOUT THIS LETTER?
NO, I DIDN'T.
I DIDN'T WANT TO SCARE HER...
...SINCE THE RESTAU-RANT IS OPENING TOMOR-ROW...
I THOUGHT YOU SHOULD DECIDE WHETHER TO WARN HER OR NOT.

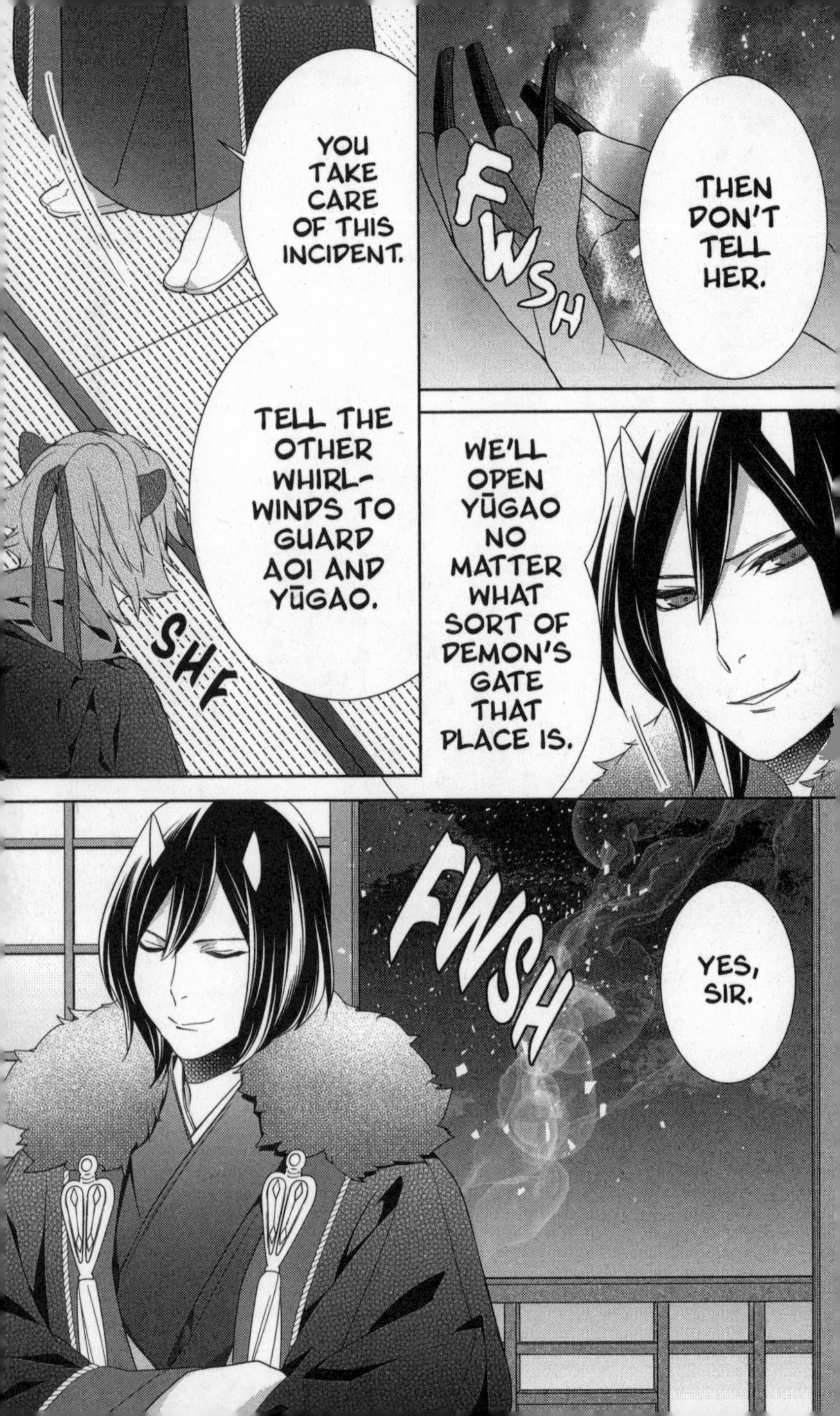
FWSH
THEN DON'T TELL HER.
WE'LL OPEN YŪGAO NO MATTER WHAT SORT OF DEMON'S GATE THAT PLACE IS.
YOU TAKE CARE OF THIS INCIDENT.
TELL THE OTHER WHIRL-WINDS TO GUARD AOI AND YŪGAO.
SHF
FWSH
YES, SIR.

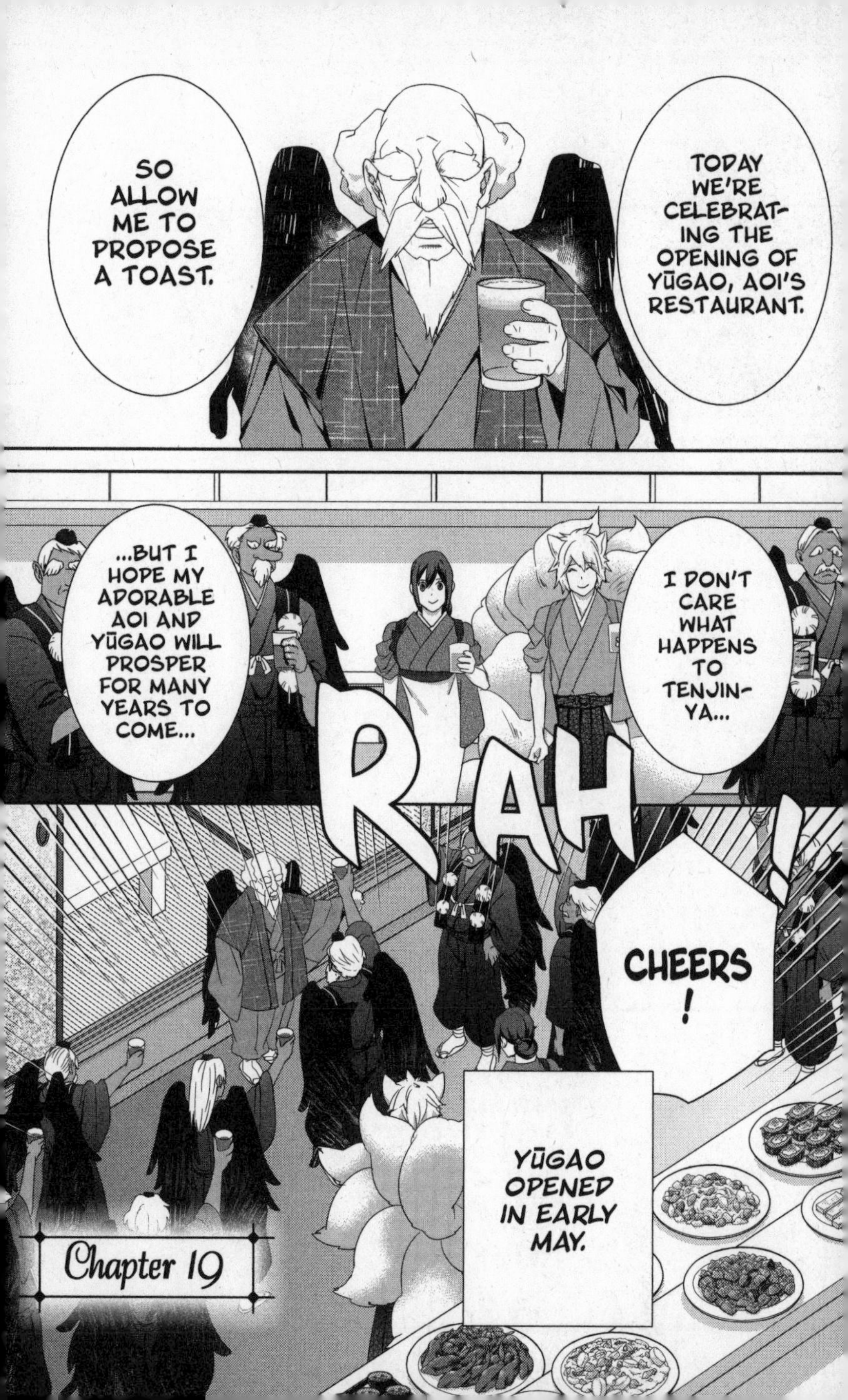
TODAY WE'RE CELEBRAT-ING THE OPENING OF YŪGAO, AOI'S RESTAURANT.
SO ALLOW ME TO PROPOSE A TOAST.
I DON'T CARE WHAT HAPPENS TO TENJIN-YA...
...BUT I HOPE MY ADORABLE AOI AND YŪGAO WILL PROSPER FOR MANY YEARS TO COME...
RAH!!
CHEERS!
YŪGAO OPENED IN EARLY MAY.
Chapter 19

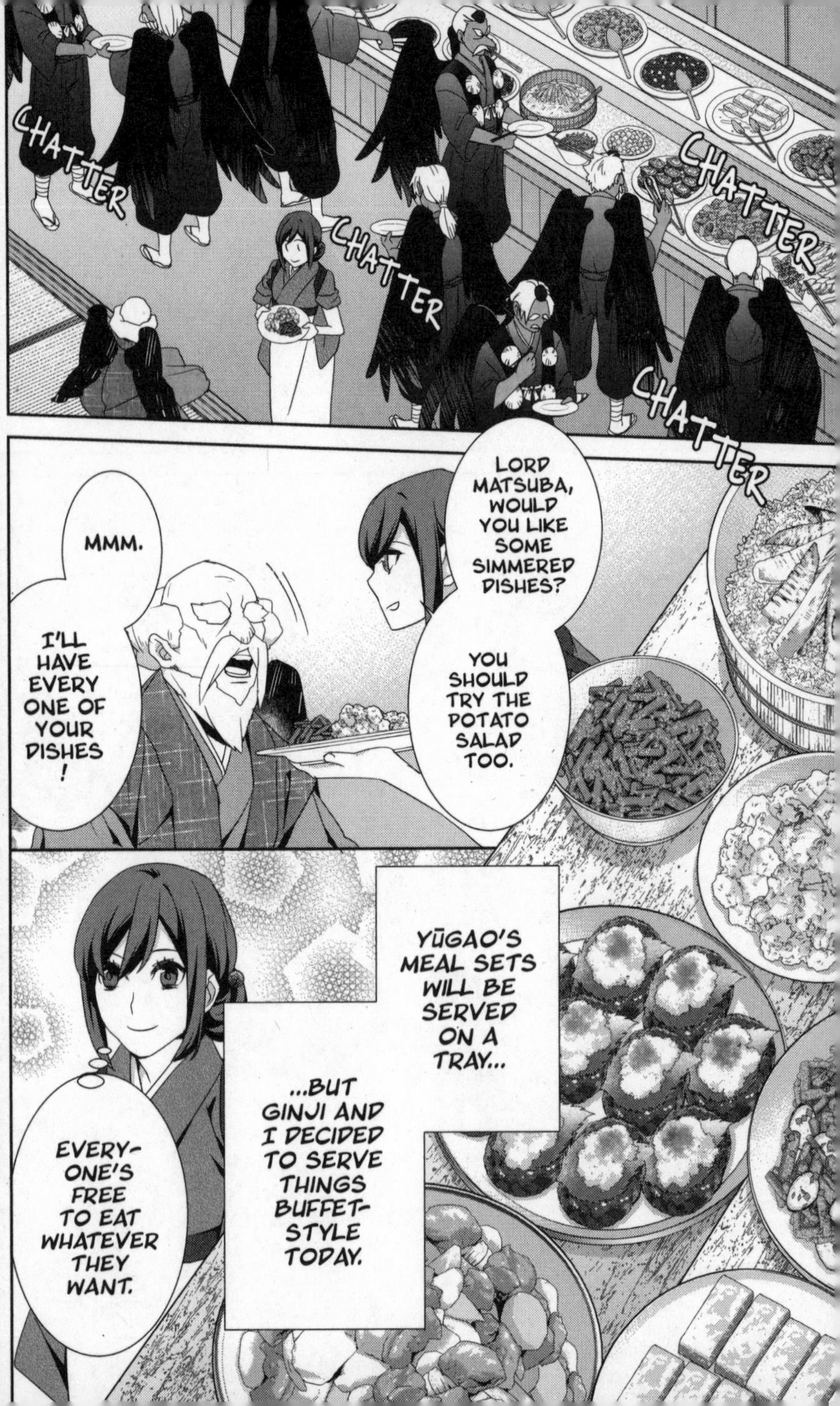
CHATTER
CHATTER
CHATTER
CHATTER
CHATTER
LORD MATSUBA, WOULD YOU LIKE SOME SIMMERED DISHES?
YOU SHOULD TRY THE POTATO SALAD TOO.
MMM.
I'LL HAVE EVERY ONE OF YOUR DISHES!
YŪGAO'S MEAL SETS WILL BE SERVED ON A TRAY...
...BUT GINJI AND I DECIDED TO SERVE THINGS BUFFET-STYLE TODAY.
EVERYONE'S FREE TO EAT WHATEVER THEY WANT.

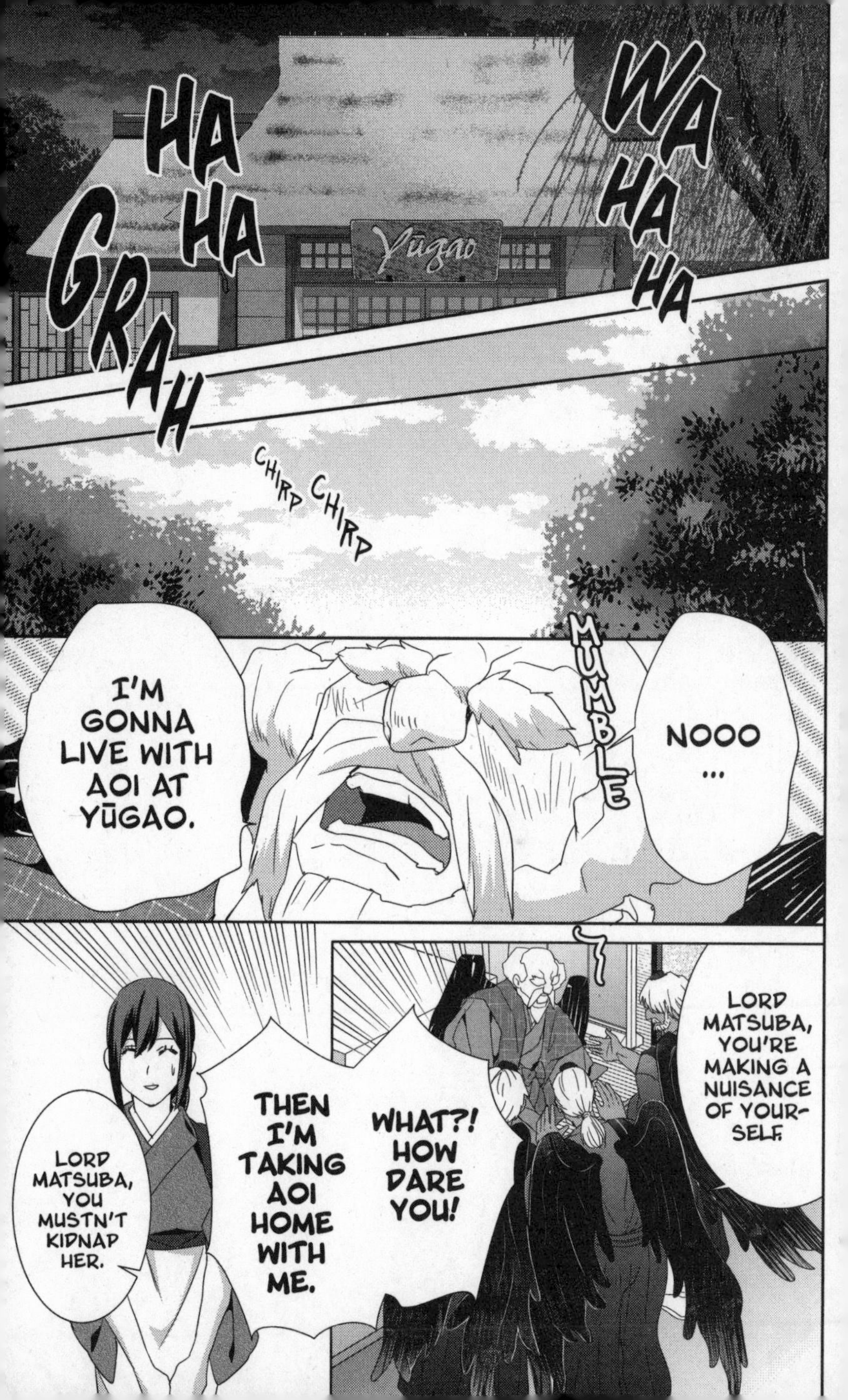
WA HA HA HA
Yūgao
HA HA GRAH
CHIRP CHIRP
NOOO ...
MUMBLE
I'M GONNA LIVE WITH AOI AT YŪGAO.
LORD MATSUBA, YOU'RE MAKING A NUISANCE OF YOUR-SELF.
WHAT?! HOW DARE YOU!
THEN I'M TAKING AOI HOME WITH ME.
LORD MATSUBA, YOU MUSTN'T KIDNAP HER.

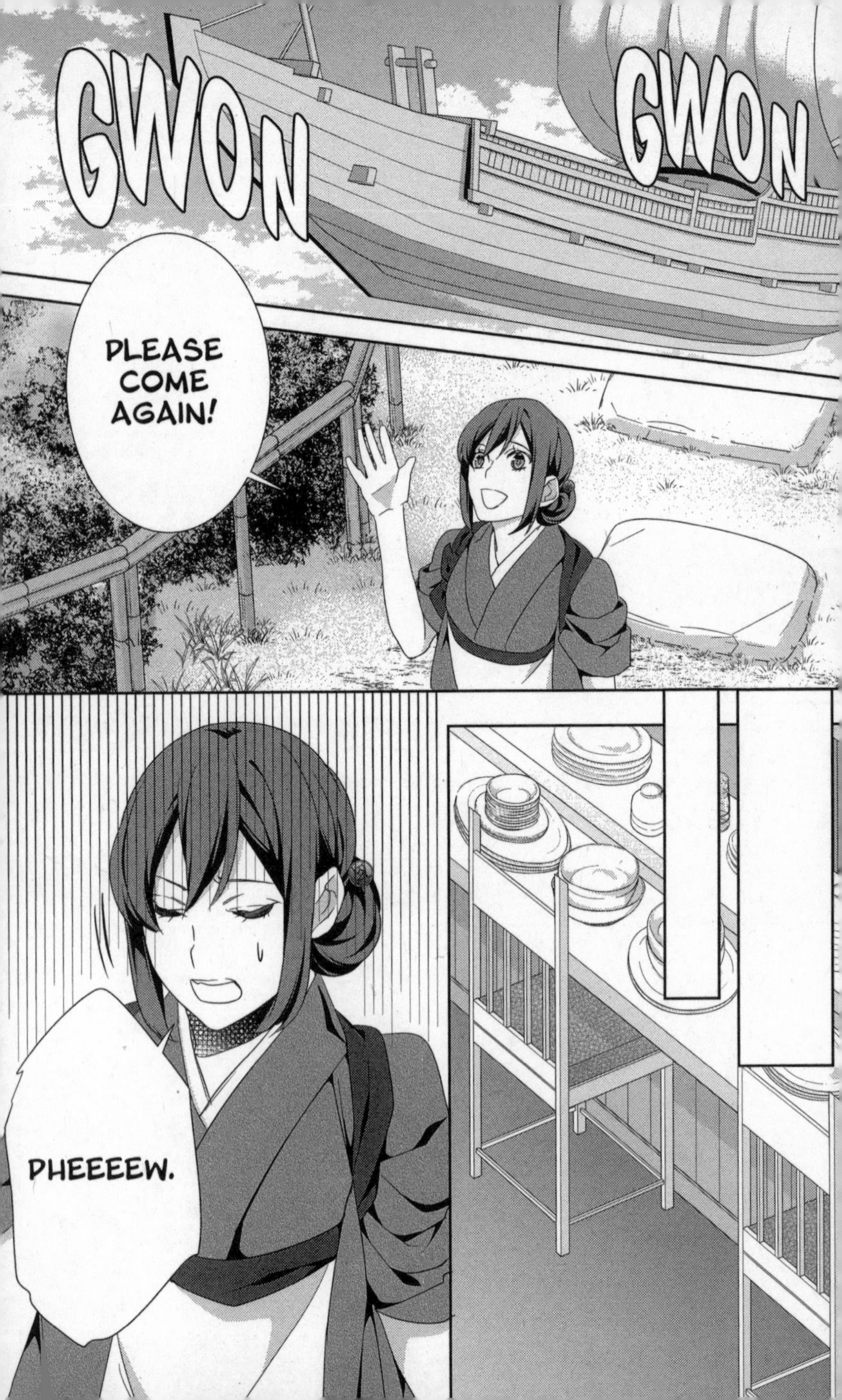
GWON
GWON
PLEASE COME AGAIN!
PHEEEEW.

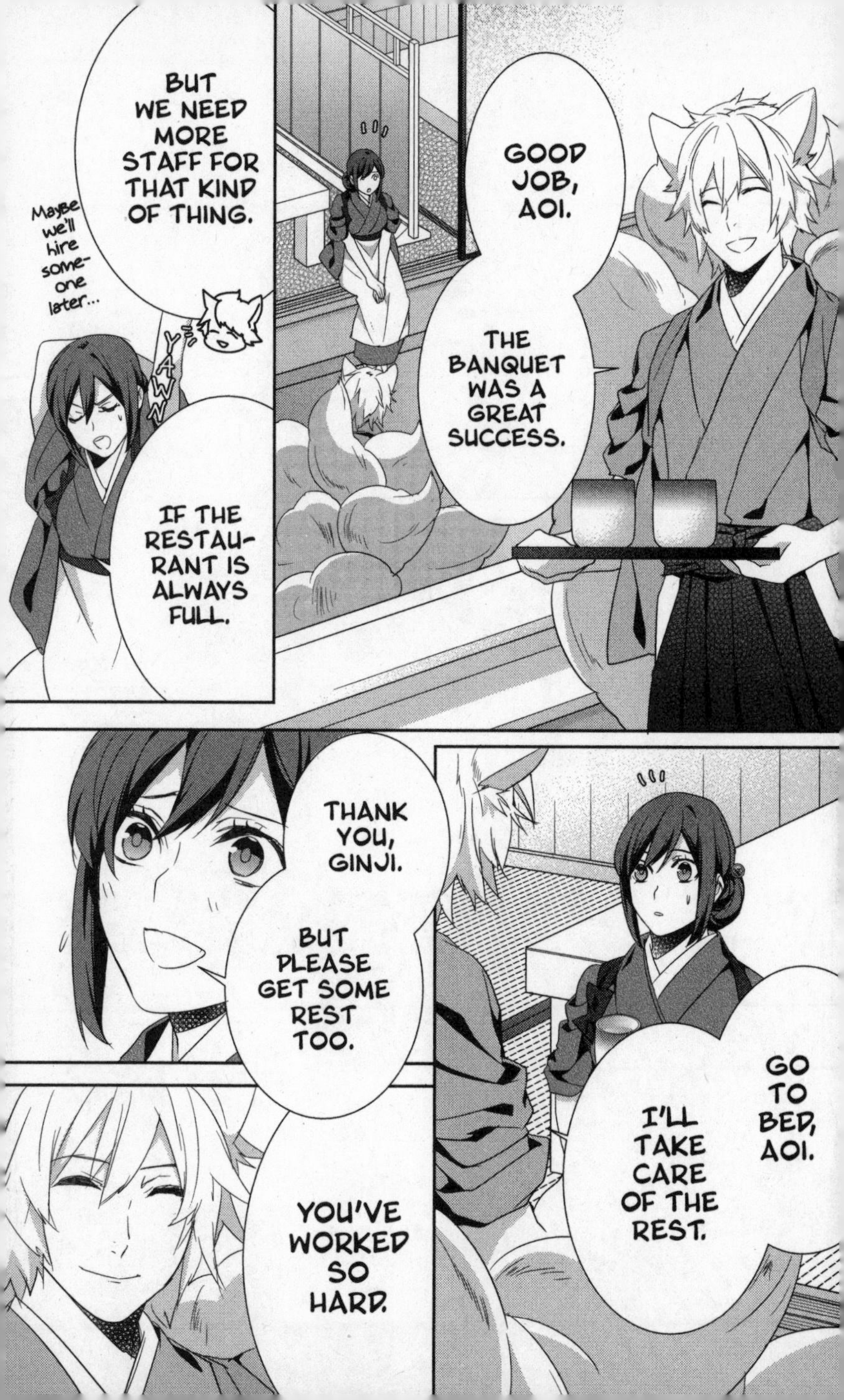
GOOD JOB, AOI.
THE BANQUET WAS A GREAT SUCCESS.
BUT WE NEED MORE STAFF FOR THAT KIND OF THING.
Maybe we'll hire someone later...
YAWN
IF THE RESTAURANT IS ALWAYS FULL.
GO TO BED, AOI.
I'LL TAKE CARE OF THE REST.
THANK YOU, GINJI.
BUT PLEASE GET SOME REST TOO.
YOU'VE WORKED SO HARD.

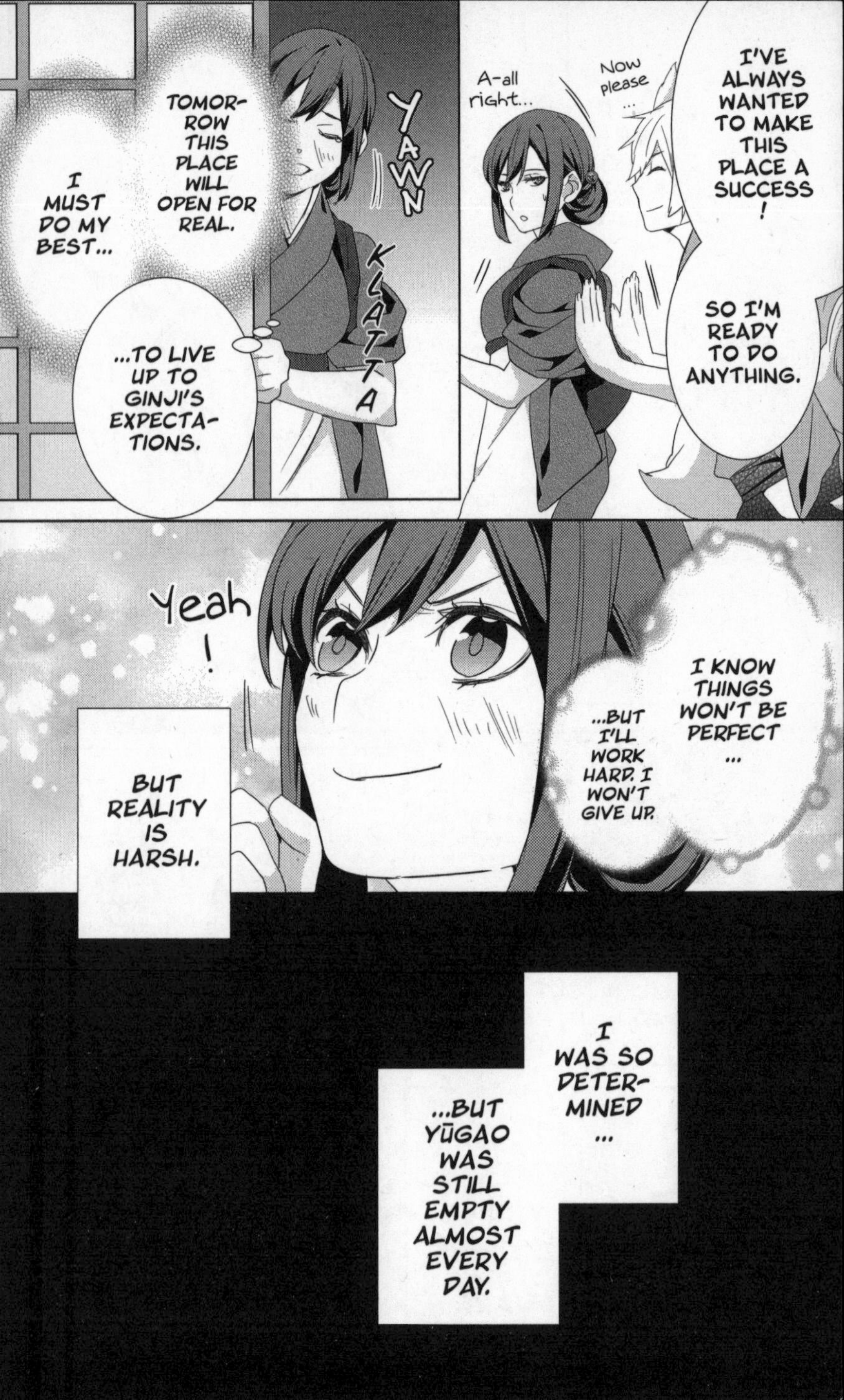
I'VE ALWAYS WANTED TO MAKE THIS PLACE A SUCCESS!
SO I'M READY TO DO ANYTHING.
Now please...
A-all right...
TOMORROW THIS PLACE WILL OPEN FOR REAL.
I MUST DO MY BEST...
YAWN
KLATTA
...TO LIVE UP TO GINJI'S EXPECTATIONS.
I KNOW THINGS WON'T BE PERFECT...
...BUT I'LL WORK HARD. I WON'T GIVE UP.
Yeah!
BUT REALITY IS HARSH.
I WAS SO DETERMINED...
...BUT YŪGAO WAS STILL EMPTY ALMOST EVERY DAY.

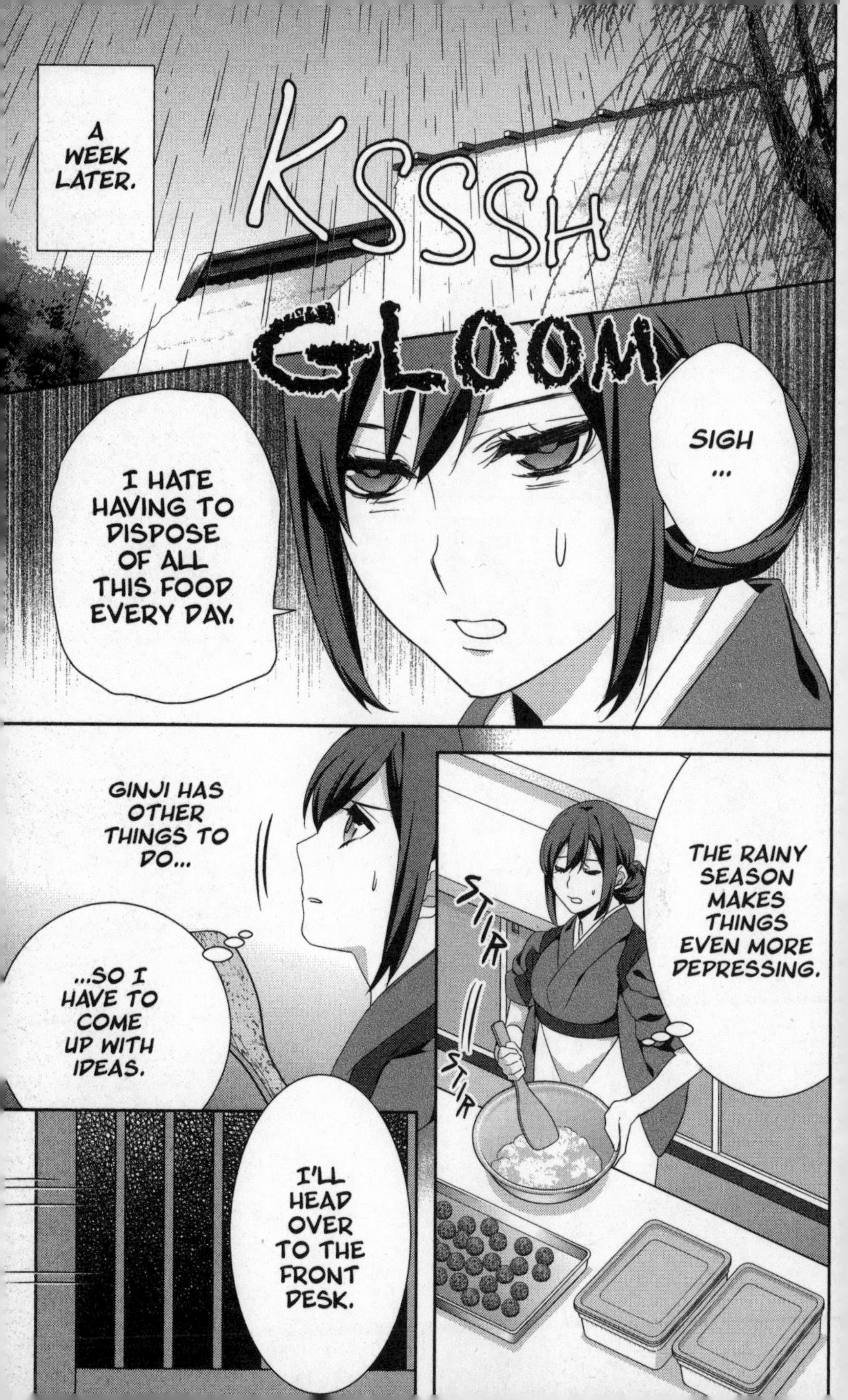
KSSSH
A WEEK LATER.
GLOOM
SIGH ...
I HATE HAVING TO DISPOSE OF ALL THIS FOOD EVERY DAY.
THE RAINY SEASON MAKES THINGS EVEN MORE DEPRESSING.
STIR
STIR
GINJI HAS OTHER THINGS TO DO...
...SO I HAVE TO COME UP WITH IDEAS.
I'LL HEAD OVER TO THE FRONT DESK.

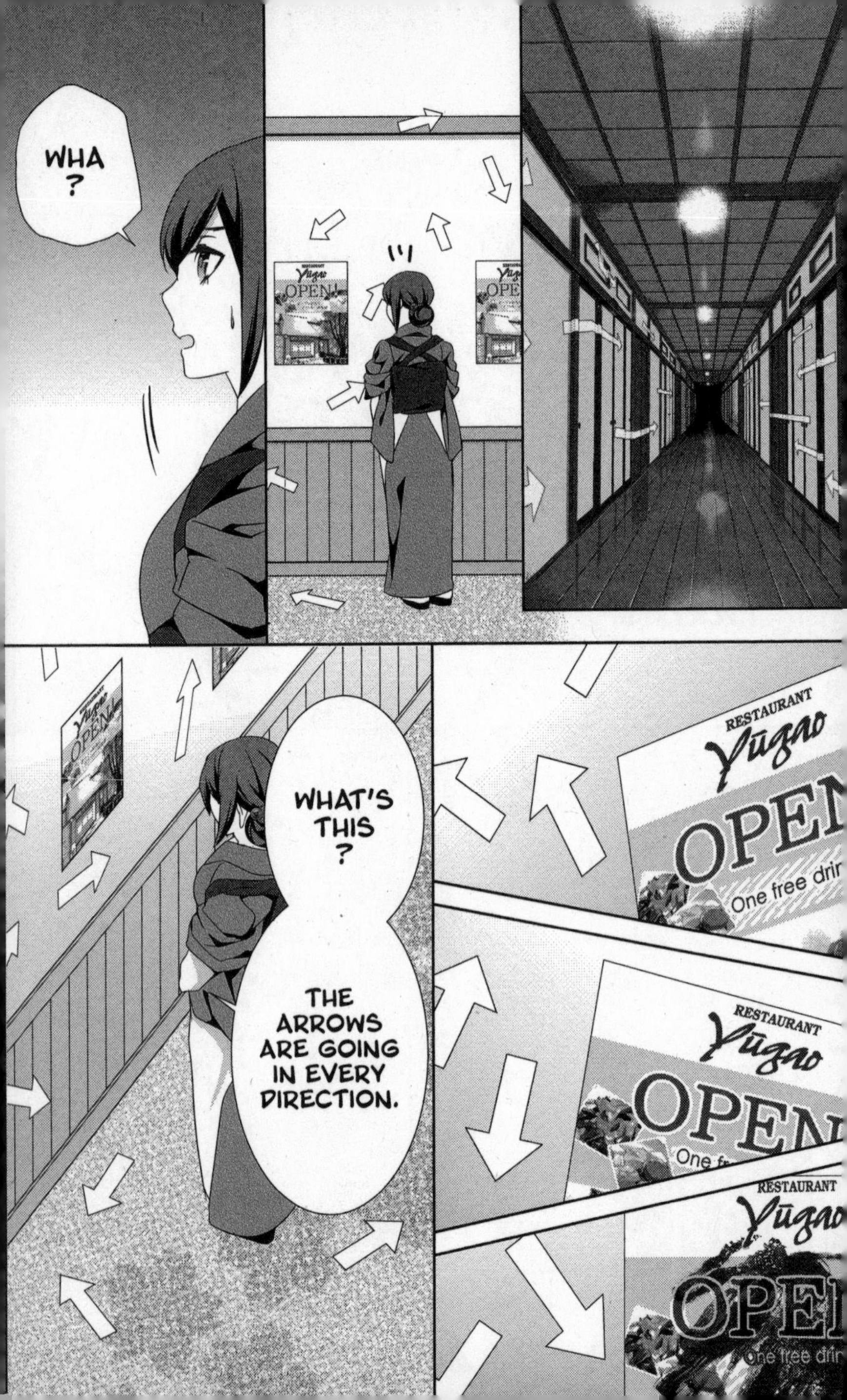
WHA ?
RESTAURANT
Yūgao
OPEN
One free dri
WHAT'S THIS ?
THE ARROWS ARE GOING IN EVERY DIRECTION.

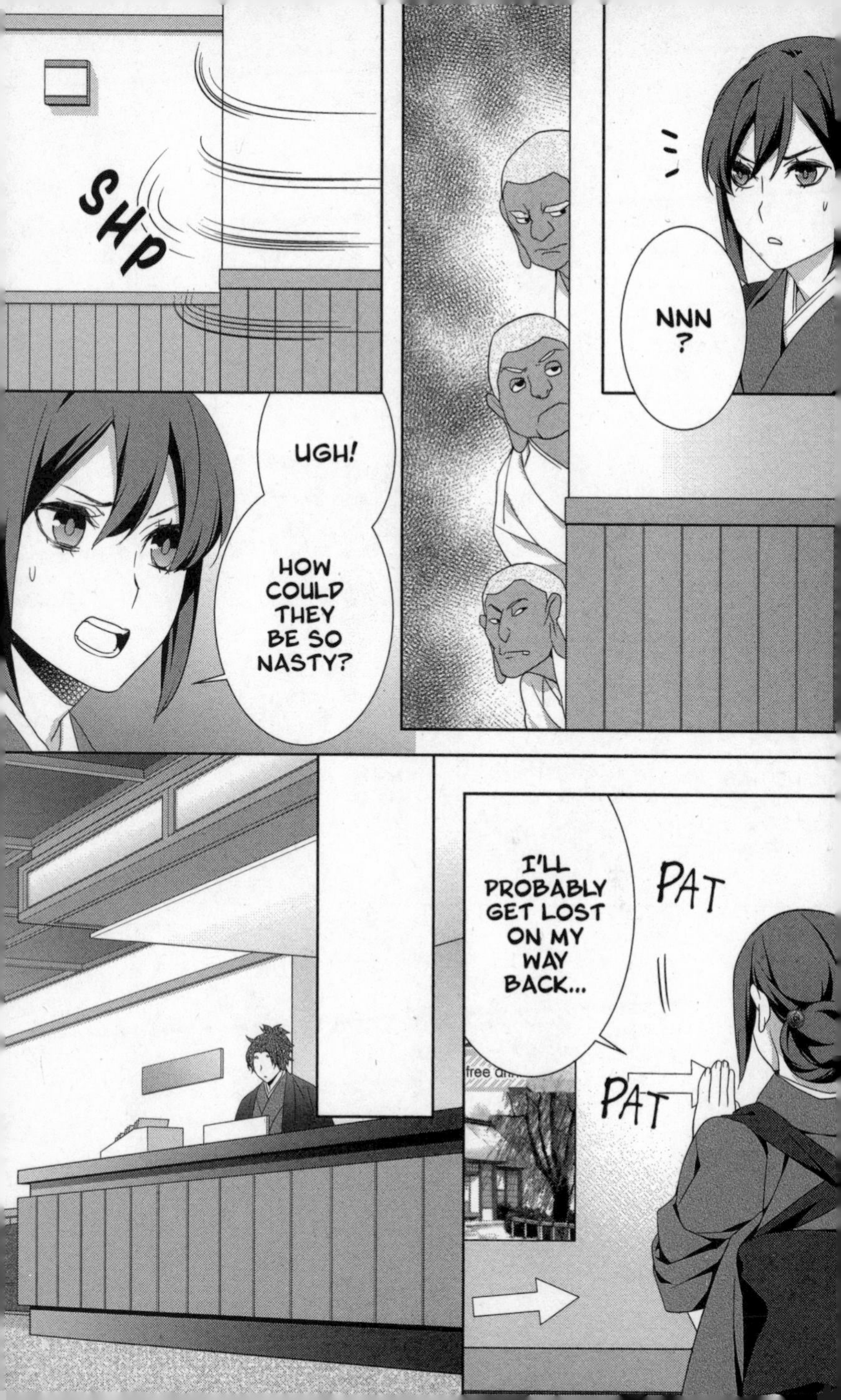
NNN ?
SHP
UGH!
HOW COULD THEY BE SO NASTY?
I'LL PROBABLY GET LOST ON MY WAY BACK...
PAT
PAT

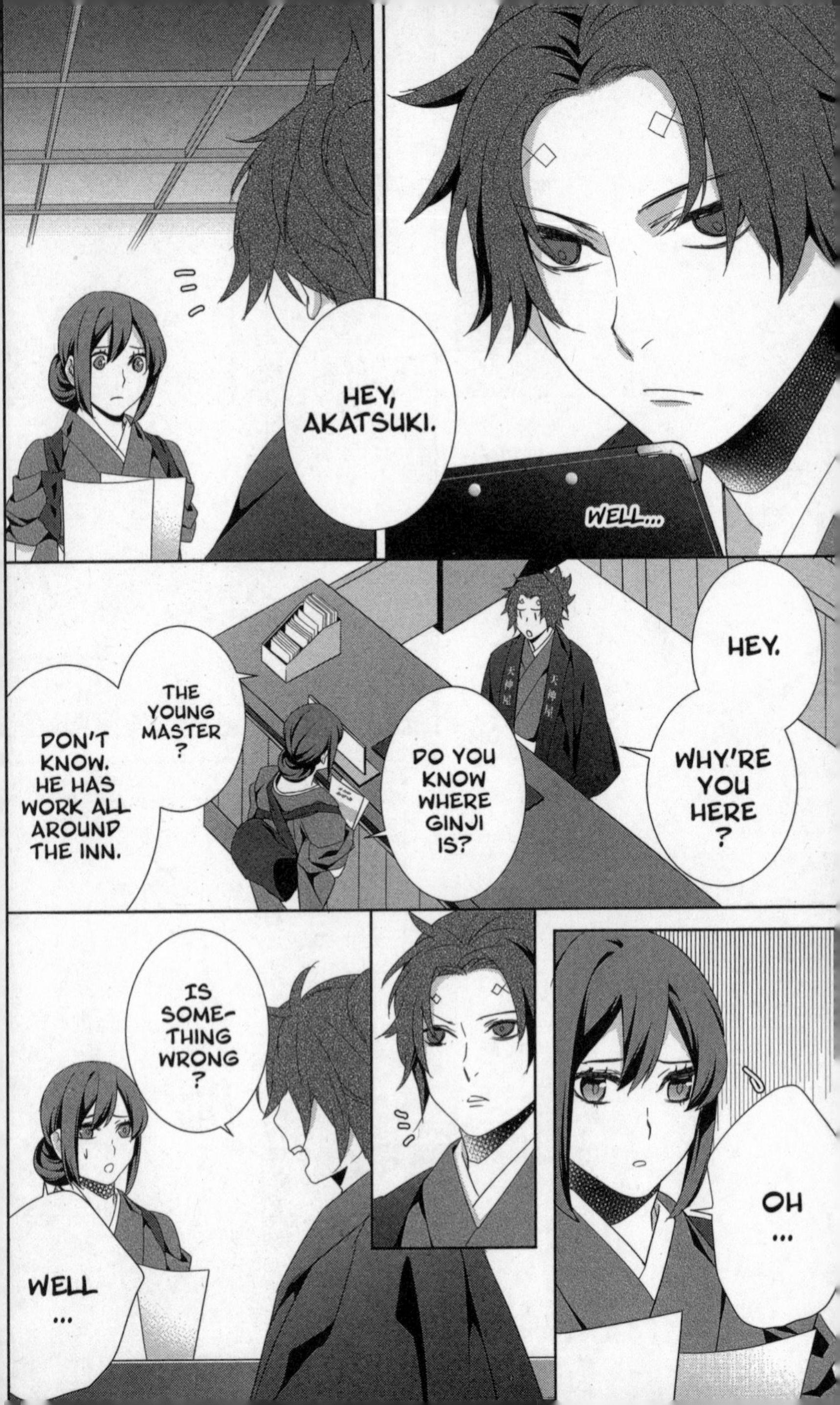
WELL...
HEY, AKATSUKI.
HEY.
WHY'RE YOU HERE?
DO YOU KNOW WHERE GINJI IS?
THE YOUNG MASTER?
DON'T KNOW. HE HAS WORK ALL AROUND THE INN.
OH...
IS SOME-THING WRONG?
WELL...

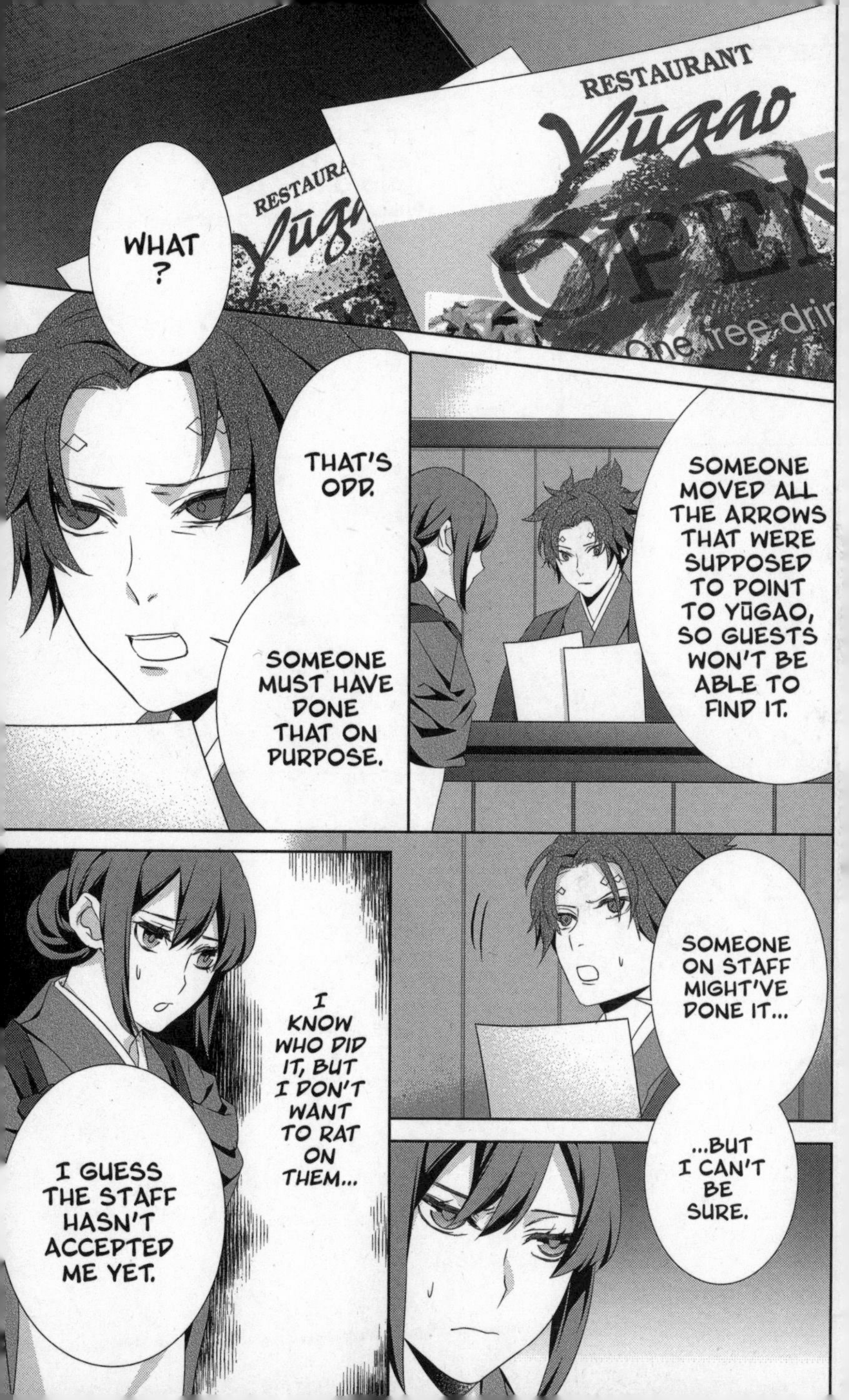
RESTAURANT
Yūgao
RESTAURANT
Yūgao
WHAT?
SOMEONE MOVED ALL THE ARROWS THAT WERE SUPPOSED TO POINT TO YŪGAO, SO GUESTS WON'T BE ABLE TO FIND IT.
THAT'S ODD.
SOMEONE MUST HAVE DONE THAT ON PURPOSE.
SOMEONE ON STAFF MIGHT'VE DONE IT...
...BUT I CAN'T BE SURE.
I KNOW WHO DID IT, BUT I DON'T WANT TO RAT ON THEM...
I GUESS THE STAFF HASN'T ACCEPTED ME YET.

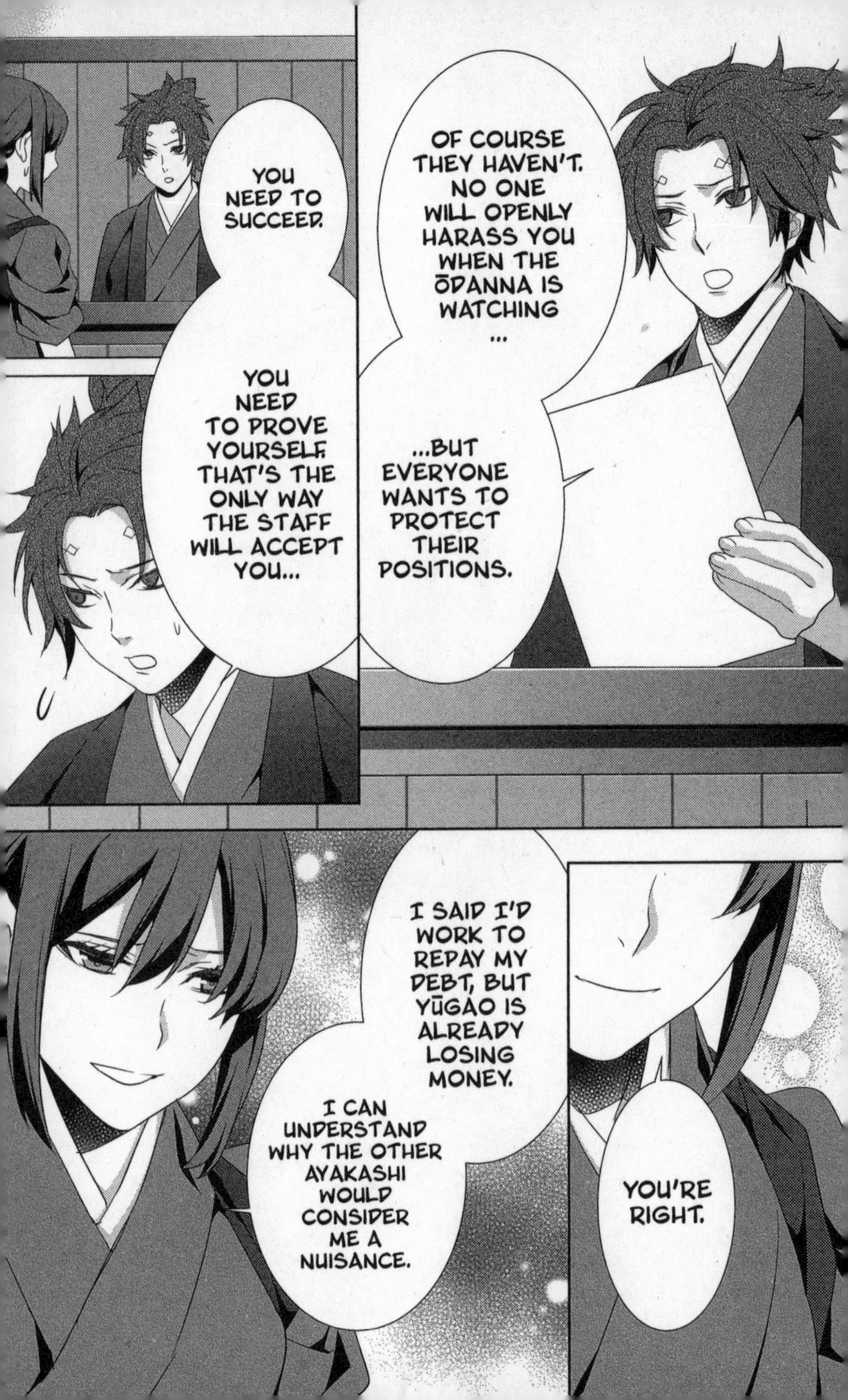

OF COURSE THEY HAVEN'T. NO ONE WILL OPENLY HARASS YOU WHEN THE ŌDANNA IS WATCHING ...
...BUT EVERYONE WANTS TO PROTECT THEIR POSITIONS.
YOU NEED TO SUCCEED.
YOU NEED TO PROVE YOURSELF. THAT'S THE ONLY WAY THE STAFF WILL ACCEPT YOU...
YOU'RE RIGHT.
I SAID I'D WORK TO REPAY MY DEBT, BUT YŪGAO IS ALREADY LOSING MONEY.
I CAN UNDERSTAND WHY THE OTHER AYAKASHI WOULD CONSIDER ME A NUISANCE.

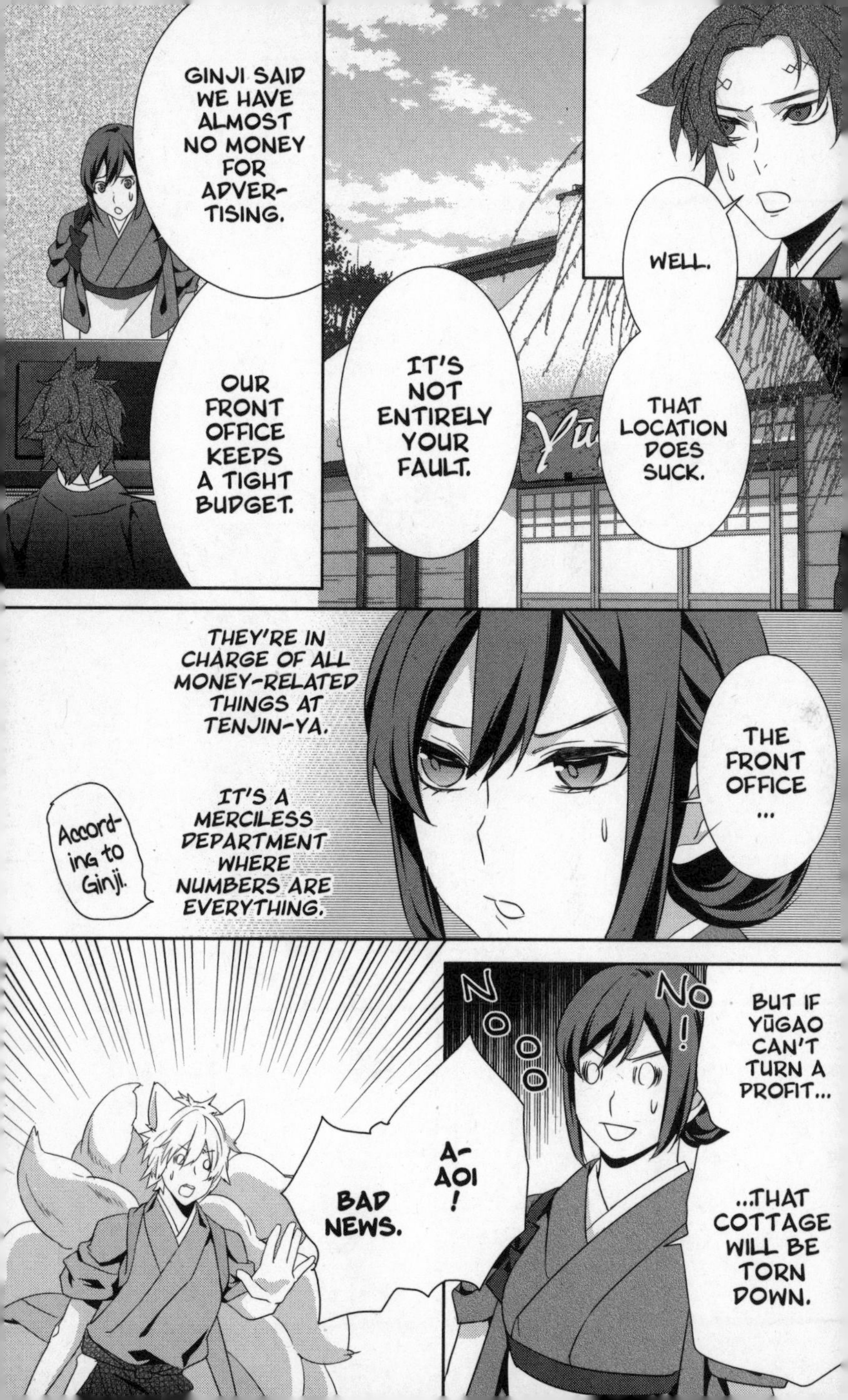
WELL.
THAT LOCATION DOES SUCK.
IT'S NOT ENTIRELY YOUR FAULT.
GINJI SAID WE HAVE ALMOST NO MONEY FOR ADVERTISING.
OUR FRONT OFFICE KEEPS A TIGHT BUDGET.
THE FRONT OFFICE...
THEY'RE IN CHARGE OF ALL MONEY-RELATED THINGS AT TENJIN-YA.
IT'S A MERCILESS DEPARTMENT WHERE NUMBERS ARE EVERYTHING.
According to Ginji.
BUT IF YŪGAO CAN'T TURN A PROFIT...
...THAT COTTAGE WILL BE TORN DOWN.
NOOOO!
A-AOI!
BAD NEWS.

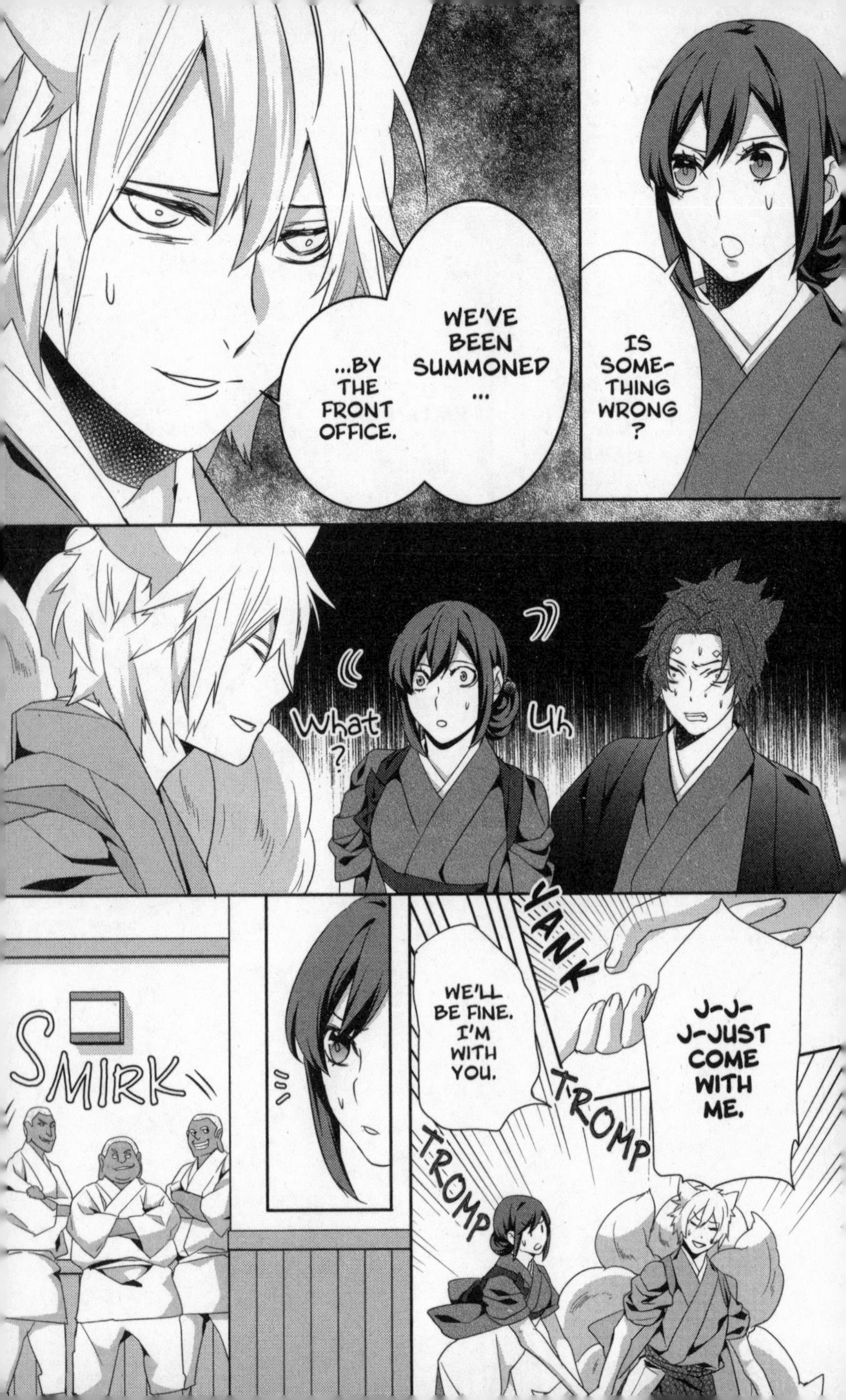
IS SOMETHING WRONG?
WE'VE BEEN SUMMONED...
...BY THE FRONT OFFICE.
Uh
What?
YANK
J-J-J-JUST COME WITH ME.
WE'LL BE FINE. I'M WITH YOU.
TROMP
TROMP
SMIRK

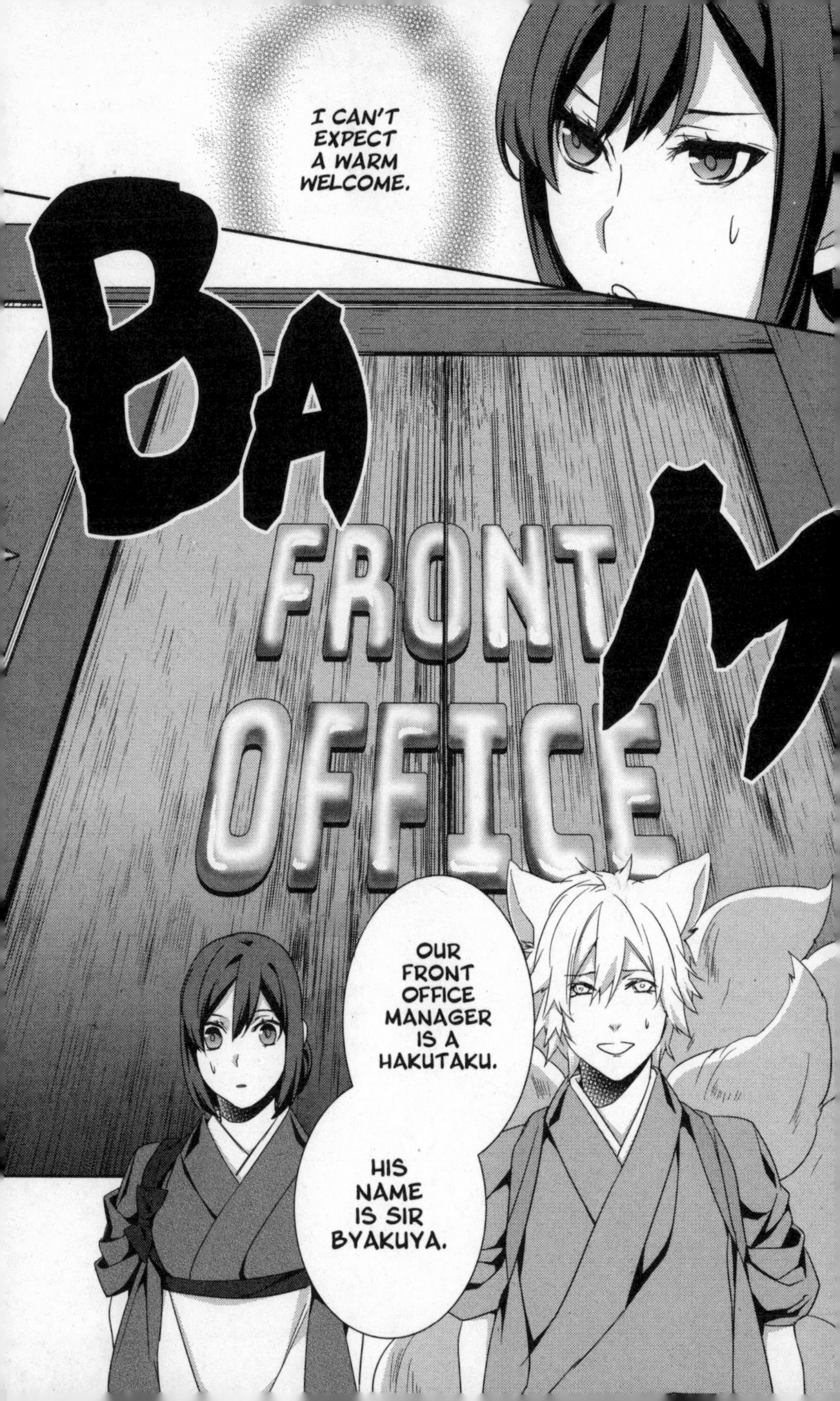
I CAN'T EXPECT A WARM WELCOME.
BAM
FRONT OFFICE
OUR FRONT OFFICE MANAGER IS A HAKUTAKU.
HIS NAME IS SIR BYAKUYA.

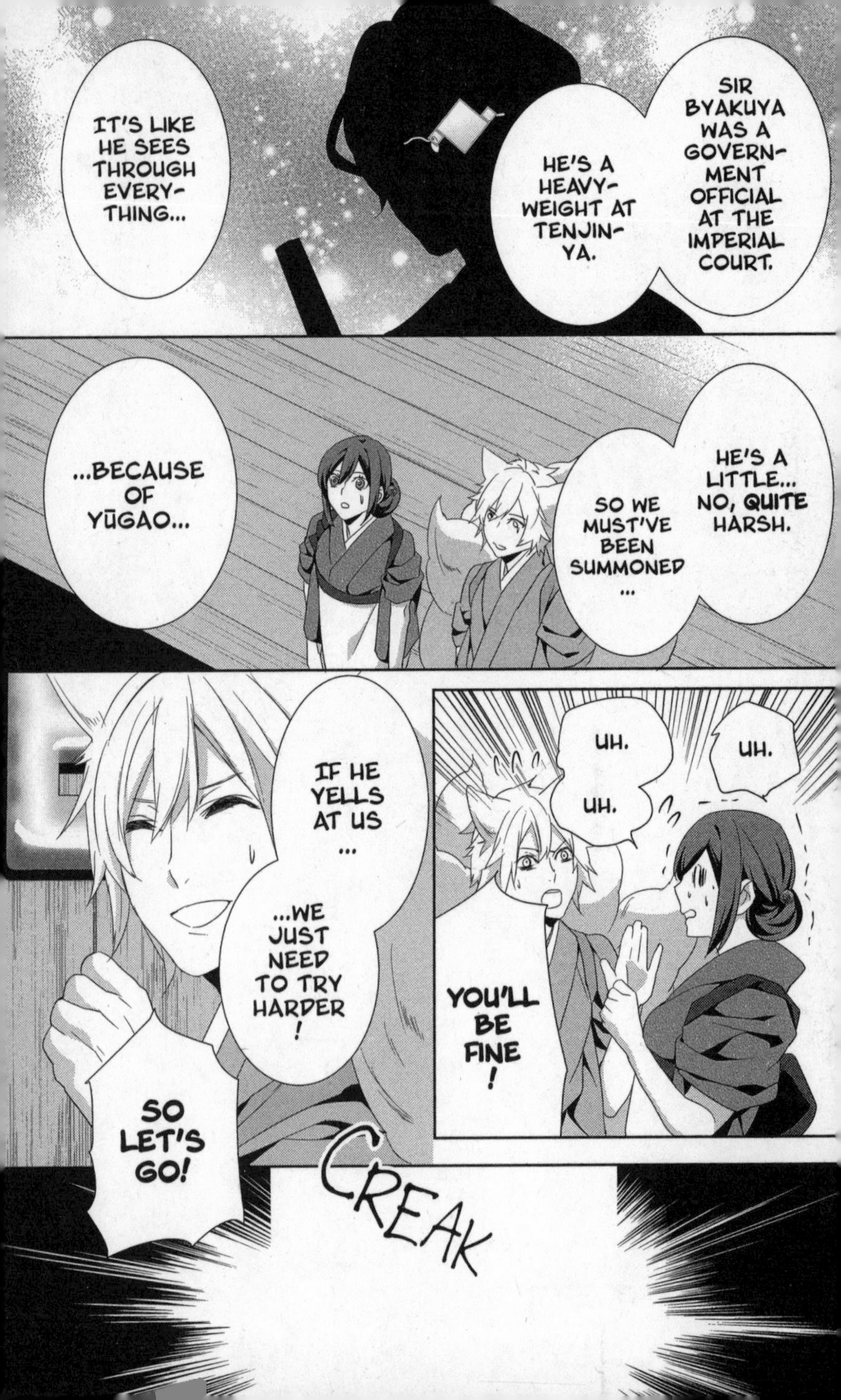
SIR BYAKUYA WAS A GOVERNMENT OFFICIAL AT THE IMPERIAL COURT.
HE'S A HEAVYWEIGHT AT TENJIN-YA.
IT'S LIKE HE SEES THROUGH EVERYTHING...
HE'S A LITTLE... NO, QUITE HARSH.
SO WE MUST'VE BEEN SUMMONED...
...BECAUSE OF YŪGAO...
UH.
UH. UH.
YOU'LL BE FINE!
IF HE YELLS AT US...
...WE JUST NEED TO TRY HARDER!
SO LET'S GO!
CREAK

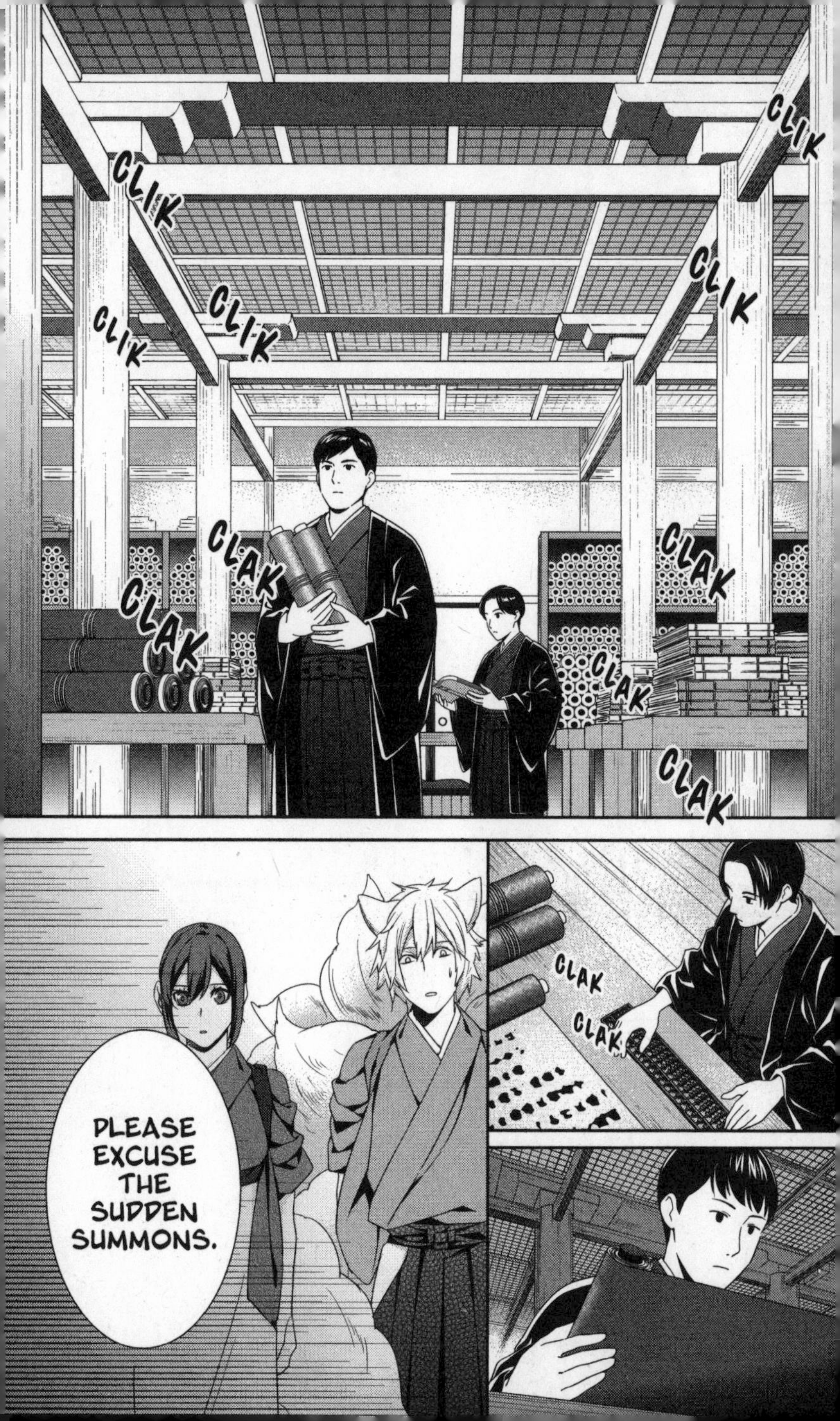
CLIK
CLIK
CLIK
CLIK
CLIK
CLAK
CLAK
CLAK
CLAK
CLAK
CLAK
CLAK
PLEASE EXCUSE THE SUDDEN SUMMONS.

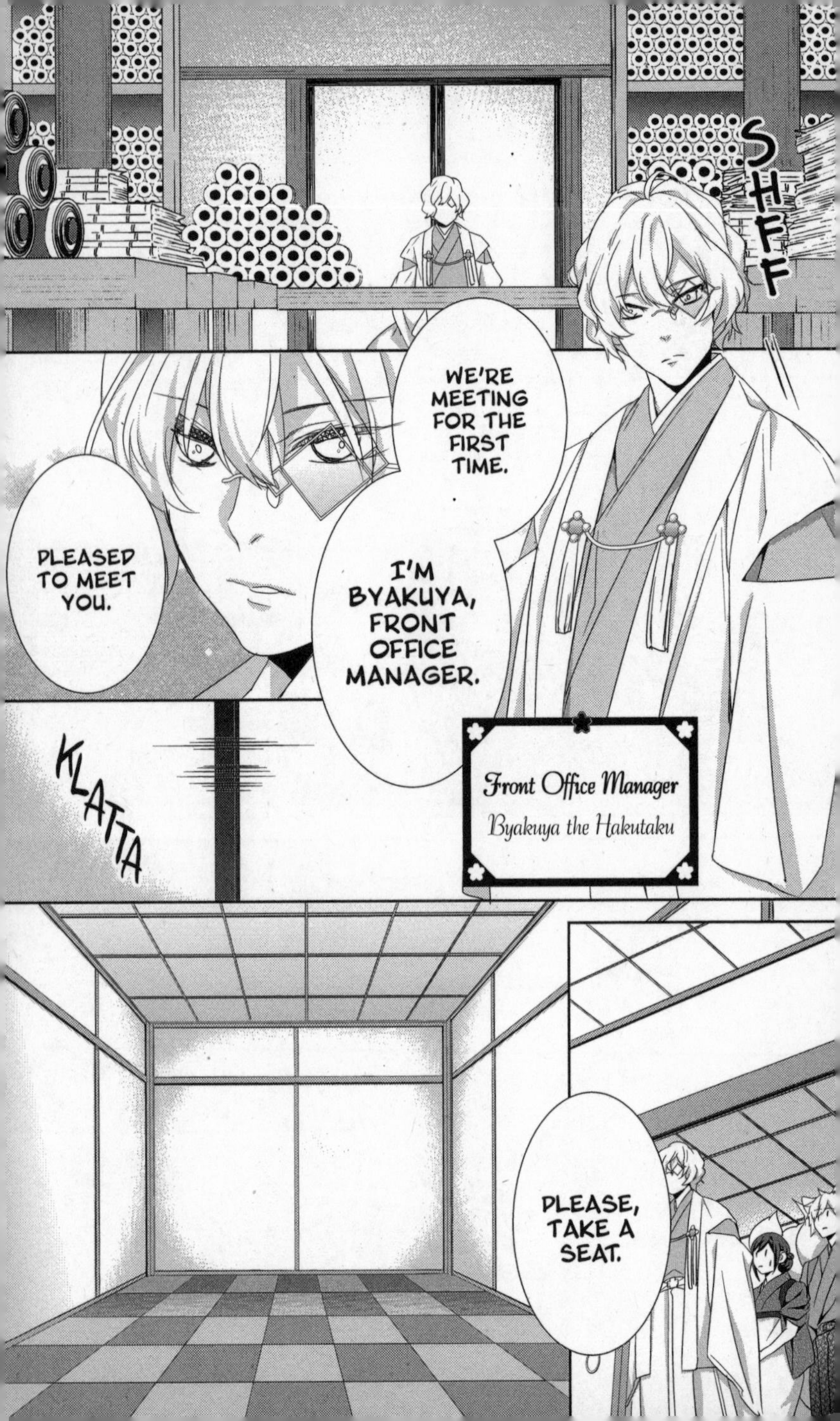
SHFF
WE'RE MEETING FOR THE FIRST TIME.
I'M BYAKUYA, FRONT OFFICE MANAGER.
Front Office Manager
Byakuya the Hakutaku
PLEASED TO MEET YOU.
KLATTA
PLEASE, TAKE A SEAT.

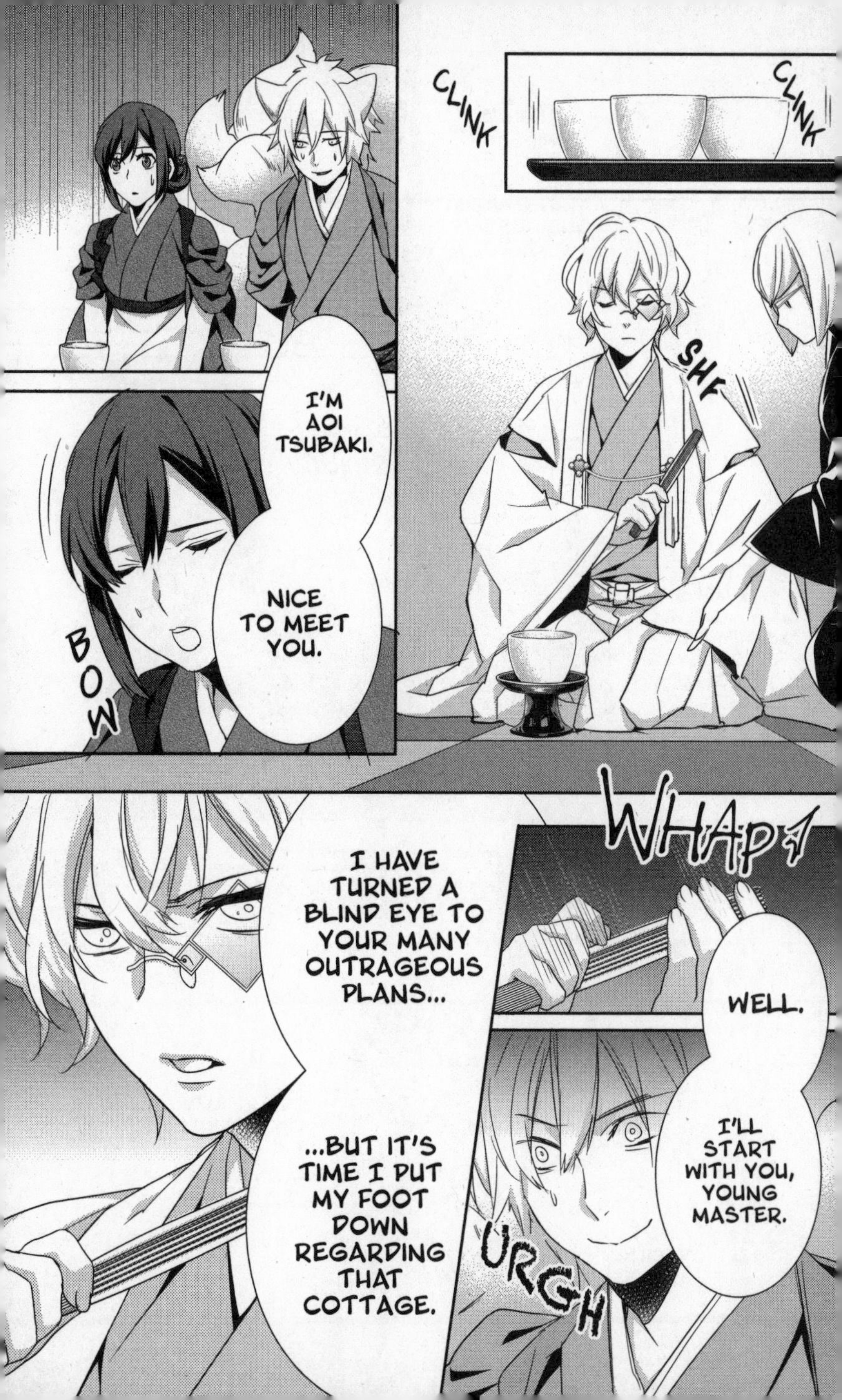
CLINK
CLINK
SHF
I'M AOI TSUBAKI.
NICE TO MEET YOU.
BOW
WHAP
WELL.
I'LL START WITH YOU, YOUNG MASTER.
URGH
I HAVE TURNED A BLIND EYE TO YOUR MANY OUTRAGEOUS PLANS...
...BUT IT'S TIME I PUT MY FOOT DOWN REGARDING THAT COTTAGE.

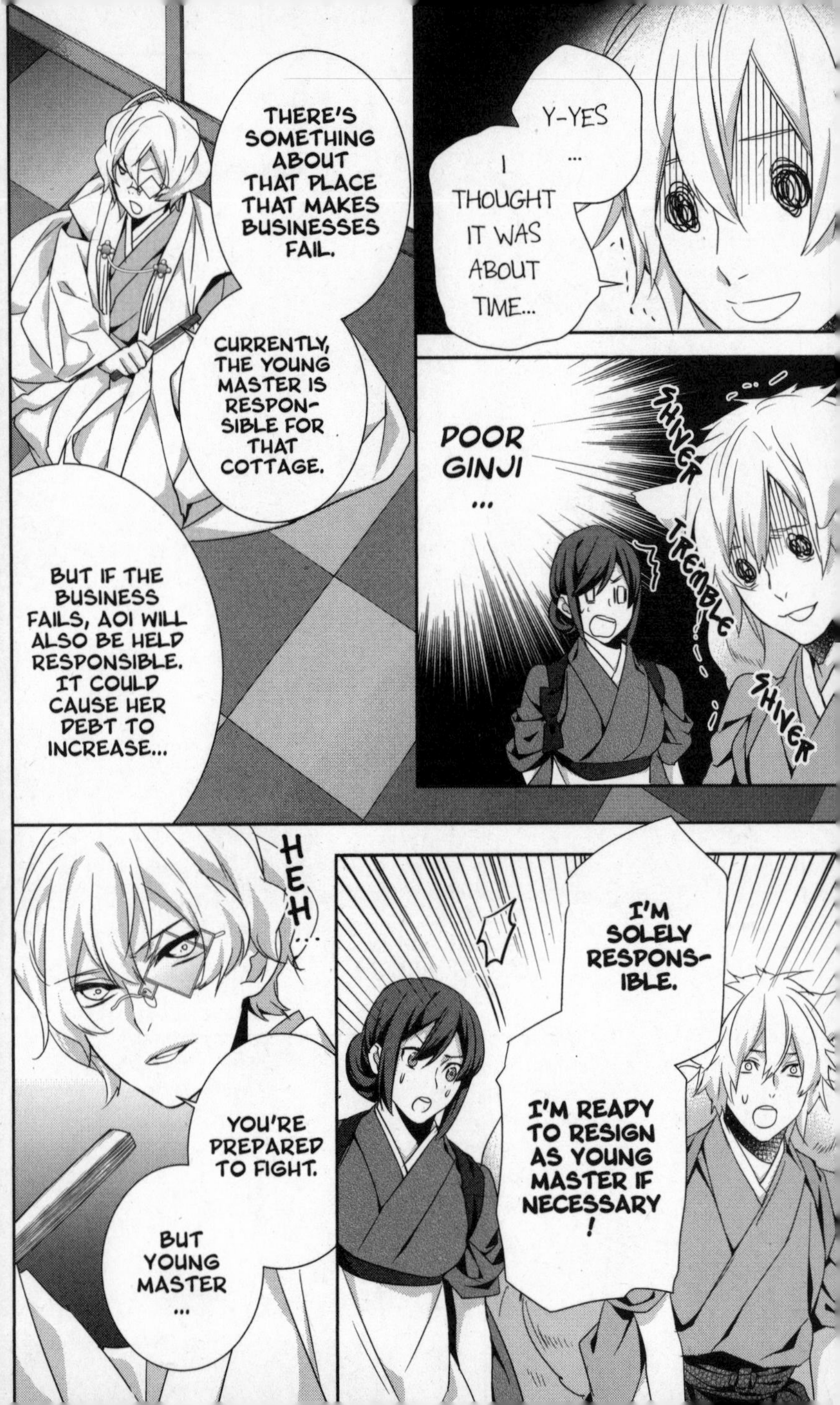
Y-YES ... I THOUGHT IT WAS ABOUT TIME...
SHIVER
TREMBLE
SHIVER
POOR GINJI ...
THERE'S SOMETHING ABOUT THAT PLACE THAT MAKES BUSINESSES FAIL.
CURRENTLY, THE YOUNG MASTER IS RESPON-SIBLE FOR THAT COTTAGE.
BUT IF THE BUSINESS FAILS, AOI WILL ALSO BE HELD RESPONSIBLE. IT COULD CAUSE HER DEBT TO INCREASE...
I'M SOLELY RESPONS-IBLE.
I'M READY TO RESIGN AS YOUNG MASTER IF NECESSARY!
HEH...
YOU'RE PREPARED TO FIGHT.
BUT YOUNG MASTER ...

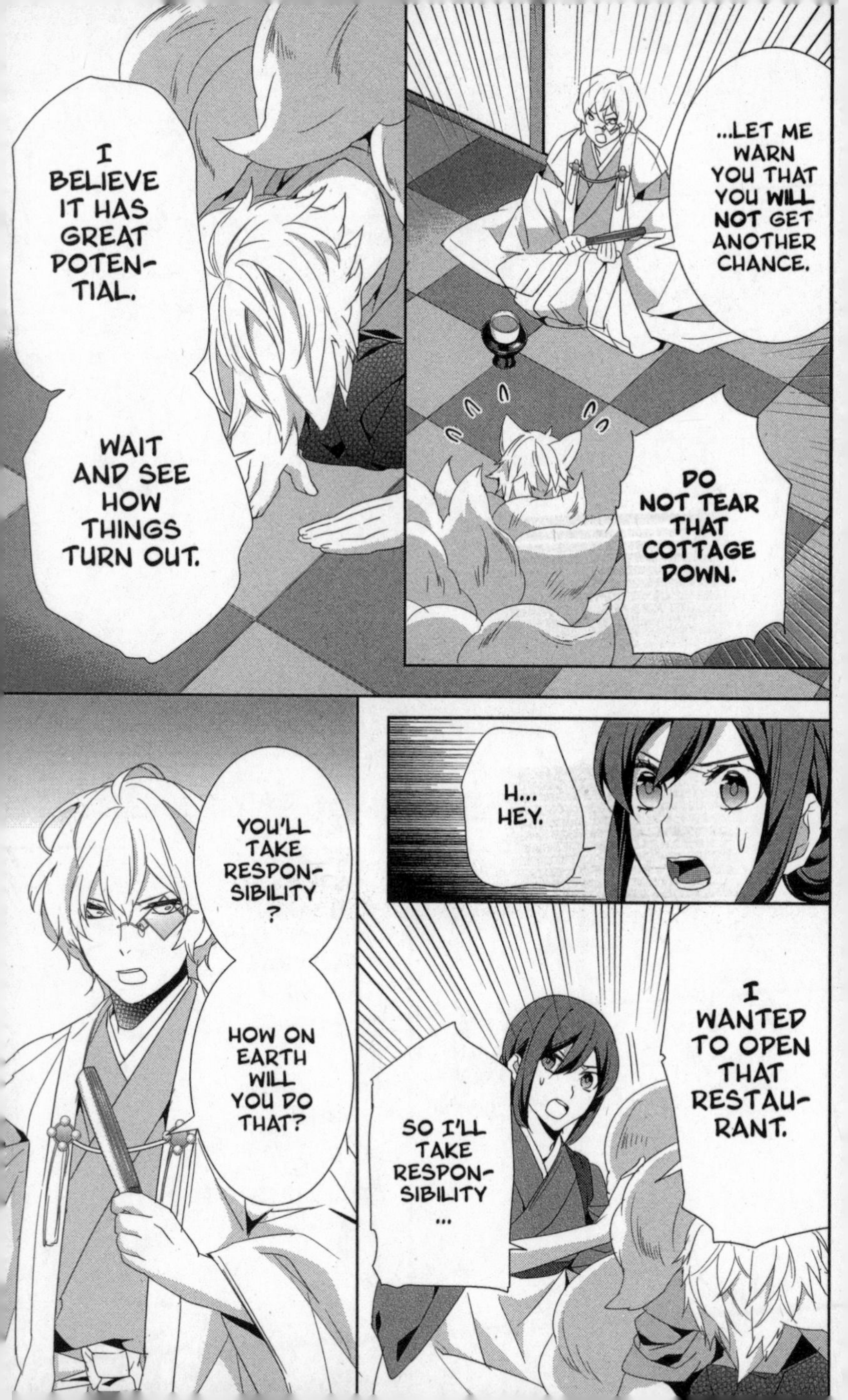
...LET ME WARN YOU THAT YOU **WILL NOT** GET ANOTHER CHANCE.
DO NOT TEAR THAT COTTAGE DOWN.
I BELIEVE IT HAS GREAT POTEN-TIAL.
WAIT AND SEE HOW THINGS TURN OUT.
H... HEY.
I WANTED TO OPEN THAT RESTAU-RANT.
SO I'LL TAKE RESPON-SIBILITY...
YOU'LL TAKE RESPON-SIBILITY?
HOW ON EARTH WILL YOU DO THAT?

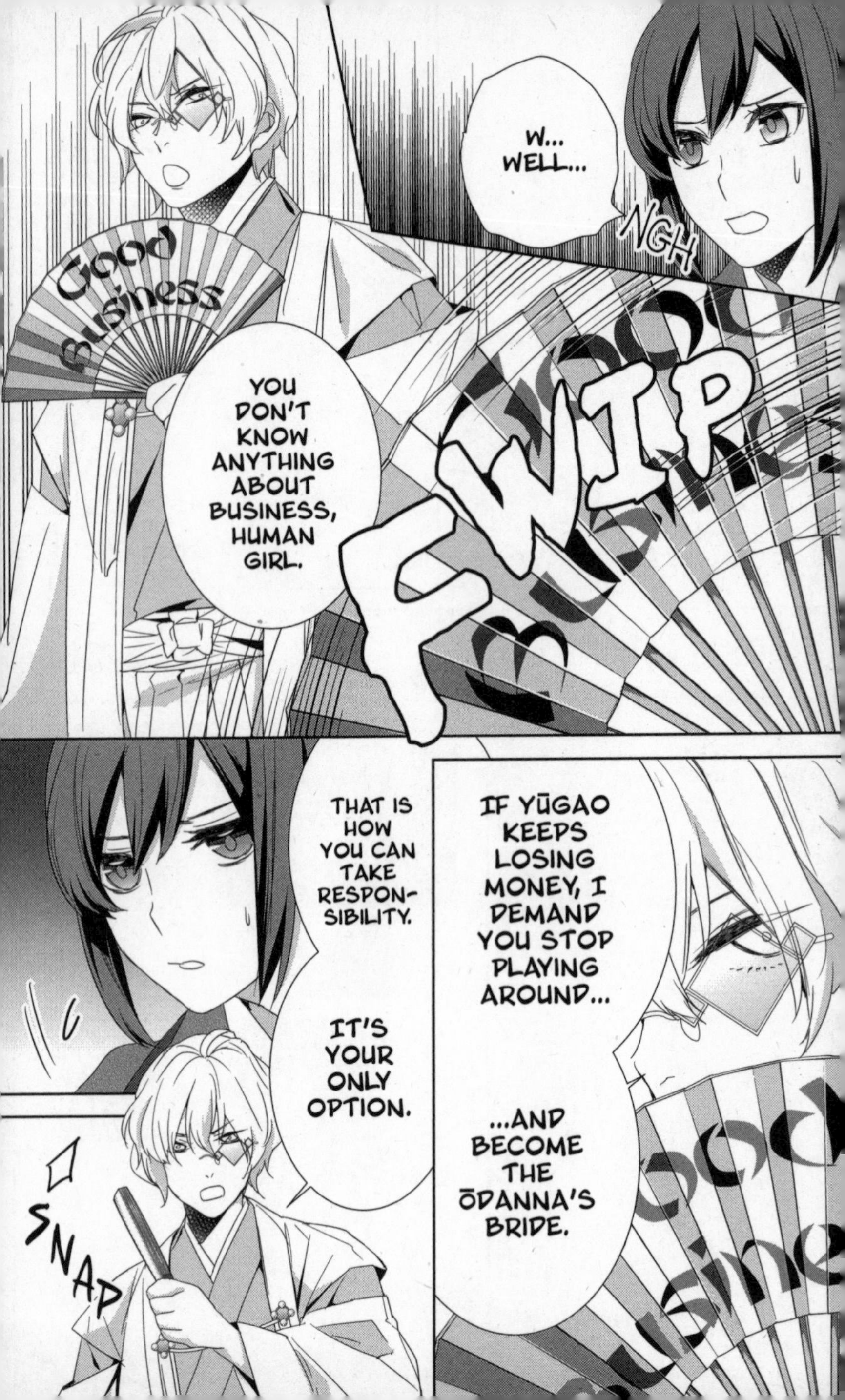
W... WELL...
NGH
FWIP
Good business
YOU DON'T KNOW ANYTHING ABOUT BUSINESS, HUMAN GIRL.
IF YŪGAO KEEPS LOSING MONEY, I DEMAND YOU STOP PLAYING AROUND...
...AND BECOME THE ŌDANNA'S BRIDE.
THAT IS HOW YOU CAN TAKE RESPON-SIBILITY.
IT'S YOUR ONLY OPTION.
SNAP

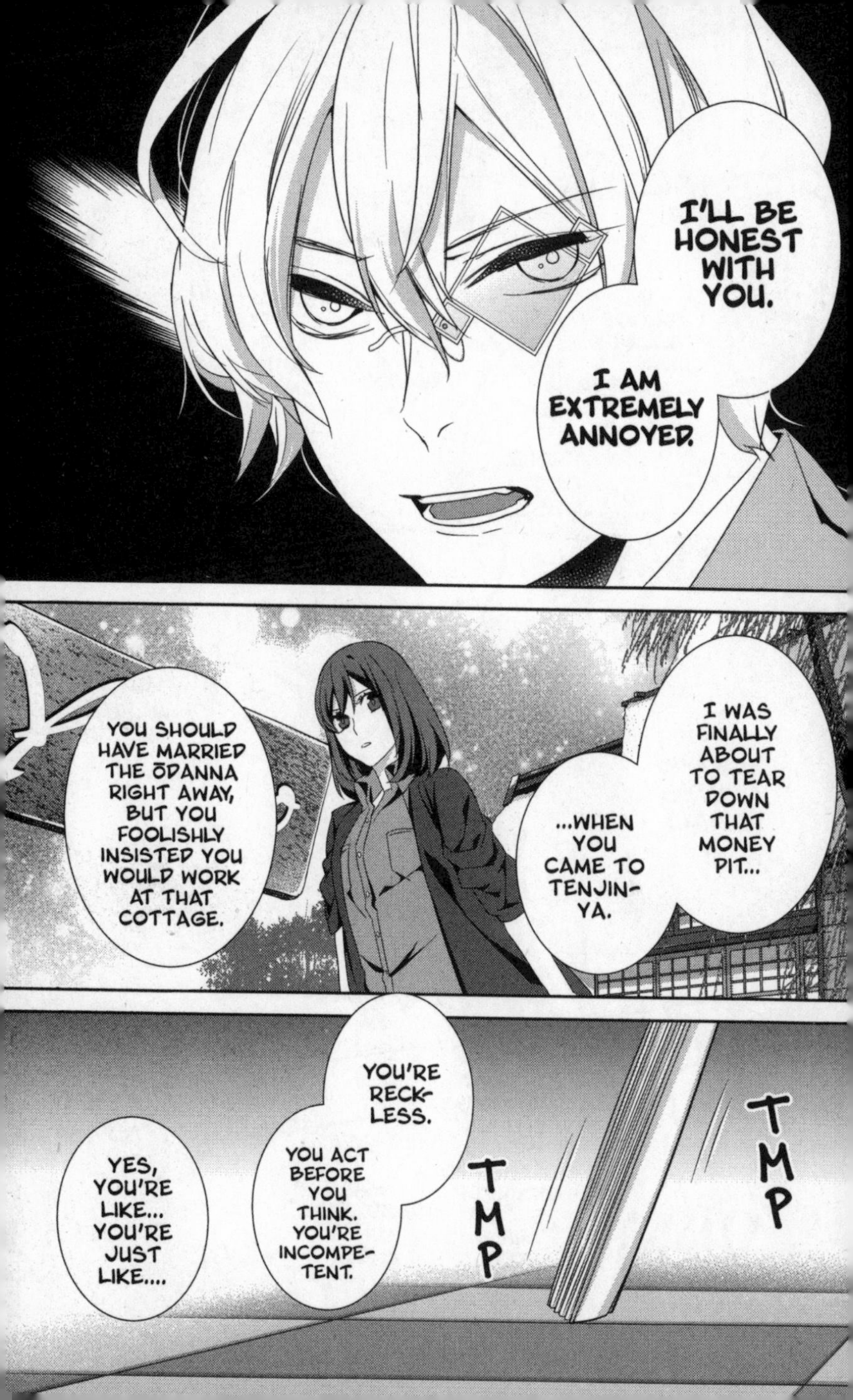
I'LL BE HONEST WITH YOU.
I AM EXTREMELY ANNOYED.
I WAS FINALLY ABOUT TO TEAR DOWN THAT MONEY PIT...
...WHEN YOU CAME TO TENJIN-YA.
YOU SHOULD HAVE MARRIED THE ŌDANNA RIGHT AWAY, BUT YOU FOOLISHLY INSISTED YOU WOULD WORK AT THAT COTTAGE.
TMP
TMP
YOU'RE RECK-LESS.
YOU ACT BEFORE YOU THINK. YOU'RE INCOMPE-TENT.
YES, YOU'RE LIKE... YOU'RE JUST LIKE....

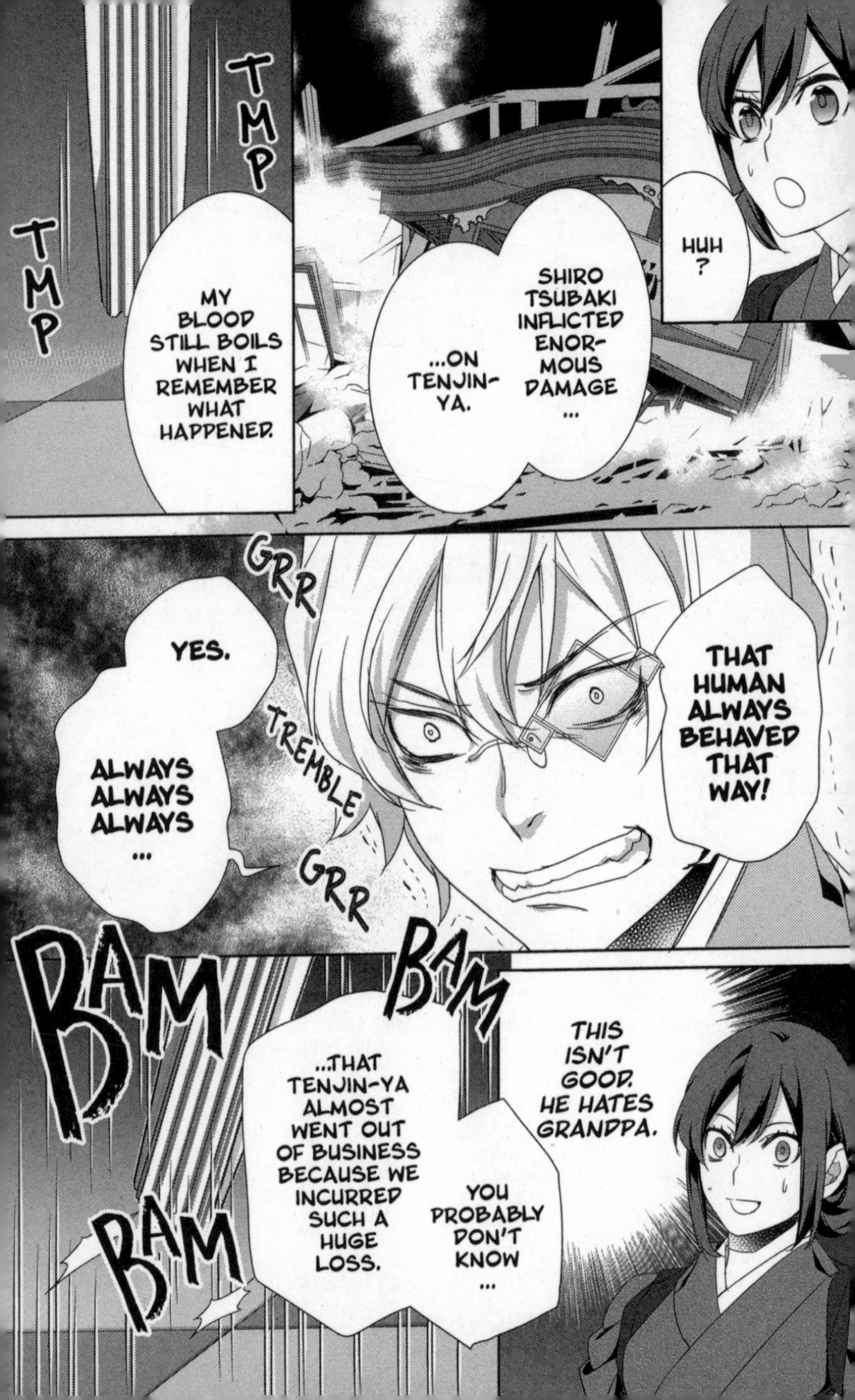
HUH?
SHIRO TSUBAKI INFLICTED ENORMOUS DAMAGE...
...ON TENJIN-YA.
TMP
TMP
MY BLOOD STILL BOILS WHEN I REMEMBER WHAT HAPPENED.
GRR
THAT HUMAN ALWAYS BEHAVED THAT WAY!
TREMBLE
GRR
YES.
ALWAYS ALWAYS ALWAYS ...
BAM
THIS ISN'T GOOD. HE HATES GRANDPA.
YOU PROBABLY DON'T KNOW ...
...THAT TENJIN-YA ALMOST WENT OUT OF BUSINESS BECAUSE WE INCURRED SUCH A HUGE LOSS.
BAM
BAM

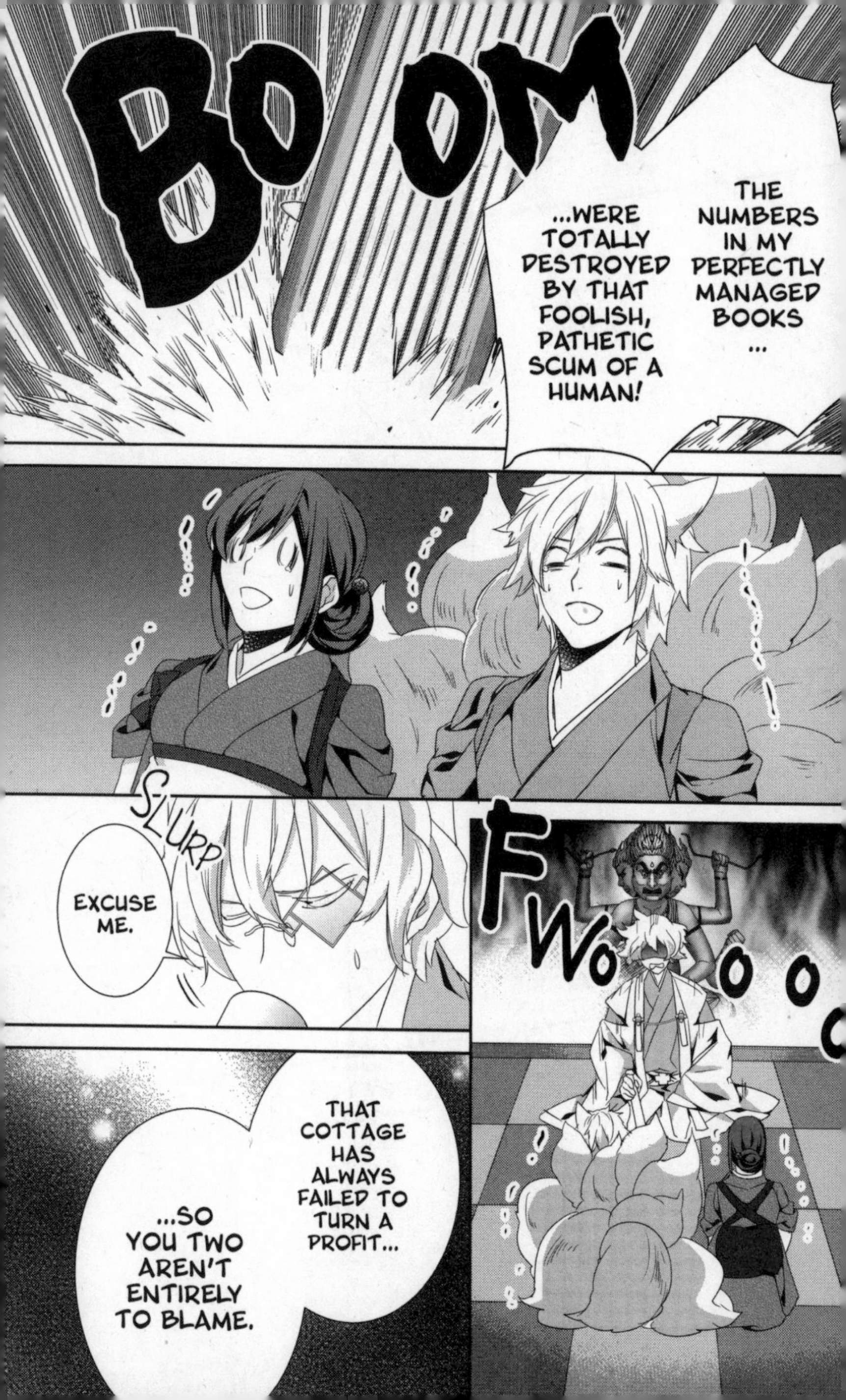
BOOM
THE NUMBERS IN MY PERFECTLY MANAGED BOOKS ...
...WERE TOTALLY DESTROYED BY THAT FOOLISH, PATHETIC SCUM OF A HUMAN!
FWOOOO
SLURP
EXCUSE ME.
THAT COTTAGE HAS ALWAYS FAILED TO TURN A PROFIT...
...SO YOU TWO AREN'T ENTIRELY TO BLAME.

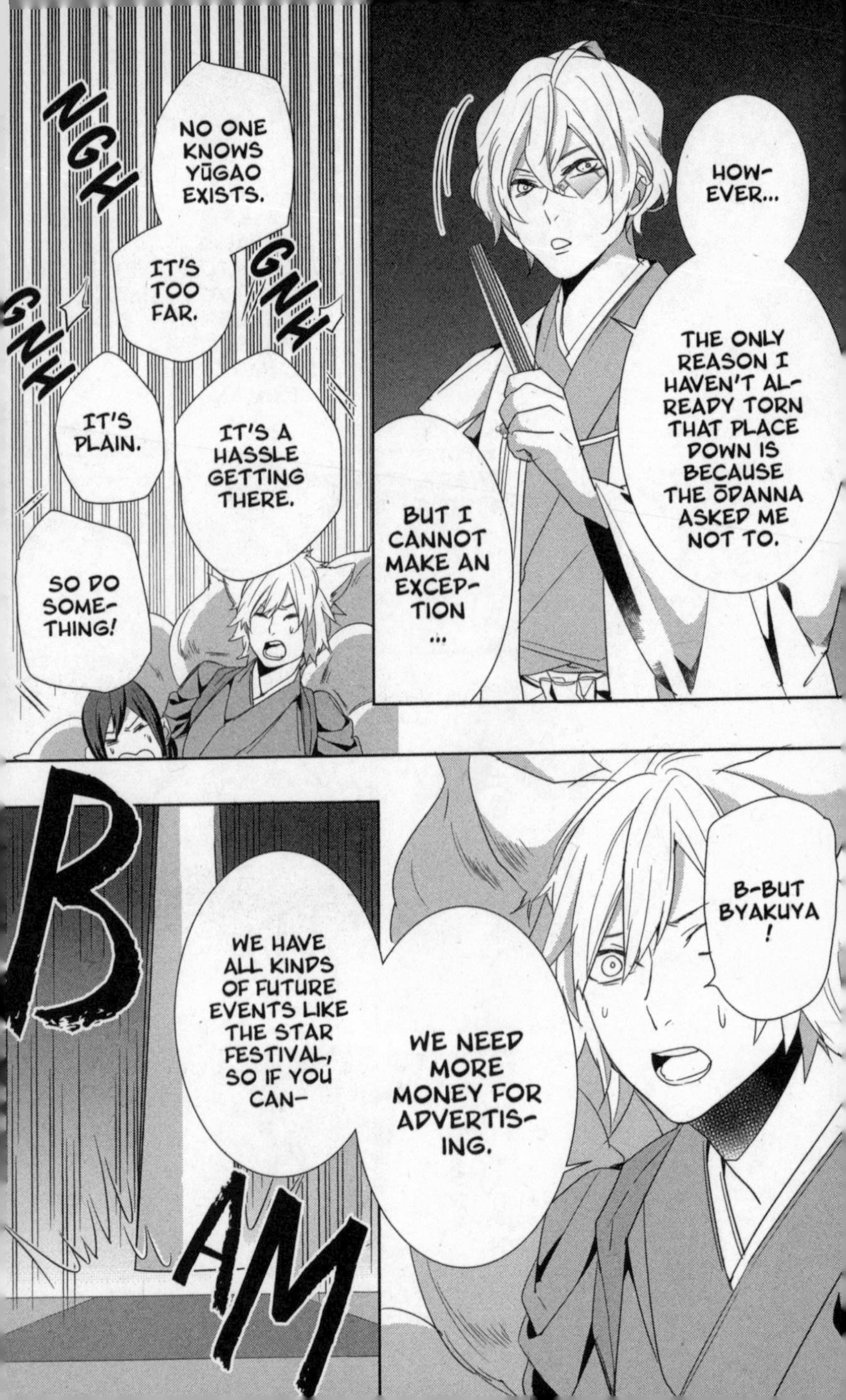
HOW-EVER...
THE ONLY REASON I HAVEN'T AL-READY TORN THAT PLACE DOWN IS BECAUSE THE ŌDANNA ASKED ME NOT TO.
BUT I CANNOT MAKE AN EXCEP-TION ...
NGH
NO ONE KNOWS YŪGAO EXISTS.
GNH
IT'S TOO FAR.
GNH
IT'S A HASSLE GETTING THERE.
IT'S PLAIN.
SO DO SOME-THING!
B-BUT BYAKUYA !
WE NEED MORE MONEY FOR ADVERTIS-ING.
WE HAVE ALL KINDS OF FUTURE EVENTS LIKE THE STAR FESTIVAL, SO IF YOU CAN-
BAM

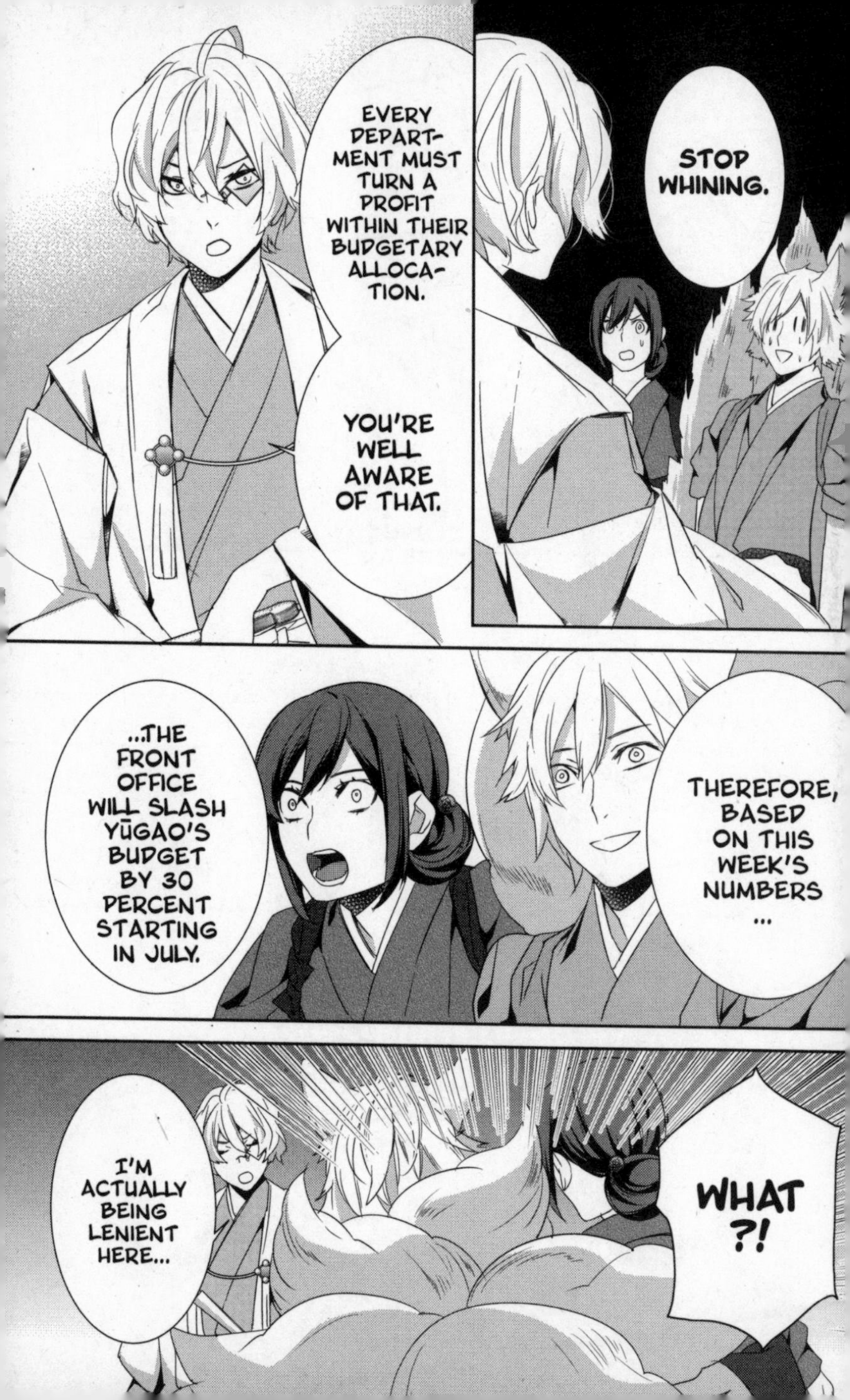
STOP WHINING.
EVERY DEPARTMENT MUST TURN A PROFIT WITHIN THEIR BUDGETARY ALLOCATION.
YOU'RE WELL AWARE OF THAT.
THEREFORE, BASED ON THIS WEEK'S NUMBERS...
...THE FRONT OFFICE WILL SLASH YŪGAO'S BUDGET BY 30 PERCENT STARTING IN JULY.
WHAT?!
I'M ACTUALLY BEING LENIENT HERE...

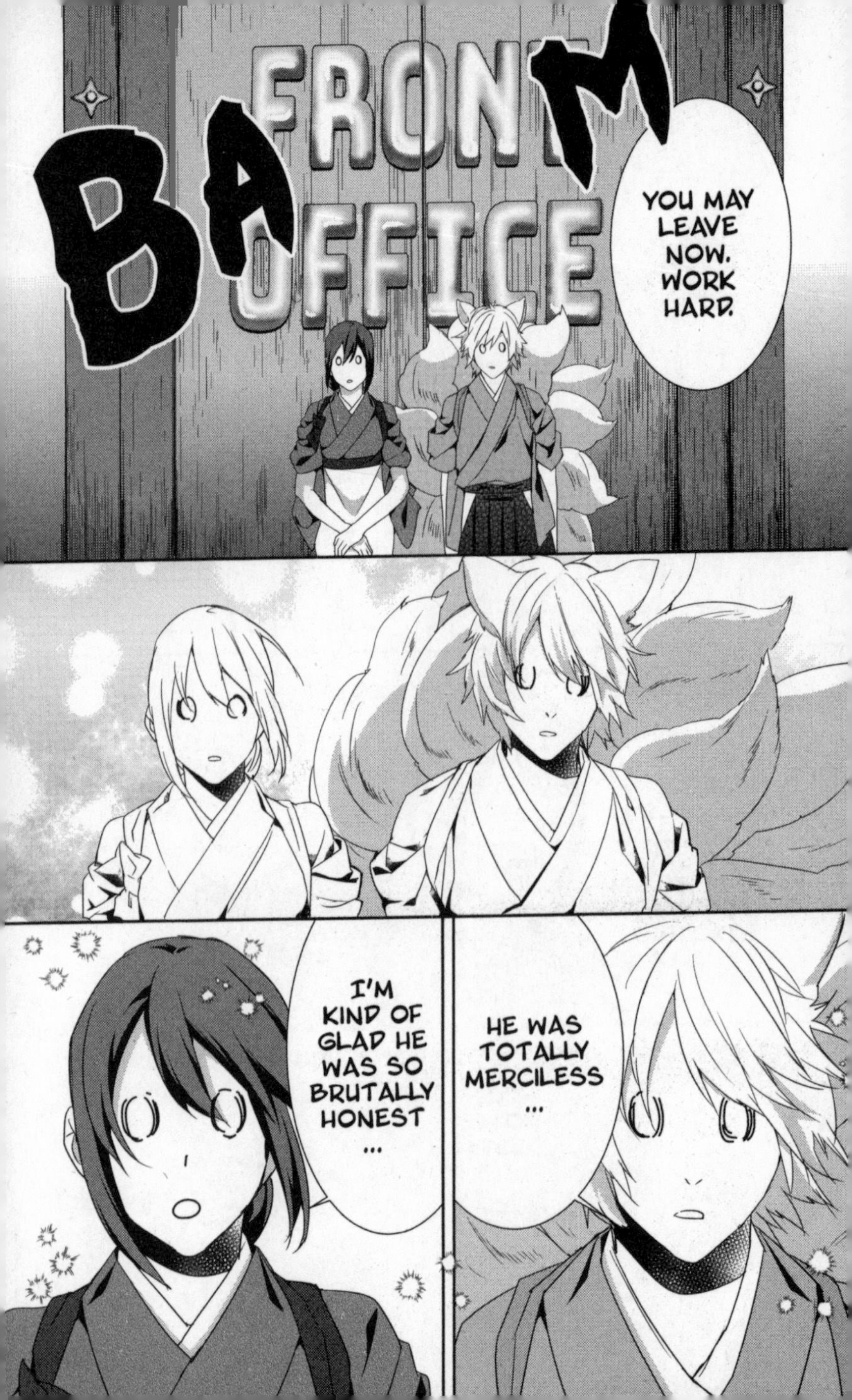
BAM
FRONT OFFICE
YOU MAY LEAVE NOW. WORK HARD.
HE WAS TOTALLY MERCILESS ...
I'M KIND OF GLAD HE WAS SO BRUTALLY HONEST ...

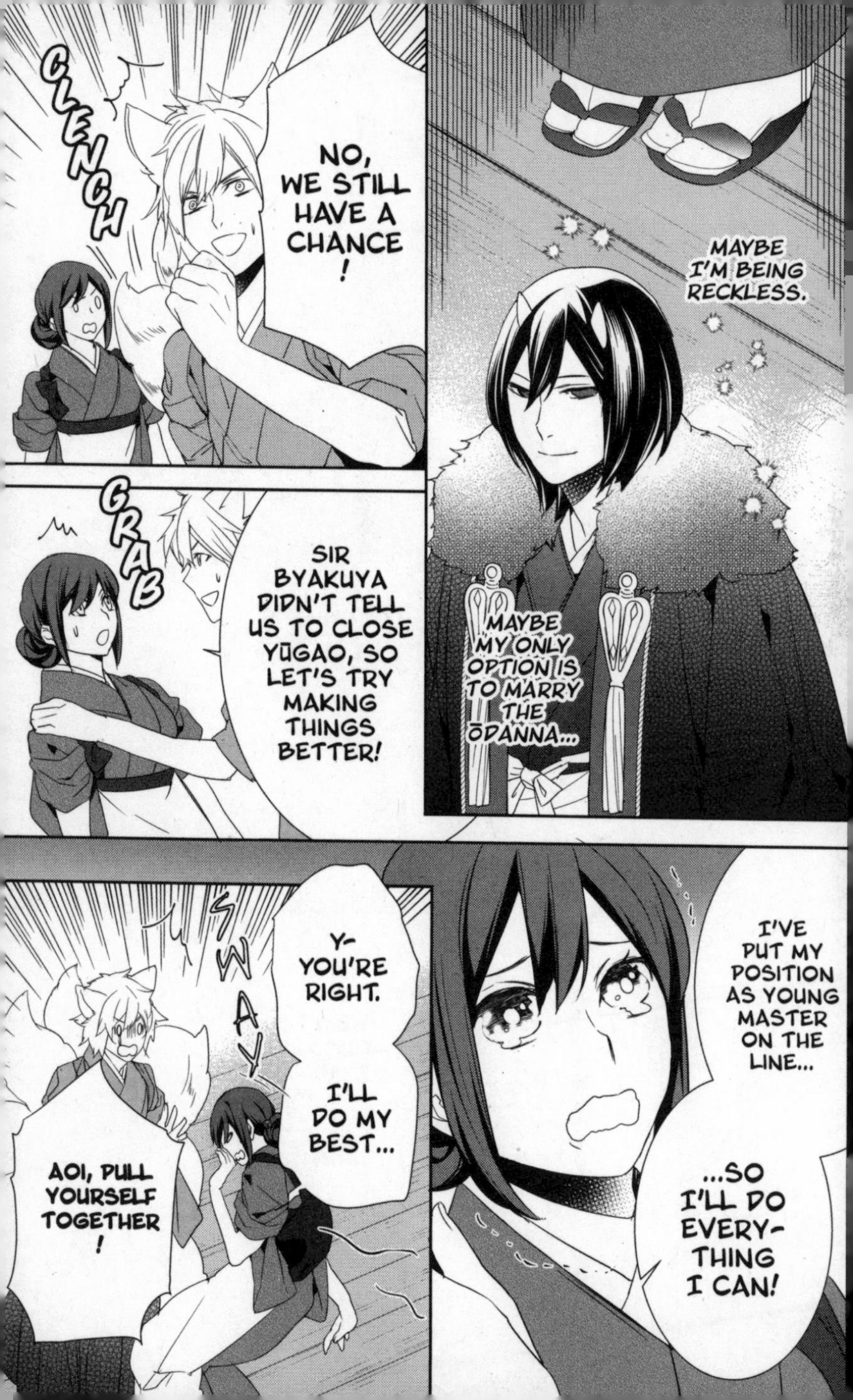
MAYBE I'M BEING RECKLESS.
MAYBE MY ONLY OPTION IS TO MARRY THE ŌDANNA...
CLENCH
NO, WE STILL HAVE A CHANCE!
GRAB
SIR BYAKUYA DIDN'T TELL US TO CLOSE YŪGAO, SO LET'S TRY MAKING THINGS BETTER!
I'VE PUT MY POSITION AS YOUNG MASTER ON THE LINE...
...SO I'LL DO EVERY-THING I CAN!
Y-YOU'RE RIGHT.
SWAY
I'LL DO MY BEST...
AOI, PULL YOURSELF TOGETHER!

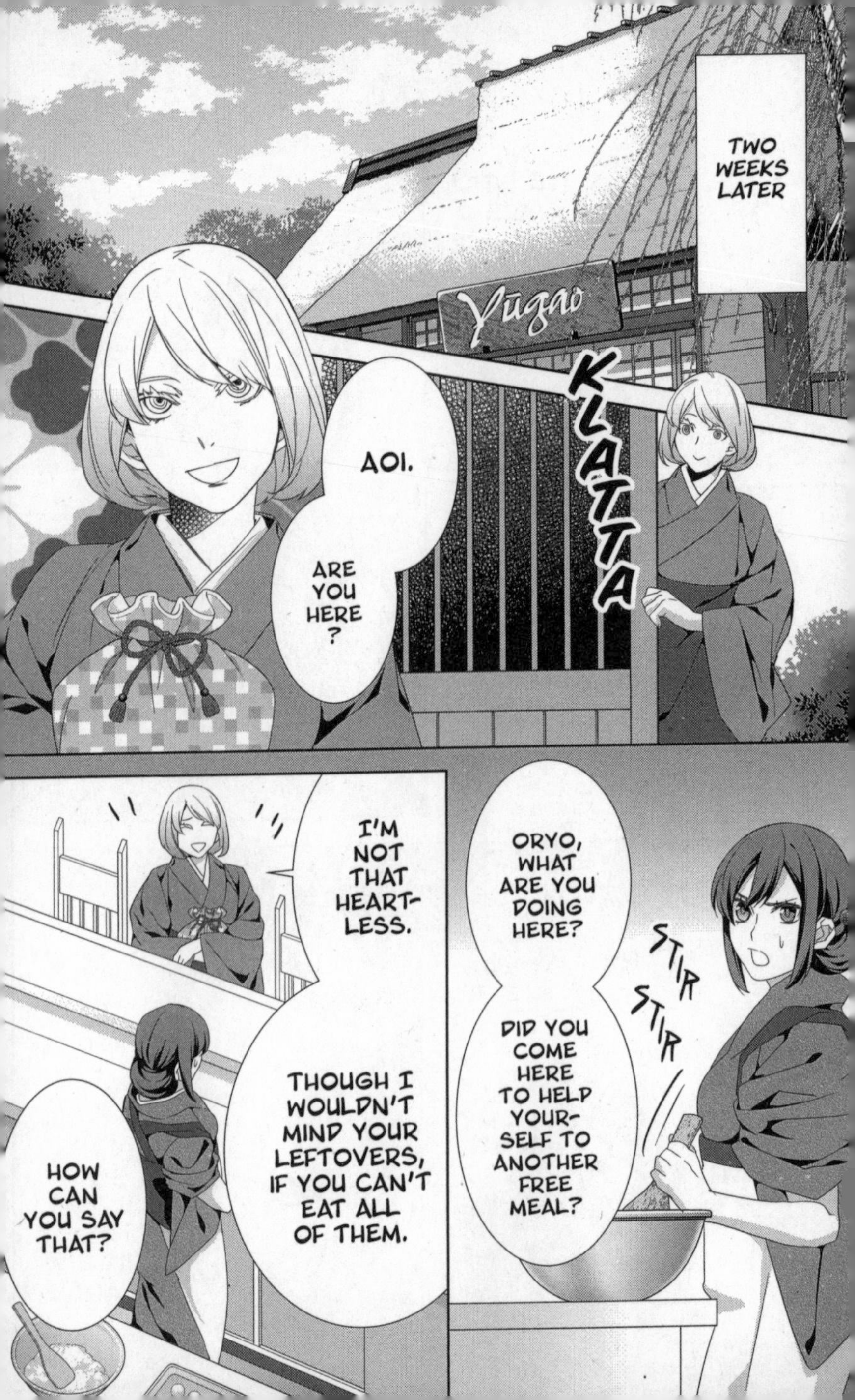
TWO WEEKS LATER
Yūgao
KLATTA
AOI.
ARE YOU HERE?
ORYO, WHAT ARE YOU DOING HERE?
DID YOU COME HERE TO HELP YOURSELF TO ANOTHER FREE MEAL?
STIR STIR
I'M NOT THAT HEARTLESS.
THOUGH I WOULDN'T MIND YOUR LEFTOVERS, IF YOU CAN'T EAT ALL OF THEM.
HOW CAN YOU SAY THAT?

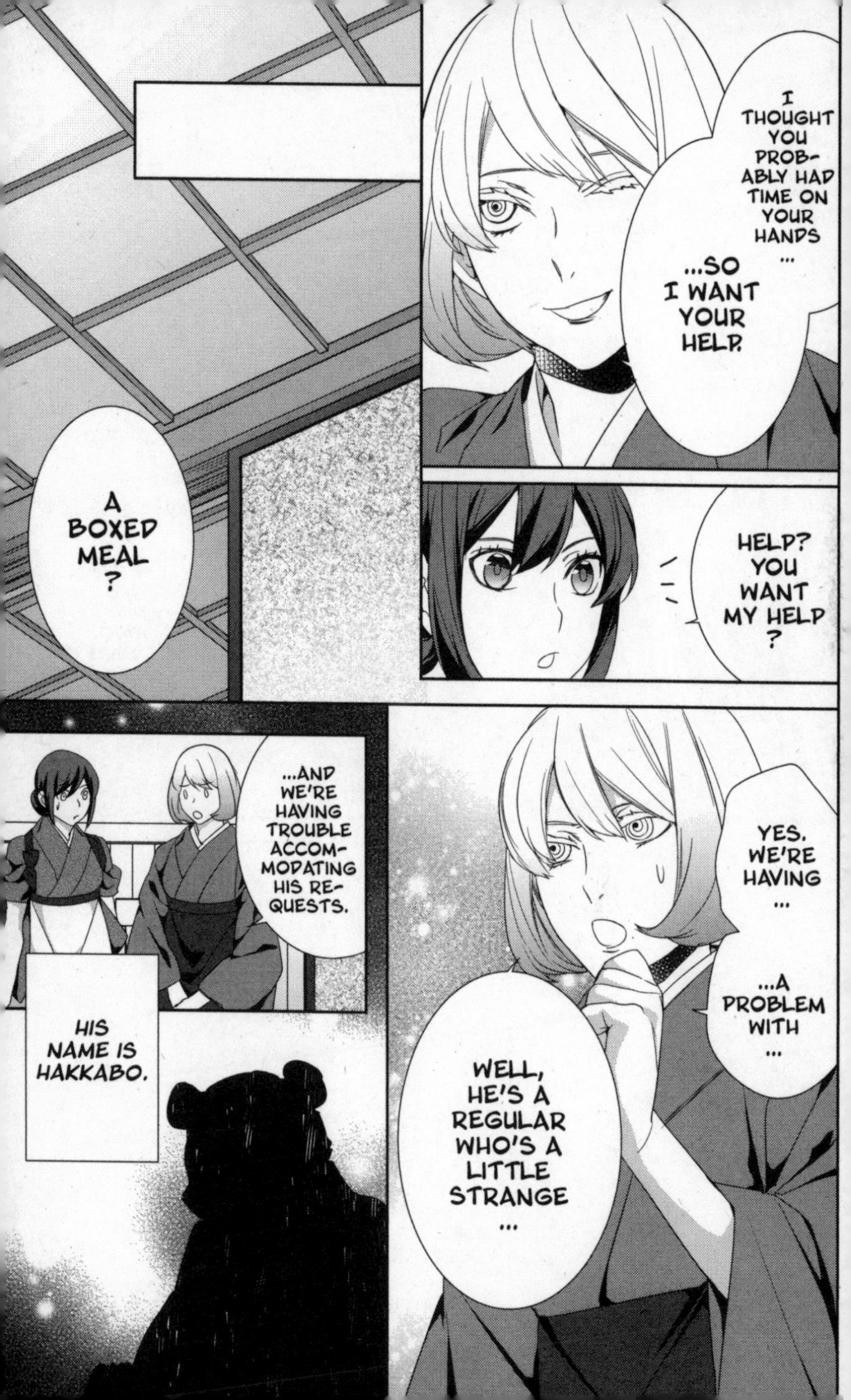
I THOUGHT YOU PROBABLY HAD TIME ON YOUR HANDS ...
...SO I WANT YOUR HELP.
HELP? YOU WANT MY HELP?
A BOXED MEAL?
YES. WE'RE HAVING ...
...A PROBLEM WITH ...
WELL, HE'S A REGULAR WHO'S A LITTLE STRANGE ...
...AND WE'RE HAVING TROUBLE ACCOMMODATING HIS REQUESTS.
HIS NAME IS HAKKABO.

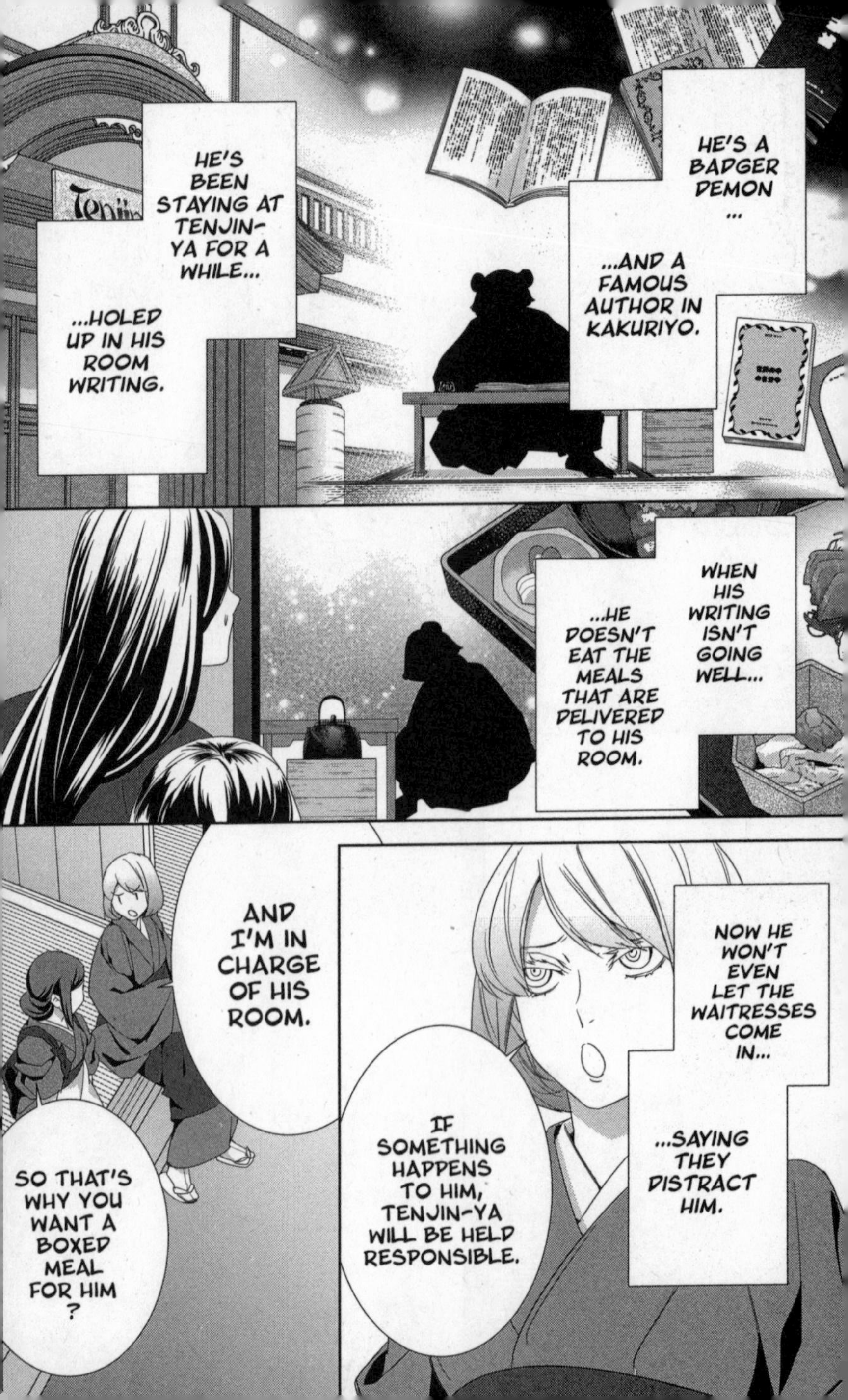
HE'S A BADGER DEMON ...
...AND A FAMOUS AUTHOR IN KAKURIYO.
HE'S BEEN STAYING AT TENJIN-YA FOR A WHILE...
...HOLED UP IN HIS ROOM WRITING.
WHEN HIS WRITING ISN'T GOING WELL...
...HE DOESN'T EAT THE MEALS THAT ARE DELIVERED TO HIS ROOM.
NOW HE WON'T EVEN LET THE WAITRESSES COME IN...
...SAYING THEY DISTRACT HIM.
IF SOMETHING HAPPENS TO HIM, TENJIN-YA WILL BE HELD RESPONSIBLE.
AND I'M IN CHARGE OF HIS ROOM.
SO THAT'S WHY YOU WANT A BOXED MEAL FOR HIM ?

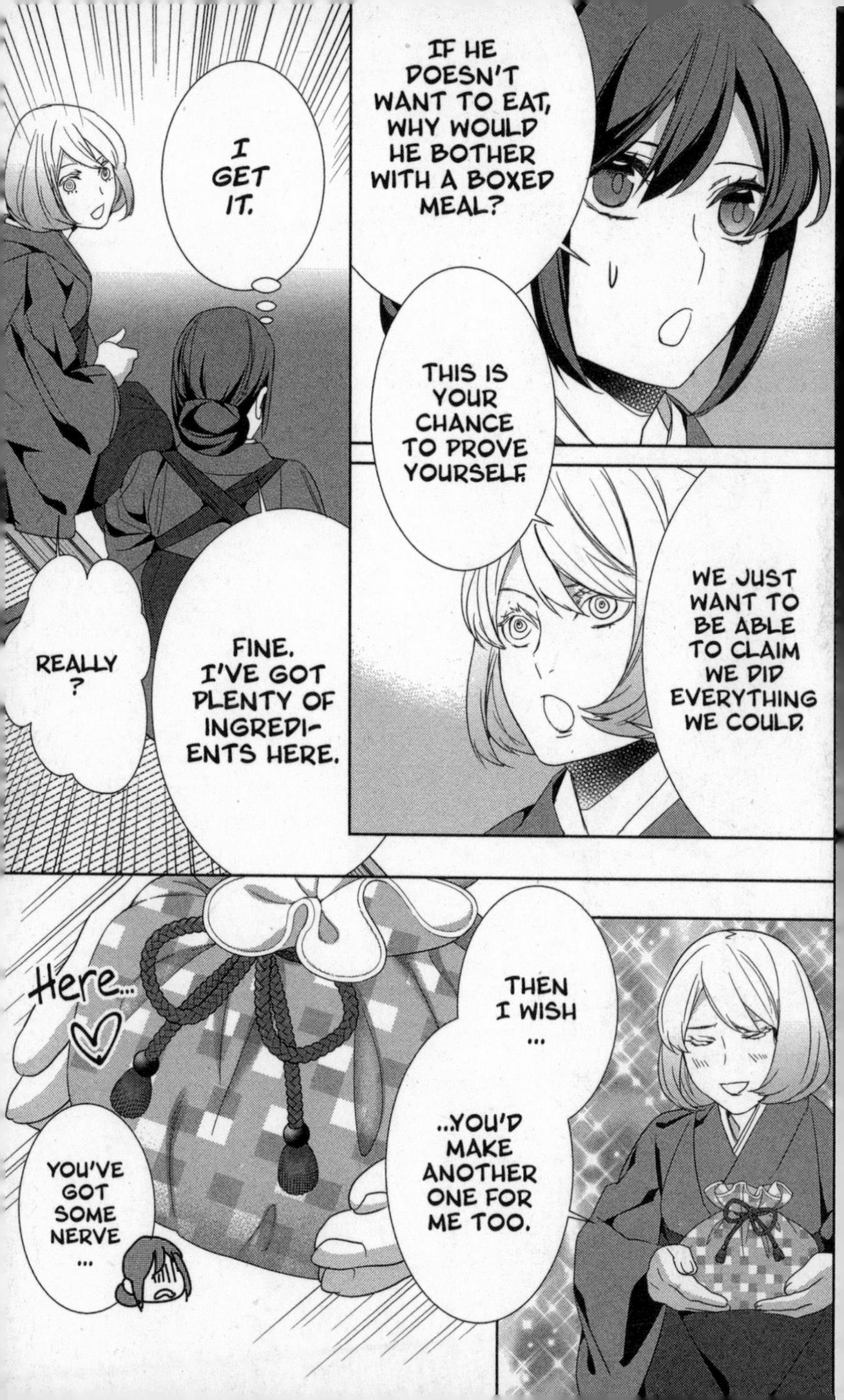
IF HE DOESN'T WANT TO EAT, WHY WOULD HE BOTHER WITH A BOXED MEAL?
THIS IS YOUR CHANCE TO PROVE YOURSELF.
WE JUST WANT TO BE ABLE TO CLAIM WE DID EVERYTHING WE COULD.
I GET IT.
FINE. I'VE GOT PLENTY OF INGREDI- ENTS HERE.
REALLY?
THEN I WISH...
...YOU'D MAKE ANOTHER ONE FOR ME TOO.
Here... ♥
YOU'VE GOT SOME NERVE...

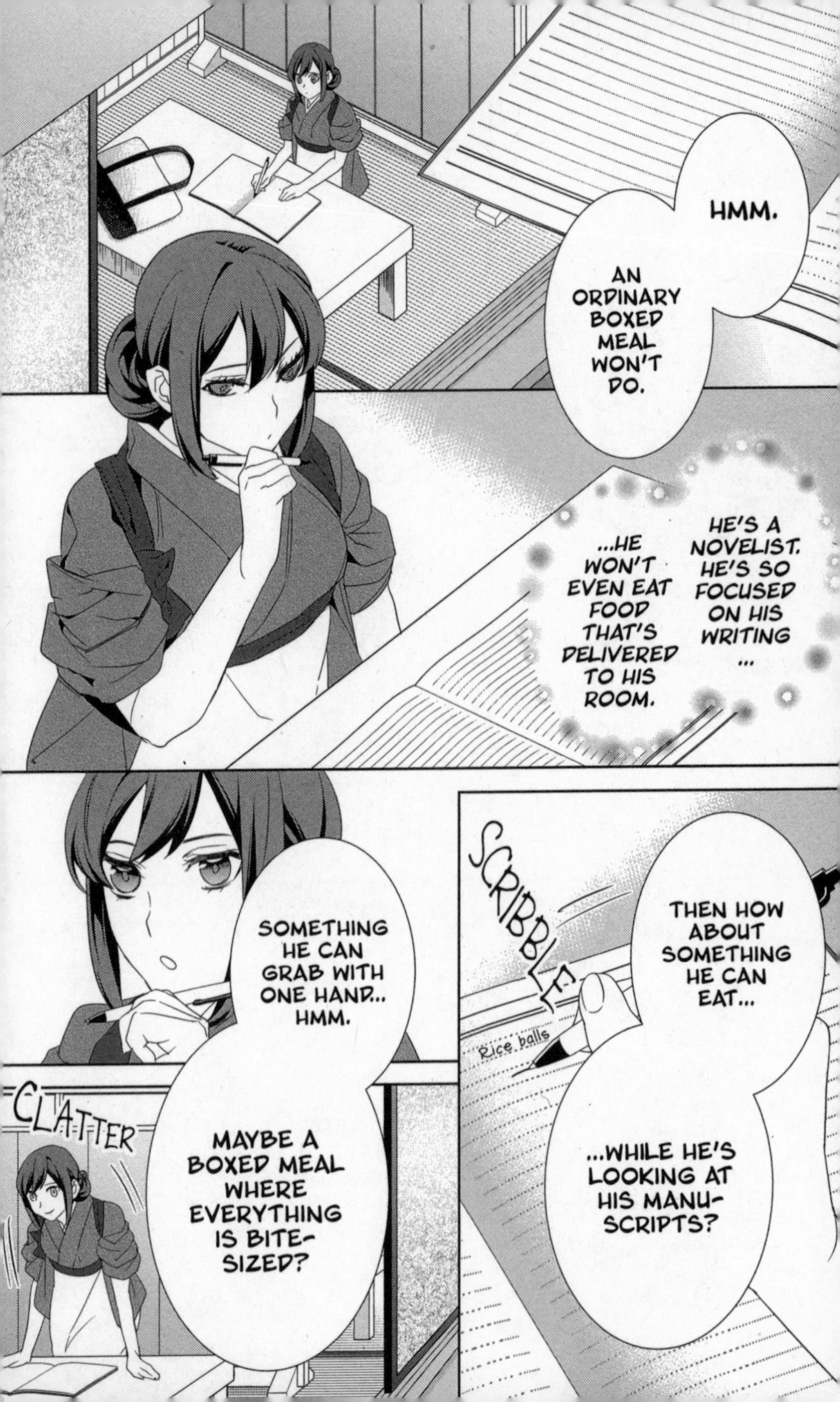
HMM.
AN ORDINARY BOXED MEAL WON'T DO.
HE'S A NOVELIST. HE'S SO FOCUSED ON HIS WRITING...
...HE WON'T EVEN EAT FOOD THAT'S DELIVERED TO HIS ROOM.
SCRIBBLE
THEN HOW ABOUT SOMETHING HE CAN EAT...
Rice balls
...WHILE HE'S LOOKING AT HIS MANUSCRIPTS?
SOMETHING HE CAN GRAB WITH ONE HAND... HMM.
CLATTER
MAYBE A BOXED MEAL WHERE EVERYTHING IS BITE-SIZED?

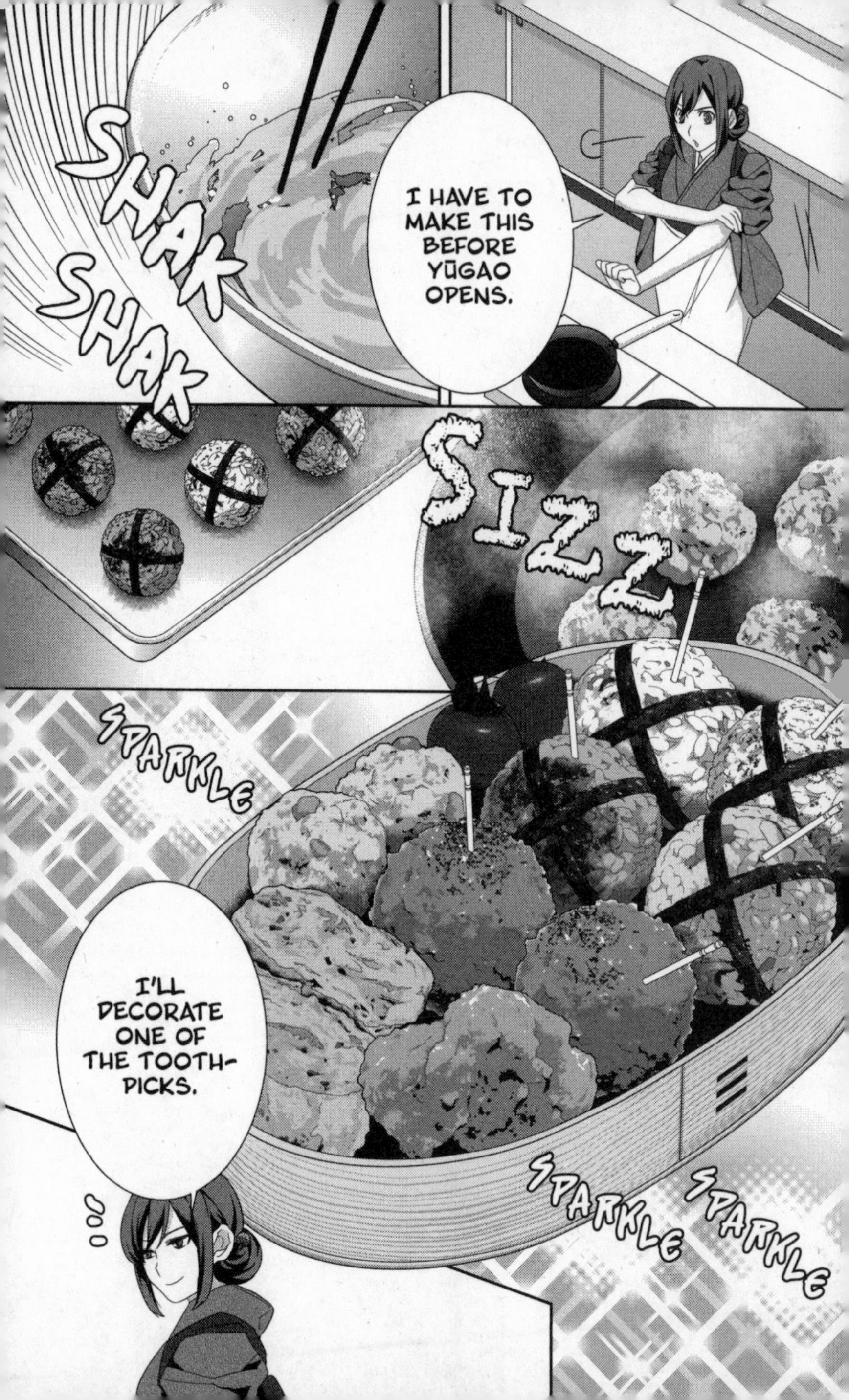
I HAVE TO MAKE THIS BEFORE YŪGAO OPENS.
SHAK SHAK
SIZZ
SPARKLE
I'LL DECORATE ONE OF THE TOOTH-PICKS.
SPARKLE SPARKLE

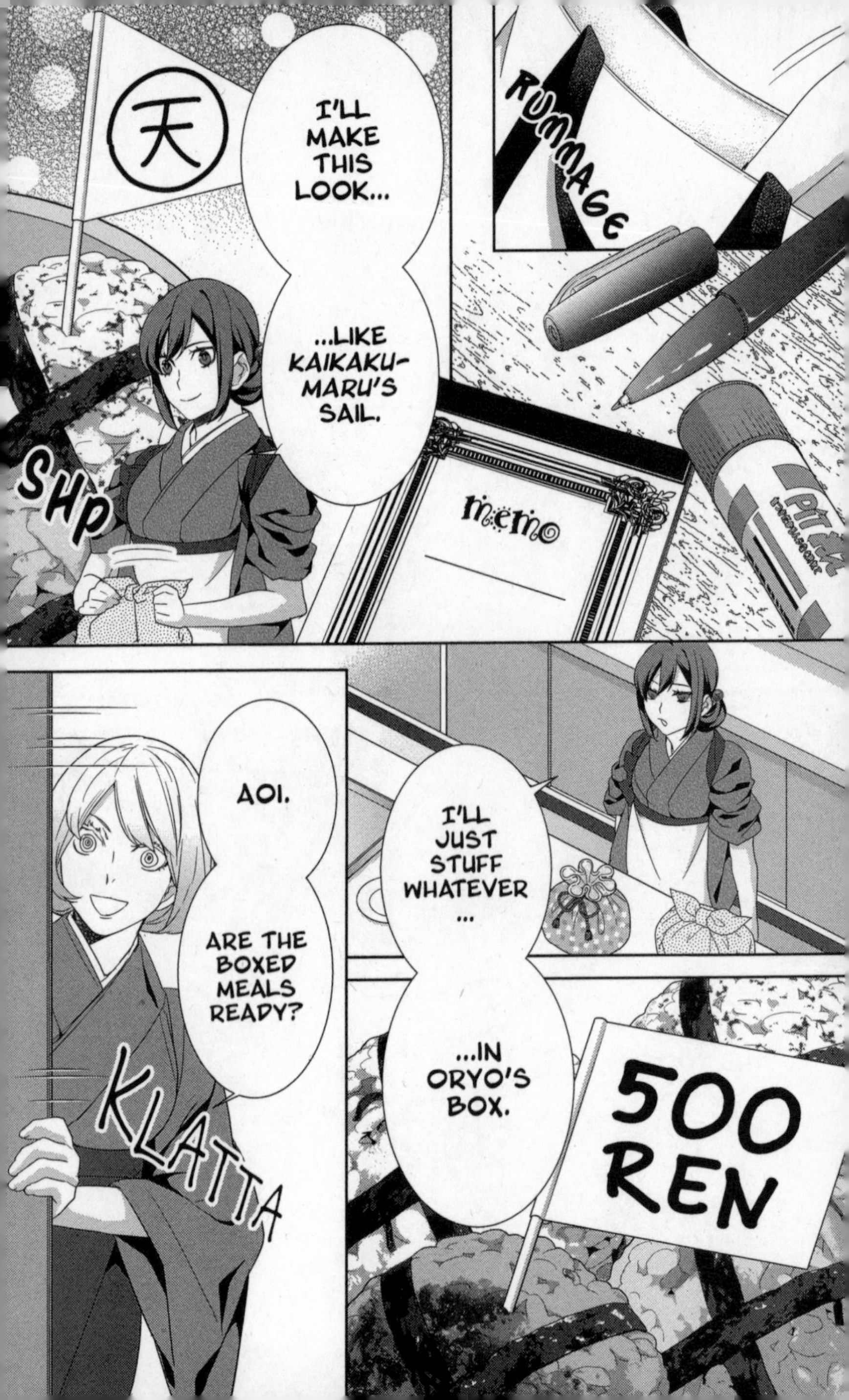
RUMMAGE
memo
天
I'LL MAKE THIS LOOK...
...LIKE KAIKAKU-MARU'S SAIL.
SHP
I'LL JUST STUFF WHATEVER ...
...IN ORYO'S BOX.
500 REN
AOI.
ARE THE BOXED MEALS READY?
KLATTA

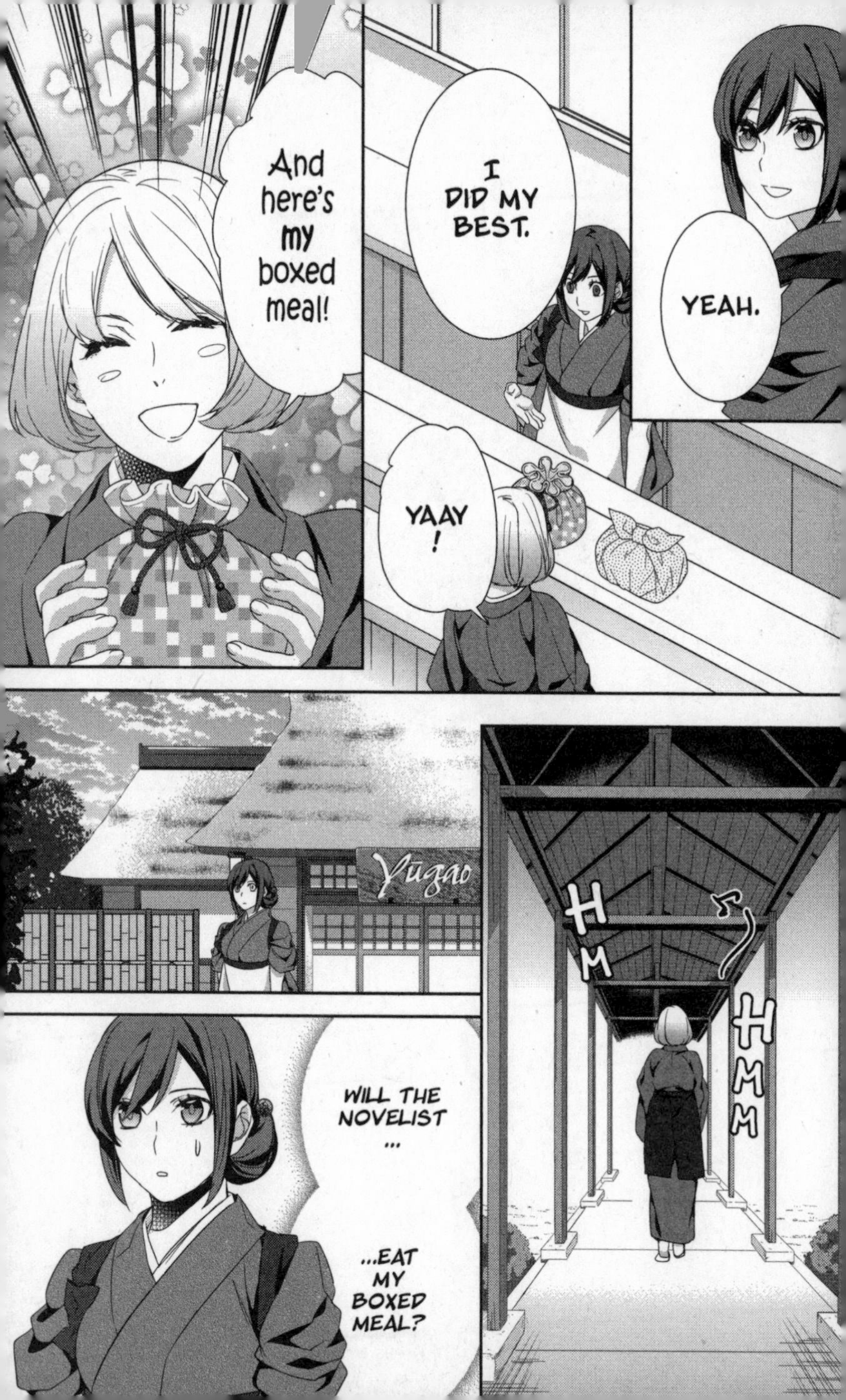

YEAH.
I DID MY BEST.
YAAY!
And here's my boxed meal!
HM
HMM HMM
Yūgao
WILL THE NOVELIST...
...EAT MY BOXED MEAL?

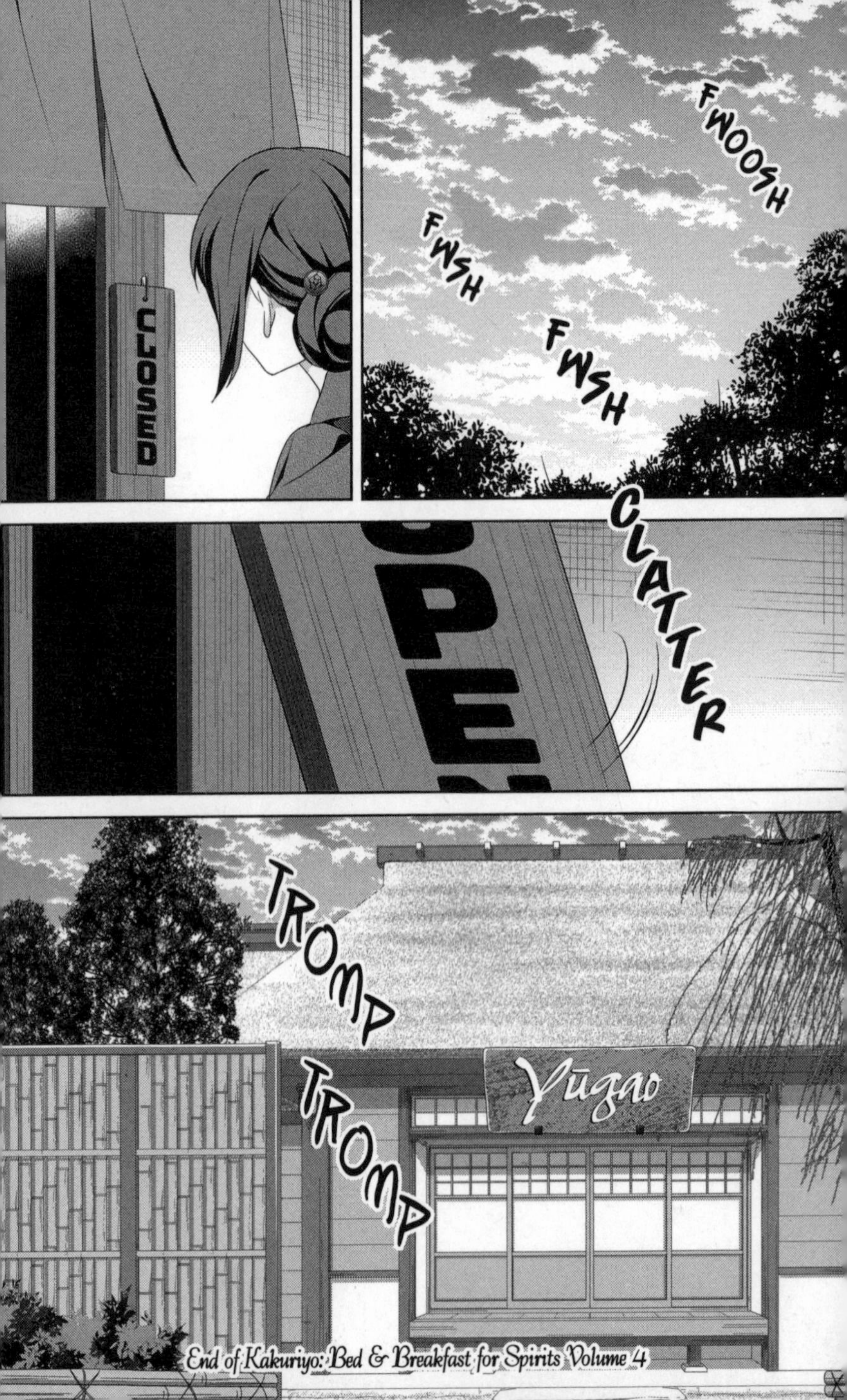
FWOOSH
FWSH
FWSH
CLOSED
CLATTER
TROMP
TROMP
Yūgao
End of Kakuriyo: Bed & Breakfast for Spirits Volume 4

Kakuriyo
Bed & Breakfast
for Spirits

END NOTES

PAGE 40, PANEL 4
Gyokuro
Partially visible on one of the tins, this is a top-quality green tea that is grown in shade and shielded from the sun until it is harvested.

PAGE 52, PANEL 1
Beppu City, Oita prefecture
A famous hot springs resort in the southern island of Kyushu. Chicken tempura is a specialty of Oita prefecture.

PAGE 119, PANEL 2
Hakutaku
A mythical Chinese animal with nine eyes and the body of a lion. They were believed to appear in the human world when a virtuous statesman was ruling the land.

PAGE 136, PANEL 1
Badger demon
Mujina in Japanese. These ayakashi look like young Buddhist priests. They are also shapeshifters and tricksters.

PAGE 4, PANEL 2
Kakuriyo, Ayakashi
Kakuriyo is the spirit realm, while Utsushiyo is the human realm. Ayakashi, also called yokai, are the spirts and demons who live in Kakuriyo.

PAGE 9, PANEL 1
Tengu
Winged mythical beings thought to be either gods or ayakashi. They are usually dressed as mountain priests and have prominent noses.

PAGE 16, PANEL 1
Inari zushi
Deep-fried tofu pockets stuffed with rice and sometimes other ingredients.

PAGE 35, PANEL 2
Bean-washing demon
Azuki arai in Japanese. These ayakashi wash *adzuki* beans in rivers. They are said to either kidnap humans or lure them into rivers with their singing.

Kakuriyo
Bed & Breakfast
for Spirits

Kakuriyo
Bed & Breakfast for Spirits

4

SHOJO BEAT EDITION

Art by **Waco Ioka**
Original story by **Midori Yuma**
Character design by **Laruha**

English Translation & Adaptation **Tomo Kimura**
Touch-up Art & Lettering **Joanna Estep**
Design **Alice Lewis**
Editor **Pancha Diaz**

KAKURIYO NO YADOMESHI AYAKASHIOYADO NI YOMEIRI SHIMASU, Vol. 4
©Waco Ioka 2018
©Midori Yuma 2018
©Laruha 2018
First published in Japan in 2018 by KADOKAWA CORPORATION, Tokyo.
English translation rights arranged with KADOKAWA CORPORATION, Tokyo.

Printed in the U.S.A.

Published by VIZ Media, LLC.
P.O. Box 77010
San Francisco, CA 94107

10 9 8 7 6 5 4 3 2 1
First printing, July 2019

VIZ MEDIA
viz.com

Shojo Beat
shojobeat.com

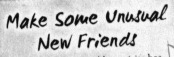

QQ Sweeper

Story & Art by
Kyousuke Motomi

By the creator of *Dengeki Daisy* and *Beast Master*!

One day, Kyutaro Horikita, the tall, dark and handsome cleaning expert of Kurokado High, comes across a sleeping maiden named Fumi Nishioka at school... Unfortunately, their meeting is anything but a fairy-tale encounter! It turns out Kyutaro is a "Sweeper" who cleans away negative energy from people's hearts—and Fumi is about to become his apprentice!

Ao Haru Ride

Futaba Yoshioka thought all boys were loud and obnoxious until she met Kou Tanaka in junior high. But as soon as she realized she really liked him, he had already moved away because of family issues. Now, in high school, Kou has reappeared, but is she still the same boy she fell in love with?

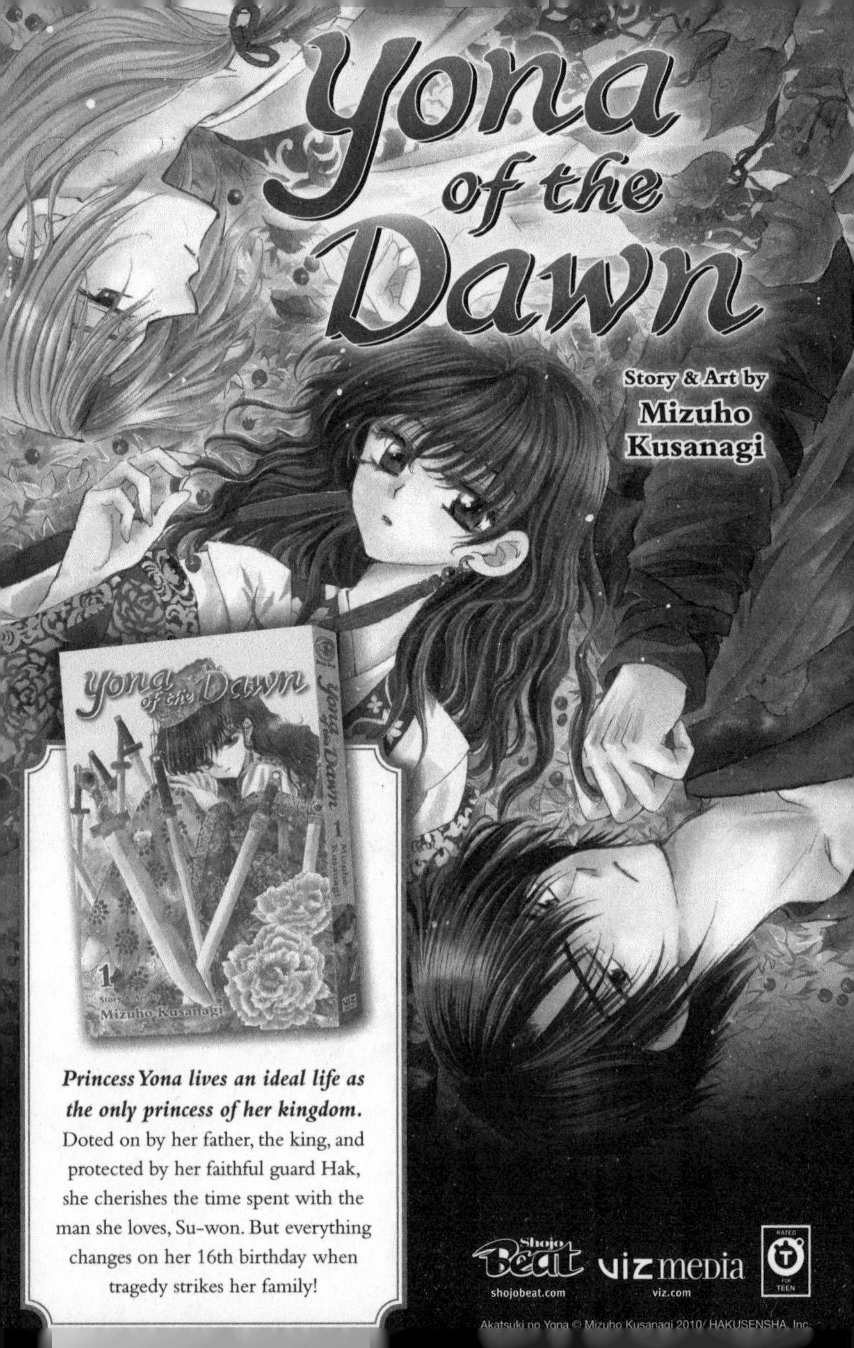
Yona of the Dawn
Story & Art by
Mizuho Kusanagi
Yona of the Dawn
1
Story & Art by
Mizuho Kusanagi
Princess Yona lives an ideal life as the only princess of her kingdom. Doted on by her father, the king, and protected by her faithful guard Hak, she cherishes the time spent with the man she loves, Su-won. But everything changes on her 16th birthday when tragedy strikes her family!
Shojo Beat
shojobeat.com
viz media
viz.com
RATED T FOR TEEN
Akatsuki no Yona © Mizuho Kusanagi 2010/ HAKUSENSHA, Inc.

This is the last page.

Kakuriyo: Bed & Breakfast for Spirits has been printed in the original Japanese format to preserve the orientation of the artwork.

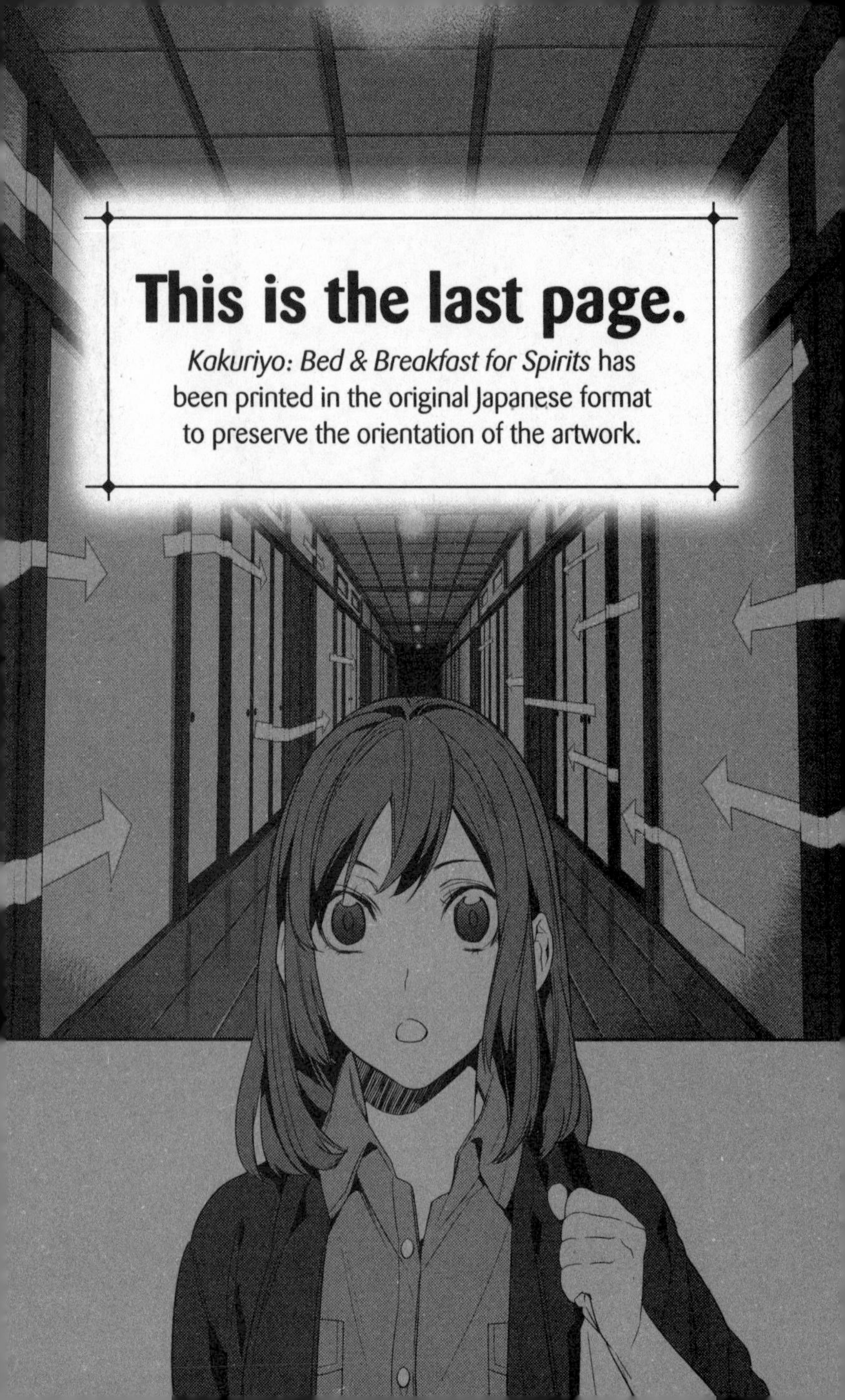